STUDIES IN HISTORY, ECONOMICS AND PUBLIC LAW

Edited by the

FACULTY OF POLITICAL SCIENCE
OF COLUMBIA UNIVERSITY

NUMBER 388

THE TERMINATION OF MULTIPARTITE TREATIES

BY

HAROLD J. TOBIN

THE TERMINATION OF MULTIPARTITE TREATIES

BY

HAROLD J. TOBIN, Ph.D.

Sometime Carnegie Fellow in International Law
Sometime Cutting Fellow of Columbia University
Licencié en sciences sociales, University of Lausanne

NEW YORK
COLUMBIA UNIVERSITY PRESS
London: P. S. King & Son, Ltd.
1933

PRINTED IN THE UNITED STATES OF AMERICA

FOREWORD

At this time when the world is already knit together by a network of treaties, and is daily becoming more so—treaties which deal with almost every conceivable subject of international interest from the migration of birds to the renunciation of war,—a scientific study such as Mr. Tobin has here given us will be most helpful not only to students, teachers, and text writers, but also to diplomats, foreign office officials, courts of justice, arbitrators, and indeed all persons or organizations who or which have to do with the interpretation or application of treaties.

In the actual operation of the complex treaty system as we have it today, an increasing variety of controversies between states is inevitable. They relate to the validity of treaties, the conditions under which they are binding on the parties, the date when they come into force, the effect of reservations, modes of interpretation, the rights and obligations of third states, the relation of posterior treaties to earlier ones, the effect of war, of political, territorial, and other changes upon them, the modes by which they are *ipso facto* terminated, and the ways by which a party may legally withdraw and free itself by unilateral action from the obligations which it has assumed. Any one of these questions and others not here mentioned might be made the subject of elaborate investigation and report.

Indeed there is an urgent need at this time for a general survey of the whole treaty system and a "codification" of the rules of international law and practice so far as there are any, which should be agreed upon by the nations as applicable in cases of controversy involving such questions as those mentioned above. Draft codes prepared by Field, Bluntschli, Fiore, Liszt, the Institute of International Law, and others including the Havana Convention of 1928 on

Treaties have proposed various rules dealing with these subjects, and the Harvard Research in International Law is now devoting itself to the preparation of a draft convention on the subject.

Among the questions concerning which controversies are most prolific and concerning which practice and juristic opinion are widely divergent are those relative to the conditions under which treaties are automatically terminated or may be terminated by action of the parties. It is with this particular aspect of the general subject that Mr. Tobin deals, and he does so in a thorough, objective and scientific manner. He examines in turn both the doctrine and the practice regarding the effect of war on multipartite treaties, termination by unilateral denunciation and termination by agreement of the parties through the conclusion of a new and superseding treaty, drawing such conclusions in each case as the practice seems to justify or which reason suggests. Incidentally he examines various related questions such as that involving the doctrine of the " separability " of treaty provisions. Altogether his work contains a wealth of facts relative to the teachings of publicists, and the practice of states in so far as they bear upon the termination of treaties, and as such it is a valuable contribution to the literature of treaty law and history.

Apart from its historical and scientific interest, this work should be of distinct practical utility to draftsmen of treaties, codifiers of treaty law, and indeed to all who are charged in any way with the interpretation and application of treaties. It is to be hoped that it will be followed by other studies of a similar scope and character dealing with other aspects of treaty law and practice upon which more light is much needed.

JAMES WILFORD GARNER

UNIVERSITY OF ILLINOIS.

PREFACE

A BRIEF discussion of the nature of the instruments included in this study is essential before proceeding with the treatment of the problems involved. Only such instruments will be considered as are drawn up between states, and signed, and, in addition, ratified, if that is necessary for their entry into force. Protocols, statutes and annexes attached to treaties, or signed and ratified similarly to treaties, will also be included. The terms "treaty", "agreement" and "convention" will be used interchangeably, as there appears to be no established distinction between these terms in the practice of states. The term "multipartite treaty" includes all agreements to which more than two states are parties. These agreements may be either bilateral,—in which case one of the parties has rights and obligations vis-à-vis the others as a group,—or multilateral, in which case there may be rights and obligations both as between each of the parties and each of the others, and as between each of the parties and the group as a whole. The principal matter of consideration will be those rules, if any, which may exist for the termination of multipartite treaties, and which may differ from those applying to bipartite instruments.

For the sake of convenience in treatment, multipartite agreements will be divided into three main categories. The first of these comprises that large and growing group whose functions, aside from that of effecting an exchange of rights and obligations between the parties, is to secure uniformity of conduct on the part of all of them for their mutual benefit. Such treaties deal with matters which can be treated uniformly for the international society as a whole, or for a large group of states having common interests. They may establish rules for the conduct of states in dealing with one another, such as those set forth in the General Act of the Congress of Vienna concerning diplomatic rank. They may set up rules for the conduct of states in dealing with each other's nationals, such as the Private International Law conventions of 1902 and 1905. They may set up international agencies which unify certain functions of the states for some international object, such as the Universal Postal Union conventions. But in each case all the stipulations apply equally to all the parties. The design of the parties in setting up these stipulations is generally not defeated by the termination of one or more of the treaty's provisions or by the withdrawal of one or more of the parties, and treaties of this legislative type frequently contain provision either for suspension or termination of certain clauses without affecting the rest, or for unilateral denunciation leaving the convention in force for the remaining signatories. The fact that a large number of states are parties to these conventions, and that international regulation of the subjects dealt with has proved useful to the parties, alone makes possible such unilateral denunciation without greatly impairing the usefulness of such arrangements.

There is also a large body of multipartite treaties containing provisions which set up differing obligations for the different parties. The rights and obligations of each of the parties to such treaties depend in most cases very closely on those of each of the others, and the effect of termination of any clause or the withdrawal of any party may be to destroy the results intended by the parties when they set up the treaty. Due to the difficulties inherent in reaching agreement among the parties to such treaties and to the fact that agreement among a few states serves their purpose, they are usually confined to a small number of states. The Washington Naval Treaty of 1922 is an example.

There is a third category of treaty combining the characteristics of the two already discussed. This category includes such treaties as those drawn up at the end of a general war, such as the Versailles Treaty, or, if drawn up in time of peace, which regulate questions possessing great political interest for a considerable number of states, such as the treaties of African partition, or the successive settlements of Near Eastern questions. Such treaties frequently include provisions setting up identical rights and obligations for all the parties, such as the provisions of the Act of Algeciras concerning equality of commercial opportunity in Morocco, as well as those imposing individual obligations on certain of the parties, such as the provisions of the same Act concerning organization of the bank and of the gendarmerie. In such treaties the balance between rights and obligations for any given party is obscured. There is rarely an indication for any of the parties as to which provisions are a consideration for its participation, and which are accepted as contributing to the general advantage of all. The design of the conferences which draw up these settlements is to settle all outstanding questions between the parties within a broad field, and they frequently take the opportunity to draw up general principles for future application, without making clear whether the inclusion of stipulations concerning the latter was a consideration for the acceptance by any of the parties of stipulations concerning the former.

The manner of drawing up these different types of convention varies also with the type. Almost all are the result of a conference of representatives of the parties concerned, but in the legislative type, provision is frequently made for subsequent signature by states which have not participated in the conference. The second type of treaty described above, dealing with matters of primary interest to a small number of states, and imposing different obligations on each party, is drawn up by a conference to which only those states are invited, goes into effect only with the exchange of ratifications among all the parties, and, if open to accession or adhesion, the privilege is confined to specified states. Treaties of general settlement, though the number of parties bound is generally larger, are drawn up in much the same manner as those described above, but are frequently put into effect on ratification by only a small number of the parties; for example, the Versailles Treaty required ratification by only three of the Principal Allied and Associated Powers and Germany. Modern treaties of general settlement rarely contain provision for accession or adhesion. The legislative type, on the other hand, sometimes goes into effect on ratification by as few as two signatories, and is usually open to accession or adhesion at any time and by any state.

Where other classifications than those mentioned above are used in this study, such as those on the basis of the subject matter—alliances, guaranties, commerce, etc.—they will be utilized chiefly to indicate the relationship between these bases for classification and the new basis adopted here, in order to indicate defects in these former classifications. These weak points are particularly notable in earlier attempts to determine the effect of war on treaties, and it is chiefly in this connection that such classifications will be mentioned.

Throughout this study the chief object of concern will be less to determine the effect on multipartite treaties of certain conditions or events than to seek to discover the design of the parties as to what that effect should be. This method finds its justification in the fact that as the parties to a treaty are sovereign states they have the right to determine in advance the effect of any condition or event on such an agreement, and it lies within their power to provide or to avoid providing against any contingency. The design is sometimes indicated in the instrument itself. Where it is not so indicated it cannot, however, be discovered merely through a determination of the nature of the event or condition. If international law is clearly defined concerning the status of treaties under such conditions, there is a presumption that the parties intend that their action should be determined by the law. But if international law is vague or uncertain, then the decisive factor in the termination of the treaty is the interpretation of the parties themselves as expressed when the treaty was in process of negotiation or in their practice in dealing with the events or conditions in question.

For constant supervision and assistance at all times, and for the personal aid which made possible the completion of this work while the writer was on foreign soil, he is indebted to Professor Philip C. Jessup. He also owes much to Professors Charles Cheney Hyde and Joseph P. Chamberlain for their cooperation and suggestions throughout the period when the work was in progress. The unfailing courtesy and helpfulness of the staff of the international law library of Columbia University has greatly lightened the burden of research. A Carnegie Fellowship in International Law enabled the writer to devote his entire time to his task without interruption.

CONTENTS

CHAPTER I

Termination in Wartime

INTRODUCTION

The attempt to determine the effect of war on treaties has occasioned great diversity of view, a diversity which appears as far from being reconciled today as at any time in the past. Principal causes of this lack of uniformity of opinion appear to be uncertainty regarding the nature of war, and the widespread and rapid development of the treaty relations between states, which render obsolete many of the conceptions of earlier periods.

The ancient Roman conception that war was the natural relation between states, with conquest of the enemy's territory and his complete absorption as the goal, left no room for any conflicting theories regarding the fate of treaties between the belligerents.[1] The problem of individual rights under treaties did not arise, as the foreigner was generally regarded as an enemy, even in peacetime, and so had no rights protected by inter-state agreements. In the Middle Ages, during the period of private war and feudalism, the state system was at a low ebb, and of so different a character from the system of today that comparison has little significance. But as the modern State commenced to develop and international commerce, both by sea and by land, commenced to grow, war gradually ceased to be regarded as the normal relationship between states, and regulation of peaceful relations became more important. When war occurred, how-

[1] Hershey, "History of International Relations during Antiquity and the Middle Ages," *American Journal of International Law*, vol. v (1911), pp. 901-920.

ever, it still involved a termination of the treaty relations between the belligerents, the practical effect being similar, for the period of the war, to that under the old Roman concept.[2]

As we come into the modern period of history, however, the relations between states become closer, and are more frequently subject to treaty regulation, not alone as between any two states, but also on the basis of regulation of general European affairs, and later even for the world as a whole. With this increasing interdependence of states the effect of complete abrogation of all treaties as a result of war would have been to leave all such fields of inter-state relations unregulated, a condition inconvenient, if not dangerous, to all the states concerned. The idea grew up that war was an exceptional condition, causing an interruption of normal relationships which must be resumed when hostilities were over, and which did not destroy the entire structure of these relationships by its mere existence, nor prevent the making of agreements even during the course of hostilities.

The result has been a conflict of intent between the parties holding these two concepts concerning the character of war; between those states believing that it is a condition destroying all normal relationships between states and therefore that their treaties with opposing belligerents are terminated, and those states who hold that it is an abnormal condition serving to destroy only certain relationships, but leaving others merely in a state of suspension or entirely unaffected. This difference of view concerning the nature of war has been at the root of most of the difference of opinion among states concerning its effect on treaties.

A second element in the difficulties attendant on the attempts to discover the rules governing the effect of war has

[2] *Cf.* Kent, *Commentaries on American Law* (Boston, 1867), vol. i, p. 177.

been the great development of the field covered by treaties. When Grotius published his great work, the treaties available for consideration were for the most part bipartite instruments of commerce, of dynasty, of alliance, or of peace at the close of a war, and generally of indefinite duration. In the course of the succeeding centuries, however, the treaty field was broadened to cover international guaranties, the setting up of the Concert of Europe, and the whole field of international legislation including such varied subjects as the conduct of war, the setting up of international unions, the protection of labor and the financial reconstruction of states.[3]

The result of this great broadening of the field has been to render partially obsolete the premises on which early authorities based the rule which they attempted to set up concerning the effect of war on international agreements. In the seventeenth century there was not the vast network of international relationships to be affected by war such as there is today. Agreements regulating commerce and navigation covered the principal fields of peacetime activity requiring common regulation at that time. In the other fields covered by treaties, those dealing with subsidies and alliances were entered into for the purpose of security against a threatened attack, and for common defense when it came, and treaties of peace reestablished affairs in these fields when war was over. But the twentieth-century industrial civilization, much more sensitive to the dislocations brought about by war, has required much more extensive and detailed regulation, and more frequently by multipartite agreements than in the earlier period. The effect of war on this treaty structure is a matter

[3] For example, during the five years following the Treaty of Utrecht there is a record of twenty-eight bipartite and four multipartite conventions; in the five years following the Napoleonic wars there were 179 bipartite and seventeen multipartite treaties, and during the five years beginning with 1920 there have been recorded 600 bipartite and 125 multipartite treaties.

of great concern, and during the period of rapid growth of world-wide agreements the feeling has grown that it would be desirable to reduce such effects to a minimum compatible with the attainment of the military objectives. For this reason the drift away from the old theory of termination of all conventions between belligerents has been marked, and the tendency to make exceptions of continually broadening groups has been noticeable.

Grotius himself held that while the written law between states was terminated by war, the unwritten subsisted.[4] Vattel accepted the theory of general termination,[5] on the ground that the aim of war was to despoil the enemy of all his possessions, including his treaty rights, but conceded that it was necessary to except treaties providing for the event of war, such as those allowing a delay for enemy subjects to leave the realm, or granting a status of neutrality to a city or a province, as well as agreements between belligerents concluded during the course of hostilities, and providing for their regulation.

For those later authorities who have accepted the theory of abrogation of treaties between belligerents with the outbreak of war, the question whether any treaties should be excepted, and if so which, has given rise to a variety of views. Most advocates of the theory of uniform termination accept the view early expressed by the Abbé Mably, which exempted those treaties providing for a state of war.[6] Others included treaties of a transitory or dispositive character, and those to which nonbelligerents were parties.[7] Others would leave it

[4] *Prolegomena*, secs. 25-7.

[5] Bk. iii, ch. x, sec. 175.

[6] Mably, *Droit public d'après les traités* (Geneva, 1768), vol. ii, p. 312. (See Kent, *Commentaries on International Law* (Cambridge, 1866), p. 420).

[7] Westlake, *International Law* (Cambridge, 1907), pt. ii, p. 31.

to the parties to decide through the peace treaty which prewar agreements they wish to revive.[8]

The judiciary has been slow to abandon the theory of uniform termination of treaties between belligerents. In the early nineteenth century the United States courts appear to have accepted this point of view, but the cases involved did not deal with the type of treaties indicated above as usually exempted, such as those concerned with the conduct of war, or dispositive conventions, but rather with treaties involving matters still frequently held to be included among those affected by the advent of war.[9] When a case came up in 1823 involving a dispositive provision, however, the provision was held to be at most suspended, and the American courts have never gone back since that time to the general termination theory.[10]

The French courts accepted the uniform termination theory during the nineteenth century, but made exceptions in favor of certain private rights under treaty provisions.[11] Even as late as 1922 the theory was affirmed, but its application was not essential to the case at bar.[12] German court decisions frequently expressed the uniform termination theory during the war of 1914-18, but made broad and general exceptions.[13]

[8] *Cf.* Keeley in *Transactions of the Grotius Society* (1927), vol. xii, p. 7.

[9] *Cf. The Rapid,* 8 Cranch, 155 (1812); also *Hutchinson v. Brock,* 11 Mass. 119 (1814).

[10] *Society for the Propagation of the Gospel v. New Haven,* 8 Wheat. 464, 494 (1823). For an abandonment of the theory, *cf. Fritz Schulz, Jr., Co. v. Raines & Co.,* 164 N. Y. Supp. 454 (1917).

[11] *Le domaine c. Meyrand, Journal du Palais,* 1843, pt. ii, p. 168.

[12] *Soc. des anciens établissements Wenger c. C.F.P.L.M.,* Sirey, *Recueil général des lois et des arrêts,* vol. ii, p. 112 (1922).

[13] Oberlandesgericht Dresden, October 2, 1917, *Niemeyer's Zeitschrift für internationales Recht,* vol. 30, p. 266; also March 20, 1923, *Juristische Wochenschrift,* 1924, p. 701.

The Japanese courts also accepted it but only as justification for holding a commercial convention invalid.[14] The British and Italian courts appear not to have subscribed to the theory.

This concept of general termination has had its advocates in the political branches of Governments as well. States have frequently stipulated in the past in their declarations of war that all treaties between themselves and the opposing belligerents were terminated. That this practice has probably not yet ceased is evidenced by the declaration of war by Serbia against Turkey in 1914, in which all treaties were denounced,[15] and China's declaration in 1917, in which the only exception made was in favor of agreements for the conduct of war.[16]

A sweeping declaration to the effect that war terminated all treaties between belligerents was made by Lord Bathurst on behalf of the British Government in 1815.[17] He tempered this view, however, by making an exception of treaty provisions testifying to an already recognized condition, such as the independence of a state, which, though specified in a treaty, had been previously acknowledged.[18] The United States, in a controversy with Great Britain over title to the Oregon country, accepted the view of general termination of all unexecuted treaties.[19] The conferences at Vienna in 1855 and in Paris the succeeding year accepted the same

[14] *Horitzu Shimbun*, June 20, 1915; Röthlisburger, "Die Schicksale des gewerblichen Eigentums im Weltkriege", *Schweizerische Juristen Zeitung*, 1916, p. 45.

[15] December 24, 1914, *British and Foreign State Papers*, vol. 109, p. 1016.

[16] August 14, 1917, *ibid.*, vol. 111, p. 680.

[17] October 13, 1815, *American State Papers, Foreign Relations*, vol. iv, p. 352.

[18] *Ibid.*

[19] Buchanan to Pakenham, July 12, 1845; *Brit. & For. State Papers*, vol. 34, p. 93.

view regarding the prewar Russo-Turk treaties.[20] Spain expressed the same opinion regarding its treaties with the United States in 1898.[21] As late as 1925, the award of the umpire in the Ottoman Debt arbitration included the statement that war terminated all treaties between opposing belligerents.[22]

A close examination of the occasions on which the theory of uniform termination has been accepted, by either the judicial or political branches of states during the past hundred years indicates that such acceptance has been limited or qualified. By the beginning of the nineteenth century there was a consciousness of the fact that the states of Europe had common interests whose bases were indicated in their treaties, and that the regulations governing these interests could not be destroyed whenever a conflict arose, leaving chaos until new arrangements were made. The problem of setting up rules governing the preservation of these relations through a period of war was extremely difficult, however, and is not yet solved. It was plain that certain treaty relations were incapable of continuance, and the old rule of uniform termination was called on when its application appeared to fit the case at issue. A brief examination of the instances cited above will show the limited application given the old doctrine even as stated in these instances. In 1815 Lord Bathurst made use of the doctrine to warrant British refusal to observe a provision of the 1783 treaty granting to Americans certain fishing privileges in Canadian waters, Lord Bathurst maintaining that the war of 1812 had terminated the 1783 treaty. But Bathurst himself excepted the first article acknowledging

[20] Protocol no. 1, March 15, 1855, *ibid.*, vol. 45, p. 8. Protocol no. 14, March 25, 1856, *ibid.*, vol. 46, p. 99.

[21] May 3, 1898, *Foreign Relations of the United States*, 1898, p. 774.

[22] April 18, 1925, *Repartition des annuités de la dette publique ottomane, Sentence arbitral*, pp. 62-3 (Borel, arbitrator), Geneva (1925).

the independence of the United States.[23] In 1830 the British Court of Chancery held that that part of the 1794 treaty between the same parties, a treaty dealing with individual property rights, which would have been equally subject to termination by the War of 1812, was nevertheless not affected, inasmuch as it was the intent of the parties that such rights should subsist in wartime as well as in peacetime.[24] It is clear that the theory of termination by war of all treaties between belligerents was not accepted by the British Government at this period.

The United States, in the course of its negotiations with Great Britain in 1845 concerning the boundary of the Oregon country, cited with apparent approval the statement of Lord Bathurst mentioned above to prove that a claim resting on a 1790 treaty between Great Britain and Spain was invalid as a result of a subsequent war. In developing the point, however the contention was modified to affect only unexecuted engagements, and the specific provision in point was a negative one providing that trading between the Indians and the nationals of the contracting states, a type of activity likely to be affected by a subsequent war, should not be disturbed. This is far from Lord Bathurst's original claim.[25]

The discussions at Vienna during the Crimean War, and at Paris after its close dealt only with the commercial treaties between Russia and Turkey.[26] There appeared to be no

[23] *Brit. & For. State Papers, loc. cit.*; Adams, then Secretary of State, forced this exception by maintaining that, if the treaty were terminated, the United States was still a dependency of Great Britain.

[24] *Sutton v. Sutton*, 1 Russel & Mylne, p. 663 (1829). But see discussion between Sir George Lewis, British Secretary of State for War, and Messrs. Baring and Bright, M. P.'s, in which the former maintained the thesis that war would terminate the Declaration of Paris; Hansard, *Parliamentary Debates*, 3rd ser., 1862, vol. 165, cols. 1383-90.

[25] *Cf.* Buchanan-Pakenham correspondence, 1845, *Brit. & For. State Papers*, vol. 34, p. 93 *et seq.*

[26] *Ibid.*, vol. 45, p. 56; vol. 46, pp. 17, 99.

necessity of adopting the sweeping doctrine applying to all treaties, and in practice the balance of the Russo-Turk pre-war treaties continued to govern their relations thereafter.

In 1898, Spain's declaration was aimed particularly at two treaties between herself and the United States granting special privileges to the nationals of each on the territory of the other.[27] These treaties had operated to render difficult the prevention of American filibustering expeditions directed against Spanish sovereignty in Cuba, and Spain was determined they should be terminated. The United States refused to accept the Spanish thesis, particularly as one provision of the earlier of these treaties, that of 1795, had allowed a year's time after the outbreak of hostilities for the merchants of either state to leave the territory of the other. In spite of the fact that Spain did not withdraw her denunciation, she did not expel American nationals. In 1899 she promised payment on an annuity due under an 1834 treaty with the United States, claiming that the treaty had been merely suspended by the war. It was not until 1902 that a new Spanish-United States treaty stated that all the treaties between the two states prior to that at the end of the war, and excepting the 1834 agreement, were abrogated. There was clearly no adoption in practice of the theory of uniform termination by either of the states concerned.[28]

The statement of M. Borel, umpire in the Ottoman Debt arbitration of 1925, that war operated to annul all treaties between opposing belligerents, although made without qualification, partakes of the nature of dictum. The Turkish Government had advanced the claim that the reason for reviving

[27] LeFur, *Revue générale de droit international public*, 1898, p. 676. Treaty of October 27, 1795, art. xiii; Moore, *Digest of International Law, etc.* (Washington, 1906), vol. v, pp. 375-6.

[28] Jacomet, *La guerre et les traités* (Paris, 1909), p. 158. Treaty of July 3, 1902, Malloy, *Treaties, etc., of the United States*, vol. ii, p. 1701.

a number of multipartite engagements between Turkey and the other European Powers by a provision in the peace treaty, was that Turkey was a new state, in the same sense as Iraq, Syria or Palestine, and that without such a provision the status of the treaties in respect to the new state would be in doubt. M. Borel, in holding that the Turkish contention was wrong,[29] chose to interpret the intent of the parties to the Lausanne treaty as being not to recognize Turkey as a new state but to revive certain treaties which had been terminated by the war, a conclusion which, as we shall later see, was not entirely correct, and in any case was not essential to prove that Turkey was not deemed to be a new state.

It appears safe to conclude, then, that during the past hundred years such expressions as we find in favor of the theory of complete termination of all treaties as between opposing belligerents have either been limited in fact to certain types of treaties by those making them, or have been controverted by the facts in the case. Further, there has been no attempt made in these cases to distinguish between suspension during wartime and termination. In the light of the greatly broadened field covered by international engagements, and the increased sensitiveness of the international economic structure, even the temporary complete absence of any rules governing the relations between states or between them and aliens works great hardships. Except where the maintenance of such relationships seriously prejudices the successful conduct of the war there is an increasing tendency to make exceptions to their general termination.

The converse of the theory of general termination, which holds that war has *ipso facto* no effect on treaties, has had much less general support. It was advocated however in the Draft Regulations concerning effects of war on treaties drawn up by the Institute of International Law at its Chris-

[29] April 18, 1925, *Sentence arbitral*, p. 61 *et seq.* (See note 22.)

tiania meeting in 1912.[30] The first article of the regulations stated that "the opening and carrying on of hostilities does not affect the existence of treaties, conventions and agreements, whatever their title or object, between the belligerent States. The same holds for special obligations derived from these treaties, conventions and agreements." As in the case of the proponents of the general termination theory, however, a large number of exceptions were made, which brought the modified view of the two theories almost to agreement regarding the classification of those treaties which survive and those which terminate.

The middle view between these two extremes is the most commonly held, that is, that war terminates certain types of treaties, suspends others and allows others to subsist. There is no approach to unanimity of view however, except concerning a very few classifications, and a variety of reasons is given for including or rejecting the different categories. There appears to be unanimity of opinion that treaties envisaging war remain in force in wartime if all the belligerents are parties to the treaty,[31] and the same holds true for treaty provisions involving transfer of territory.[32] There appears to be equal unanimity in the opinion that alliances are terminated.[33] But there is a marked difference of view regarding treaties of commerce, guaranty, transportation, and private rights, and also concerning those treaties which supposedly testify to the existence of an international law, or set up

[30] Project of the Institute of International Law, Christiania, August, 1912, *Annuaire de l'Institut de Droit International* (1912), vol. 25, p. 648; also in *American Journal of International Law* (1913), vol. vii, p. 149.

[31] *Cf.* Kent, *Commentaries on International Law* (Cambridge, 1866), p. 420.

[32] For a representative view see Baker and McKernan, *Selected Topics connected with the Laws of Warfare as of August 1, 1914* (Washington, 1919), p. 259.

[33] Bonfils, *Manuel de droit international public* (Paris, 1905), pp. 480-1.

international unions, or which, at the end of a general war, settle a combination of several of these questions.

In the course of the nineteenth century various classifications were attempted by the courts of different states, in an effort to make more precise the distinction between those conventions which might be applied even as between belligerents during wartime and those which were suspended or even terminated by war. Among those held to be abrogated were treaties of friendship and commerce and political treaties generally.[34] Another classification appears in the statement that "treaties stipulating for permanent rights, and general arrangements, and professing to aim at perpetuity, and to deal with the case of war as well as of peace do not cease on the occurrence of war, but are at most only suspended while it lasts. . . ."[35] A later conception placed even commercial treaties in the "suspended" category, and included also treaties dealing with private interests.[36] A continental judicial decision set up the criterion of the will and intent of the parties to the treaty, but where that could not be determined it was held that private or judicial rights incompatible with the state of war were at most suspended.[37]

In determining the effect of war on treaties a considerable group of writers have attempted a division of treaties into those dealing with private as opposed to those dealing with public rights, the former surviving and the latter being at least suspended. The basis for this classification lies in the conception that war is an affair between states, and does not

[34] December 23, 1854, *Featherstonehaugh c. Boffi*, Sirey, Cassation criminelle, *Recueil général des lois et des arrêts*, vol. i, p. 811.

[35] *Society, etc., v. New Haven*, 8 Wheat. 464 (1823).

[36] December 2, 1858, *Isnard Blanc c. Pezzales*, cour d'Aix, *Journal du Palais*, 1860, p. 333.

[37] October 30, 1885, *Bicci c. hospices de St. Quentin*, Tribunal de St. Quentin, Clunet, *Journal du droit international*, 1888, p. 99.

involve individuals except in their capacity as citizens, and the rights of the individual as stipulated by treaty are thus not affected by war.[38] Grotius recognized the distinction in declaring that the King might make and terminate treaties without affecting his subjects, but added that such treaties as were published as law bound the subject.[39] He did not however, make any specific reference to the effect of war on either published or unpublished treaties. Rousseau spoke of war as a contest between armies, and not between peoples, and held that it was only in his capacity as a soldier that the individual's rights might be affected.[40] Montesquieu suggested the same idea in his theory that men should in wartime do each other the least harm possible compatible with the interest of the state.[41]

A number of later continental writers have adopted similar views, among them Holtzendorf, Despagnet, Bonfils [42] and Jacomet.[43] Westlake approximated the view of Montesquieu, maintaining that it was only lawful to do harm to the individual where such an act constituted an important means of breaking down the enemy's resistance. The scope which he gave to the state in its dealing with enemy nationals, however, weakened his contention to a point where it resembled more closely the theory that war involves the interests of individuals as well as those of states.[44]

The latter rule is the conception of the common law, and

[38] Despagnet, *Cours de droit international public* (Paris, 1910), p. 827.

[39] Grotius, *De jure belli ac pacis,* lib. ii, ch. xiv, sec. ix.

[40] *Contrat social,* i: sec. 4.

[41] Cited by Westlake, *op. cit.*, p. 33.

[42] Holtzendorff, *Handbuch des Völkerrechts* (Hamburg, 1889), vol. iv, sec. 90, p. 371. Despagnet, note 38, *loc. cit.* Bonfils, *Manuel de droit international public* (Paris, 1912), p. 693.

[43] *La guerre et les traités* (Paris, 1909), p. 170.

[44] Westlake, *op. cit.*, pp. 33-4.

lies at the root of English practice. It has not been confined to England, however; the theory was generally accepted in the Middle Ages and down to the eighteenth century on the continent as well. During that period France was in the habit of forbidding even postal communication between her own and enemy nations in her declaration of war, or by special decree immediately after its outbreak. By the beginning of the nineteenth century, however, both in the United States and on the continent, the courts frequently maintained that private rights were at most suspended.[45]

Though in modern times continental writers have generally opposed the theory of the involvement of individual rights in war, as a matter of practice during the recent war there appeared a tendency among continental governments toward modifying unfavorably the treaty rights of individuals, on the basis of a lack of reciprocity. The theory itself, however, appears not to have been abandoned.[46] The United States did not adopt either the common law or the continental law completely, modifying certain rights of enemy aliens but carefully preserving others which England denied under the common law concept. In practice those states holding either theory tended to approximate the same standard of conduct. Where the common law concept was held, its rigors were softened by special provision of the government. On the other hand where the continental theory was held, the government frequently adopted the common law practice in those cases where unrestricted exercise of private rights appeared

[45] *The Rapid,* 8 Cranch, 1812; *Severyns case,* June 30, 1838, Cour d'appel, *Pasicrisie belge,* 1838, 186; *Guyot c. Rosetti,* Cour royale de Nimes, August 14, 1839, *Journal du Palais,* tome 2, p. 550, cited by Jacomet, *op. cit.,* p. 170; *Isnard Blanc c. Pezzales,* December 2, 1858, Cour d'Aix, *Journal du Palais,* 1860, p. 333.

[46] *S. H. H. v. L. Ch. in Paris,* Reichsgericht, Zivilsachen, October 26, 1914, vol. 85, p. 374. See also Oberlandesgericht Dresden, October 2, 1917, *Niemeyer's Zeitschrift für internationales Recht,* vol. 30, p. 266.

to be prejudicial to the successful conduct of the war. The practice of different states in this connection will be considered in detail.

A number of writers have based their views concerning termination on the relation of the treaty to the cause of the war. Lawrence maintains that in the case of multipartite conventions where the origin of the war is not connected with the treaty, the latter remains unaffected.[47] Temperley takes the same view.[48] Baker and McKernan consider that the treaty may nevertheless [49] under certain conditions be affected. Lawrence holds that if the origin of the war is connected with the treaty the non-belligerent signatories must assist in determining its fate.[50] Westlake considers that if the treaty is the cause of the war it is terminated.[51] Baker and McKernan hold the same view with an exception when the peace treaty stipulates revival.[52]

There have been very serious obstacles in the way of classifications such as those mentioned above. For the most part they are based on the treaties existing in a period when their number was much smaller than it now is, when the subjects dealt with in treaties were less varied and numerous than at present, and when the machinery for drawing up treaties, and provisions for their determination, offered less guidance for such a study than is now available. There is still a great lack of uniformity in the practice of states, as evidenced by their action during and after the war of 1914-18,

[47] Lawrence, *Principles of International Law* (New York, 1923), p. 339.

[48] *History of the Peace Conference* (London, 1920), vol. i, p. 360.

[49] Baker and McKernan, *op. cit.*, p. 241.

[50] *Loc. cit.*

[51] *International Law* (1924), vol. ii, p. 419.

[52] *Op. cit.*, p. 241. See also, *Project of the Institute of International Law*, Christiania, 1912, cited *supra*, note 30, art. ii, sec. ii.

to be considered later. Some confusion of thought appeared at the Peace Conference due to the attempt to fit previously accepted doctrine into the frame of the specific conditions to be dealt with, but in the end the Conference settled the problem of the postwar status of former treaties without dealing with the wartime status at all.

The period since the war has been only slightly more fruitful than the years preceding, in expressing through the medium of the treaties themselves the attitude of the contracting parties in regard to the effect of war. The solution of the question, in view of the conflicting or ambiguous views expressed above, must be sought in the practice of states as indicated in the diplomatic history of individual treaties, and in court decisions hinging on the questions of termination, suspension and survival.

The attempt to determine the present design of states, as expressed in the acts of their political and judicial branches, regarding the effect of war on their multipartite treaties will concern itself with three periods of time:—the period during which hostilities are in progress, the period between the time when they have ceased and before the peace treaty at the end of the war goes into effect, and the period thereafter. The principal matters of concern will be to discover (1) how multipartite treaties have actually been affected by the wars to which they have been subjected; (2) whether the categories into which they generally are divided in determining the effect of war furnish useful bases of classification; (3) whether all parts of these treaties are equally affected, and if not whether in fact the clauses may be separated; and (4) whether the nature and extent of the war modifies the effect on a given treaty.

TREATIES REGULATING THE CONDUCT OF HOSTILITIES

It appears to be the unanimous opinion of authorities in international law that stipulations providing for the conduct of war come immediately into force at the outbreak of hostilities; any other conception would seem to render the making of such stipulations useless. Violations of these agreements have frequently been charged in wartime, but there appears to have been no case where any party to a convention providing for the conduct of hostilities has declared itself not bound except according to the terms of the convention itself, or where there has been a general denunciation of all treaties with the opposing belligerent.

The most important of these agreements are the Declaration of Paris of 1856,[53] the Red Cross Conventions of 1864 [54] and 1906,[55] the 1904 Convention Exempting Hospital Ships from Harbor Dues and Taxes in Wartime,[56] and the two sets

[53] April 16, 1856, *Brit. & For. State Papers*, vol. 146, p. 56. In 1862, on a proposal in the British House of Commons to modify the Declaration in regard to the principle that a neutral flag covers enemy goods except contraband of war, Sir George Lewis, then Secretary of State for War, stated that in any case the declaration would not be binding as between belligerents in case of war. He held that while the declaration had the same character as a treaty and was subject to the same law, treaties were not binding as between opposing belligerents, when in derogation of a principle of international law. International law at that time, he held, did not prevent search and seizure of non-contraband enemy goods on neutral ships. His views were sharply contested by several of the members, on the ground that the Declaration of Paris was a declaration of a new principle for the conduct of nations, and a breach of it would call down on the offending party the condemnation of the whole world. The proposed modification was not made.

During the war of 1914-18 the Declaration of Paris was frequently invoked in prize court decisions, so it would appear that the early doctrine of suspension found little favor.

[54] August 22, 1864, Malloy, *Treaties, etc., of the United States*, vol. ii, p. 1903.

[55] July 6, 1906, *ibid.*, p. 2183.

[56] December 21, 1904, *ibid.*, p. 2135.

of Hague Conventions, signed in 1899[57] and 1907.[58] The war of 1914-18 subjected these conventions to a great strain, but in no case were they suspended in spite of the fact that with the exception of the Declaration of Paris they all contained clauses permitting non-application in wartime, either on the ground that all the belligerents were not parties to the convention, in which case all the parties were relieved of their obligations,[59] or on the ground that the convention was not being observed by one of the parties, in which case it might be suspended in dealing with that party.[60]

Of the earlier conventions, the Declaration of Paris appears to have been accepted as binding in 1914. At the outbreak of the war all of the belligerents were parties to it, and during the course of the war the United States was the only belligerent non-signatory, and even the United States had observed its provisions in both the Civil and Spanish wars.[61] The fact that the Declaration did not make plain what was contraband of war, or what constituted an effective blockade, reduced the value of the Declaration during the war of 1914-18, so that when protest was made against supposed violations of the rules regarding the matters dealt with in the Declaration, they were made usually under one of the Hague Conventions or under the Declaration of London of 1909, although the latter had no obligatory force.[62]

[57] July 29, 1899, *ibid.*, pp. 2017-42.

[58] October 18, 1907, *ibid.*, pp. 2220-2366.

[59] *Cf.* art. ii of 1907 Hague convention concerning Laws and Customs of War on Land; *ibid.*, p. 2269.

[60] *Cf.* art. xiv of 1868 Additional Articles to 1864 convention concerning the Amelioration of the Condition of the Wounded in Armies in the Field, *ibid.*, p. 1907.

[61] Garner, *International Law and the World War* (London, 1920), vol. i, p. 13.

[62] *Cf. The Roumanian*, December 7, 1914, *Times Law Report*, vol. 31, p. 111; also *The Miramichi*, November 23, 1914, *ibid.*, p. 72.

The fact that the 1906 Convention for the Amelioration of the Condition of the Wounded in Armies in the Field replaced as between the signatories the convention of similar title of 1864 resulted in a more general application of the later convention during the period from 1914 to 1918. The amendments to the earlier pact applying it to naval warfare, while never ratified, were incorporated in one of the Hague Conventions,[63] but, as has been observed, these Hague Conventions of 1907 were not binding. The French Government, however at the commencement of the war announced its intention to observe both the 1906 Convention and the Hague adaptation of it to naval warfare,[64] and in the course of the war Germany,[65] France,[66] Great Britain,[67] Russia,[68] Turkey[69] and Austria-Hungary[70] all indicated their acceptance of one or both of these conventions, usually as a basis for registering a protest against violation by one or another of the enemy Powers.

Of the Hague Conventions only two, that respecting the Laws and Customs of War on Land, and that adapting the Principles of the Geneva Convention to Naval Warfare, both signed in 1899, were in force, all the 1907 agreements being

[63] Hague, 1907, Convention for the Adaptation to Naval Warfare of the Principles of the Geneva Convention.

[64] *Avis, Ministère de la guerre*, August 18, 1914, *Revue générale de droit international public*, 1915, Documents, p. 17.

[65] Brochure, "Violations of Geneva Convention of July 7, 1906, by French Troops and francs-tireurs", cited by Garner, *op. cit.*, p. 502.

[66] *Communiqué*, September 18, 1914, *Ministère de la guerre, Revue générale de droit international public*, 1915, Docs., p. 80.

[67] Protest against submarine attacks, *ibid.*, p. 137.

[68] Similar protest, *New York Times* of April 5, 1916.

[69] *Ibid.*, April 17, 1916.

[70] Garner, *op. cit.*, p. 503.

legally suspended due to the presence among the belligerents of non-signatories.[71]

At the outbreak of the war France notified the representatives of the Powers at Paris that she " proposed to observe the principles of the law of nations ", and " assuming that reciprocity will be observed, would act in accordance with the International Conventions signed by France concerning the law of war on land and sea." It is interesting to note in this connection that France by this declaration abandoned the legal ground for suspension of these conventions—namely, the participation in the war of a non-signatory, Serbia,—on condition that the opposing belligerents should reciprocate. The fact remains, however, that though she resorted to reprisals for alleged violations of the conventions[72] and although she frequently modified her interpretation of the nature of her obligations under the conventions, her policy throughout the war remained one of maintaining the conventions in force.[73] France also maintained in force the Hague Convention providing for the Status of Merchant Ships at the Outbreak of Hostilities, excepting those pro-

[71] In spite of this fact, a number of the signatories of the latter conventions indicated that they would observe the terms of one or more of them, sometimes stating that such observance was due to the fact that these agreements embodied existing international law.

[72] In a case before the Tribunal of the Seine it was maintained that " one cannot think of according to German nationals the benefit of the law of nations or of the treaties which Germany has violated at every opportunity " (*Daude c. Faber*, Clunet, *Journal de Droit International*, 1916, p. 1304). But a later decision under the same convention held that its espionage provisions were binding on the French courts (*Affaire Krug*, May 6, 1918, Clunet, *Journal de Droit International*, 1919, p. 1108). In 1915, by way of reprisal, France suspended application of the provision for the internment of officers on parole.

[73] *Cf. Avis du ministère de la marine*, October 7, 1914, *Revue générale de droit international public*, Docs., 1915, p. 85; also Clunet, *Journal de Droit International*, vol. 43, p. 1131, 1484, and vol. 42, p. 567.

visions to which Germany had made reservations when ratifying, and again conditioned her observance on reciprocity by her enemies.[74] In the course of the war she announced her intention to maintain in force the provisions of the Convention regarding Automatic Contact Submarine Mines, at the same time protesting alleged Austro-Hungarian violations.[75]

The British prize courts consistently applied the Convention regarding the Status of Merchant Ships at the Opening of Hostilities where the ships of the other signatories of the convention were concerned, but refused to apply it in dealing with the ships of non-signatories. Early in the war the convention was held to be applicable pending a declaration by the political branch, on the grounds that, although it had not been ratified by all the belligerents, of the two which were not parties,—Montenegro and Serbia,—the former " has no navy, and . . . no merchant marine; it has a coastline, but only of about thirty miles; and Serbia is a purely inland state, having no seaboard at all." It was felt to be undesirable that the non-ratification by these Powers should prevent the application of the maritime conventions.[76]

In 1915 the British Prize Court in Egypt stated that " there is no doubt that the Hague Convention has received such assent from the chief civilized states of Europe that it is an international law promulgated by virtue of agreement of such states ", but tempered the statement by limiting its application to those states granting reciprocity.[77] In 1916 a plea was allowed based on the same convention, but damages

[74] *Revue générale de droit international public*, vol. 22 (1915), Docs. pp. 9-10, cited by Garner, *op. cit.*, vol. i, p. 154.

[75] *Revue générale de droit international public, loc. cit.*

[76] *The Möwe*, November 9, 1914; *Brit. & Col. Prize Cases*, vol. i, p. 60.

[77] *The Bärenfels*, Prize Court in Egypt, January 21, 1915, *British and Colonial Prize Cases*, vol. i, p. 122.

were not awarded, not on the ground that the convention was not in force but because the ships in question were not engaged in commerce.[78]

The Thirteenth Convention of 1907, concerning the Rights and Duties of Neutrals in Naval War, was invoked by Great Britain in the case of the " Appam ", in a protest against the use of a United States harbor as an asylum by a German vessel bringing that ship in as a prize. To the German protest that the British Government had not ratified the convention and therefore could not invoke its provisions, counsel for the British Government replied that the article in question was merely declaratory of existing law as recognized by the United States and other nations generally, and was therefore as binding as any other established customary rule of the law of nations.[79] In 1914 Great Britain protested to Germany against the German method of sowing mines in the North Sea, invoking the provisions of the Eighth Convention dealing with this subject, to which both states were parties, thus indicating her belief that it was in force.[80] She also expressed her intent to maintain in force the principles of the Convention for the Adaptation to Naval Warfare of the Principles of the Geneva Convention of 1864.[81]

On the other hand, Great Britain appears at times to have taken the view that she was not bound by the Hague Conventions. During her discussions with the United States regarding stoppage of the mails she stated that although the Allies expected to be governed in their actions by the prin-

[78] *The Kronprinzessin Cecilie*, March 23, 1916; *Law Times Reports*, May 20, 1916, vol. 114, no. 2949, p. 521 (see Clunet, *Journal de Droit International*, vol. 44, p. 1083).

[79] Brief of British counsel, p. 7; see Garner, *op. cit.*, vol. i, p. 21 (note).

[80] *Ibid.*, p. 23 (note).

[81] *Cf. The Ophelia, Lloyd's Prize Cases*, vol. iii, p. 13; cited in Garner, *Prize Law During the World War* (New York, 1927), p. 244.

ciples of the Eleventh Convention dealing with this matter, it was of doubtful validity, not having been ratified by all the belligerents.[82] Again, when the Dutch Government interned the crew of a British submarine according to the terms of the Tenth Convention, Great Britain protested that the convention was not binding, not having been ratified, and therefore could not be invoked.[83] She was not a party to, and apparently never invoked, the Convention concerning the Right of Capture in Naval Warfare, and there is no indication that she considered herself bound. Yet under the same conditions she proposed to observe the Convention for the Adaptation to Naval Warfare of the Principles of the Geneva Convention,[84] as indicated above. She invoked against Germany the provisions of the Convention regulating Automatic Contact Submarine Mines to which she was a party,[85] yet protested Holland's attempt to apply the convention regulating naval warfare, mentioned above, although the Netherlands was a party, and Great Britain had announced her intent to be governed by its principles.[86]

At the outbreak of the war, certain German writers attempted to defend the violation of Belgian neutrality on the ground that some of the belligerents had not ratified the 1907 Convention concerning the Rights and Duties of Neutrals in War on Land, articles one and two of which relate to the inviolability of neutral territory.[87] But Germany officially failed to avail herself of the ground for suspension specified in the convention, that is, that a non-signatory was participating.[87]

[82] October 12, 1916, Cmd. paper, 8438: Misc. 2:(1917).

[83] Garner, *International Law and the World War*, vol. ii, p. 427.

[84] See note 81 *supra*.

[85] Garner, *op. cit.*, vol. i, p. 23 (note).

[86] Note 81 *supra*.

[87] *Cf.* von Mach, *New York Times*, November 1, 1914, cited by Garner, *loc. cit.*

This accords with her stand the succeeding year that the Fourth Convention of 1907, dealing with Laws and Customs of War on Land, was binding on Germany in spite of the fact that all the belligerents were not parties. The basis for her statement was that the convention expressed principles resulting from an agreement as to what constitutes international law on the subject, and which conserved its force in wartime.[88] Under this same convention, too, Germany maintained the right of enemy aliens to sue and recover in the German courts, though she claimed that she was granting the privilege without reciprocity, as Great Britain was not adopting this policy.[89] Germany further stoutly maintained that she observed this convention during her occupation of Belgium, though the Belgians as stoutly objected to Germany's interpretation of her obligations thereunder.[90]

The German attitude toward the Sixth Convention concerning the Status of Merchant Vessels at the Outbreak of Hostilities was as favorable to its maintenance in force as was the British. In 1914 it was held that the convention "would only cease to be binding if there were among the belligerents any non-signatory which was at the same time a maritime state", and in support of this theory the British interpretation quoted above was cited.[91] Before the declaration of war between Germany and Italy, the two states, after

[88] Supreme Court of Military Justice, August 10, 1915, *Deutsche Juristen Zeitung*, 1916, p. 136, cited in Clunet, *Journal de Droit International*, 1917, p. 257.

[89] Soergel, *Kriegsrechtssprechung und Kriegsrechtslehre* (Berlin, 1916), pp. 99, 111.

[90] *Le magistrature belge contre le despotisme allemand*, pp. 76-84, cited by Garner, *op. cit.*, vol. i, p. 77.

[91] *The Fenix*, Oberprisengericht, December 17, 1914, *Zeitschrift für Völkerrecht*, vol. ix, p. 103.

interpreting its provisions, reached an agreement to apply the convention in case of war between them.[92]

In response to the British protest against alleged violations of the Eight Convention concerning Submarine Mines, and the Ninth Convention, concerning Naval Bombardment, Germany claimed her acts were within the terms of the conventions.[93] She replied to a protest from the United States concerning an alleged violation of the Convention Applying the Rules of the Geneva Convention to Naval Warfare by maintaining that the violation was an error, and did not disavow the convention.[94] But as in the case of Great Britain she sometimes contended that the conventions were not in force; in the case of the "Appam", mentioned above, because Great Britain had not ratified the convention involved,[95] and in the case of a dispute with Norway regarding stoppage of the mails, on the ground that none of the 1907 conventions was binding, as all of the belligerents had not ratified.[96]

Among the other Powers there were frequent manifestations of an intent to give effect to the Hague agreements. The Belgian courts consistently applied the Convention regarding the Laws and Customs of War on Land,[97] and there

[92] Agreement of May 21, 1915; *Revue générale de droit international public*, 1917, Docs. p. 151.

[93] January 4, 1915, *Norddeutsche Allgemeine Zeitung*; Garner, *op. cit.*, vol. i, p. 430 (note).

[94] March 10, 1915, Declaration de l'ambassade de l'Allemagne à Washington, *Revue générale de droit international public*, 1915, p. 137.

[95] Communication to the Secretary of State of the United States, February 22, 1916, Department of State, *Diplomatic Correspondence with Belligerent Governments Relating to Neutral Rights and Duties, European War*, vol. iii, p. 334.

[96] Cmd. paper, 8332: Misc. 28 (1916), p. 9.

[97] *De Brabant et Gosselin c. T. & A. Florent*, July 22, 1920, Cour d'appel de Bruxelles, *Pasicrisie belge*, 1921, vol. ii, p. 182. Also *Procureur général*

appears to have been no disposition on the part of the German authorities to object. China in her declaration of war against Germany and Austria announced her intent to observe the conventions.[98] Guatemala[99] and Salvador[1] in their declarations of neutrality announced their observance of the two neutrality conventions. Austria-Hungary agreed to act under the provisions of the conventions regarding Merchant Ships at the Outbreak of Hostilities,[2] and regarding the Laws and Customs of War on Land.[3]

Even a number of states which were not parties to the conventions accepted as binding the principles expressed in them. The Argentine Republic in its decree relative to the maintenance of neutrality, stated that "the principles of international law accepted by the opinion of writers on the subject and by the practice of nations, are found condensed in the clauses of the convention subscribed to at the Hague", and added that even though the Argentine had not yet ratified the neutrality convention, "such circumstances do not lessen in the least its value as a body of doctrine."[4] Other states while not acknowledging the conventions as statements of international law accepted one or more of them as a rule of action. Both Venezuela[5] and Cuba,[6] in their proclama-

pour la cour d'appel de Liège c. Marteaux, Michaud et consorts et Comte Charles de Borgrave d'Altena, May 20, 1916, Cassation première, *ibid.*, 1917, vol. i, p. 110.

[98] *Brit. & For. State Papers*, vol. 111, p. 680.

[99] August 12, 1914, *ibid.*, vol. 108, p. 822.

[1] December 4, 1914, *Revue générale de droit international public*, 1917, Docs., p. 228.

[2] *Revue générale de droit international public*, 1915, Docs., p. 154.

[3] February, 1915, *Ordonnance du ministère de la guerre, Revue générale de droit international public*, 1915, Docs., pp. 151-2.

[4] August 5, 1914, *Brit. & For. State Papers*, vol. 108, pp. 795-6.

[5] August 8, 1914, *ibid.*, p. 863.

[6] August 5, 1914, *ibid.*, p. 814.

tions of neutrality, embodied the rules of the Convention on the Rights and Duties of Neutral Powers and Persons in Naval Warfare, though Venezuela had not ratified any of the conventions. Uruguay went further and added most of the provisions of the Conventions regarding the Adaptation to Naval Warfare of the Principles of the Geneva Convention, the Conversion of Merchant Ships into Warships, and the Right of Capture in Naval Warfare, although she was not a party to the latter two.[7] Italy, which was not a party to any of the 1907 conventions, announced her intention to observe the provisions of the last two mentioned, insofar as the laws in force in the Kingdom and the other measures taken by the Government permitted.[8] Greece in her neutrality proclamation stated that though she was not a party to either of the neutrality conventions on this subject she would observe them,[9] and Ecuador [10] and Honduras [11] announced their intention to observe them, without mentioning the fact that they were not parties.

But though the Netherlands was a party to both conventions, she made no mention of either in her neutrality proclamation.[12] The United States, which was a party to the convention concerning Rights and Duties of Neutrals in Land Warfare, while not mentioning that fact in her neutrality proclamation, did state that "the laws and treaties of the United States . . . impose . . . an impartial neutrality." [13]

It will be observed that in many cases the principles em-

[7] August 4, 1914, *ibid.*, p. 854.

[8] May 30, 1915, *Brit. & For. State Papers*, vol. 109, p. 965.

[9] July 31, 1914, *Brit. & For. State Papers*, vol. 108, p. 821.

[10] August 17, 1914, *ibid.*, p. 817.

[11] October 5, 1914, *Neutrality Proclamations*, p. 32.

[12] July 30, 1914, August 4, 1914, *Brit. & For. State Papers*, vol. 108, p. 830.

[13] August 4, 1914, November 6, 1914, *ibid.*, pp. 846-854.

bodied in these conventions appear to have been considered as possessing a validity apart from their status as treaty provisions. In some cases there has been a direct statement that the convention is conceived of as a statement of international law, but more often there is merely a declared intent to observe the provisions of the convention without any admission of an obligation to do so. The fact of the very general acceptance at the beginning of the war of the Declaration of London of 1909, which was never in effect as a convention, indicates how valuable such conventions may be as expressions of the general will of states even when they have no legal force whatever as treaties.[14] In the case of the Hague Convention, it would appear to have been the intent of the parties to them that they should be observed as accepted rules governing war operations, so long as conditions remained such as might have been foreseen when the conventions were drafted. The time came, however, when the war assumed proportions and characteristics which could not have been contemplated by the negotiators, and some of the states which were parties to these conventions were thereafter less inclined to observe them and therefore more inclined to avail themselves of the technical excuse provided by the universality clauses of the conventions themselves.

It is difficult to conceive of a possibility of revising such conventions during the course of hostilities, and so long as war continues, its very violence and the sudden and drastic changes it brings are bound to give rise to a sentiment among the parties that the conventions were not intended to meet the strain put upon them. There is an evident disposition to refrain from denunciation during war, but charges of violations of the Hague agreements make it clear that the value of these conventions diminishes as they progressively fail to

[14] Garner, *op. cit.*, vol. i, p. 30.

take account of new methods of warfare and as the war increases in length and intensity. There has been but slight interest taken in these conventions by the new states since the war.

In 1929 a new convention was drawn up restating principles governing the treatment of prisoners of war and setting up new administrative rules, constituting an amendment to the 1907 Convention concerning the Laws and Customs of War on Land.[15] This convention recognized the weakness in the Hague Conventions which rendered their status uncertain during the last war. It stipulates that its provisions shall always be binding as between the parties, regardless of whether non-signatories are included among the belligerents or not,[16] and at the same time by recognizing changes in warfare as indicated by the last struggle, makes enforcement of the convention more feasible. It remains to be seen, however, whether the parties would continue to consider themselves bound in case a non-signatory belligerent should refuse to abide by the convention's provisions. The tendency as noted in the past war to resort to reprisals or even to abide by conventions only where reciprocity was observed would indicate that the new provision may prove little more satisfactory than the old.

TREATIES AUTHORIZING SUSPENSION IN WARTIME

In view of the divergency of opinion concerning the possibility of treaties remaining in force between belligerents in wartime, it is interesting to note that a number of recent treaties contain provisions authorizing suspension either by belligerents alone or by both belligerents and neutrals in wartime.

[15] July 27, 1929; *U. S. Treaty Series,* no. 846.

[16] Art. lxxxii.

The former have in view specific situations which relieve the belligerent from certain of his obligations under the treaty. Such is the Washington Convention for the Limitation of Naval Armament, which states that:

Whenever any Contracting Power shall become engaged in a war which in its opinion affects the naval defense of its national security, such Power may after notice to the other Contracting Powers suspend for the period of hostilities its obligations under the present Treaty . . . provided that such Power shall notify the other Contracting Powers that the emergency is of such a character as to require such suspension. . . .[17]

The Lausanne Treaty of 1923 providing a Régime for the Straits declares that Turkey and Greece shall have the right to suspend their obligations under the treaty. It states that:

If, in case of war, Turkey or Greece, utilizing their right as belligerent states, should be led to modify the state of demilitarization provided above, they would be held to reestablish, as from the conclusion of peace, the régime provided in the present Convention.[18]

The Washington Naval Treaty cited above, also contains a provision releasing neutral signatories in case one of the belligerents invokes a suspension for itself:

The remaining Contracting Powers shall in such case consult together. . . . Should such consultation not produce agreement . . . any one of said Contracting Powers may, by giving notice to the other Contracting Powers, suspend for the period of hostilities its obligations under the present Treaty. . . .[19]

[17] February 6, 1922, art. xxii, Malloy, *Treaties, etc. of the United States*, vol. iii, p. 3100. *Cf. Conference on the Limitation of Armament* (Washington, 1922), 5th Plenary Session, p. 246.

[18] July 24, 1923, *British Treaty Series*, 1923, no. 16, annex 1, art. ix.

[19] Art. xxii, *loc. cit.*

More frequent are the provisions for suspension during wartime by either belligerents or neutrals. Such a provision has been included in many of the postwar communication and transit conventions,[20] in the 1919 Aerial Navigation Convention [21] and the 1928 Pan-American Commercial Aviation agreement,[22] and the 1922 Convention regulating Navigation on the Elbe River.[23] The usual provision states that: "the convention shall, however, continue in force in time of war so far as the rights and duties [of belligerents and neutrals] permit." [24]

The Briand-Kellogg pact provides in its preamble for its own non-application in the relations between a violator and the other signatories, in the following terms:

> Any signatory Power which shall hereafter seek to promote its national interests by resort to war shall be denied the benefits furnished by this treaty.[25]

There are also a few treaties which provide specifically that they shall not be suspended in wartime. Such are the Cape Spartel Convention of 1865, which provides that the neutrality of the light and the contributions for its upkeep are to

20 April 4, 1921, Régime of Navigable Waterways of International Concern, Statute, art. 15, *League of Nations Treaty Series*, vol. vii, p. 36. Similar clauses may be found in the conventions for the Development of Hydraulic Power, the Transmission in Transit of Electric Power, etc.

21 October 13, 1919, art. 38, *League of Nations Treaty Series*, vol. xi, p. 174.

22 February 20, 1928, art. xxix, *U. S. Treaty Series*, no. 840.

23 February 22, 1922, art. xlix, *Brit. & For. State Papers*, vol. 116, p. 598.

24 The convention of June 28, 1930, regulating the Hours of Work in Commerce and Offices, states in art. ix that its provisions may be suspended by any country "in the event of war or other emergency endangering national safety." (*International Labor Conf.*, vol. i, pt. iii, p. 877).

25 August 27, 1928, *U. S. Treaty Series*, no. 796, preamble.

continue even in case of war between the parties, or between any of them and Morocco.[26] Parts IV and V of the General Act of Berlin of 1885 stipulate that "the provisions of the present Act of Navigation shall remain in force in time of war", and freedom of navigation for all nations, whether neutral or belligerent, is preserved on the Congo and Niger Rivers, for purposes of trade.[27]

The important question in the case of the treaties cited is whether the parties considered it necessary to provide as they did for or against suspension; or in other words whether they conceived of these treaties as being exceptions to a general rule on the subject, and therefore believed some provision was necessary in order to exempt these conventions from the operation of that rule.

In the case of the Straits Convention the provision cited was inserted in order to reassure Turkey, whose constant preoccupation during the conference was that there might be an attempt to diminish her sovereign right of self-defense. Lord Curzon, the British delegate, stated that the provision "embodied the sacred right of national defense in the event of war", that in such an event Turkey should "enjoy complete freedom to utilize all the means at its disposal for the purpose of assuring the safety of its territory." He emphasized throughout the discussion Turkey's "right" to modify the regime, and none of the other delegates appear to have taken any exception to his view.[28]

In the case of the Washington naval treaty there is less leeway for the belligerent. Suspension is not described as a

[26] May 31, 1865, art. iii, Malloy, *Treaties, etc. of the U. S.*, vol. i, p. 1217.

[27] February 26, 1885, art. xxxiii, *Brit. & For. State Papers*, vol. 76, p. 4.

[28] *Lausanne Conference on Near Eastern Affairs*, Cmd. Paper 1814: Turkey, no. 1 (1923), pp. 139, 149, 233, 264.

" right ", and can take place only after notification and when the belligerent considers that an emergency requires such suspension. In the Pact of Paris discussions, however, the original parties to that instrument expressed themselves unequivocally to the effect that every treaty implied the right to act in self-defense, and that every State had the right to determine whether circumstances called for recourse to war.[29] The German Government considered it "self-evident that if one state violates the pact the other contracting parties regain their freedom of action with reference to that state." It was considered unnecessary to provide for such a contingency " in a pact of this kind." [30] The United States held the same view, but specified that such suspension applied to a " multilateral anti-war treaty " rather than to the more vague German phrase, " a pact of this kind." [31] Japan,[32] Czechoslovakia,[33] Canada [34] and South Africa [35] expressed agreement with the conception that violation by a signatory released the others from their obligations to that signatory, but failed to express themselves on the necessity of including such a clause in the treaty. The French urged its inclusion for the sake of precision of the obligation of the signatories, and the British Government was " not satisfied that if the treaty stood alone the addition of some such provision would

[29] *Cf.* United States note of June 23, 1928 to other Governments, *Notes Exchanged between the United States and Other Powers on the subject of a Multilateral Treaty for the Renunciation of War* (U. S. Govt. Printing Office, 1928).

[30] April 27, 1928, *ibid.*, p. 20.

[31] *Ibid.*, p. 27.

[32] July 20, 1928, *Ibid.*, p. 49.

[33] *Ibid.*, p. 48.

[34] May 30, 1928, *ibid.*, p. 31.

[35] June 15, 1928, *ibid.*, p. 33.

not be necessary."[36] It was finally included in the preamble, without settling the question whether it was merely explanatory or actually did modify the extent of the obligations of the signatories.[37]

The clause commonly used in the communication and transit conventions, quoted above, occasioned some little discussion at the Barcelona Conference in 1921. "The rights and duties of belligerents and neutrals" had been defined to a limited extent by the Hague Conventions of 1899 and 1907, but as has been indicated the definitions even in a limited field had proved unsatisfactory. As in the case of the discussions of the Pact of Paris, France was anxious for greater precision. The French delegate claimed that the negotiators of the convention had always had in mind a state of peace, and he did not think that there was an intent to maintain the convention in force on the outbreak of war. He described the physical difficulties of maintenance in view of the widespread character of modern warfare and of the fact that transportation passed under military control in wartime. He felt, however, that while release from the treaty's obligations was to be supposed in the case of belligerents, and of those neutrals near the seat of war, neutrals which by reason of distance from the war area were not affected should not be so released.[38] The Swedish delegate also felt that more

[36] *Ibid.*, p. 24.

[37] In interpreting a clause in the 1884 Submarine Cables Convention (Malloy, *Treaties, etc. of the U. S.*, vol. ii, p. 1949), to the effect that a belligerent was free to act as if the convention did not exist, the representative of the British Government stated that "... he was not prepared to say that a belligerent on the ground of military necessity would under no circumstances be justified in interfering with cables between the territory of the opposing Power and any other part of the world." This liberty of action, however, is confined to belligerents (art. xv of the convention).

[38] Barcelona Conference, *Verbatim Report* (Geneva, 1921), p. 105.

precision was essential. He contended that either the clause merely stated the existence of obligations already acknowledged, and was therefore redundant, or it involved fresh obligations, and in that case their exact scope should be known.[39]

The subject was referred to a subcommittee, which left the clause in its original state, but recommended that the League of Nations draw up new conventions defining the rights and duties of belligerents and neutrals in wartime, and in this form the clause was adopted.[40] In the case of the 1923 conventions regarding the International Regime of Railways,[41] of Maritime Ports,[42] the Development of Hydraulic Power,[43] and the Transmission in Transit of Electric Power,[44] the clause was inserted without discussion or explanation.

It appears from the discussion at the Barcelona conference that the parties intended that these conventions should survive in wartime, but that observance of their provisions might be suspended to as great a degree as required by the rights and duties of belligerents and neutrals. It is also evident that there was no agreement as to what extent those rights and obligations would warrant suspension and that there was a desire to arrive at a more complete understanding on the subject.

The 1919 Aerial Navigation Convention stipulates that " in case of war the provisions of the present Convention shall not affect the freedom of action of the Contracting States

[39] *Ibid.*, p. 107.

[40] *Ibid.*, p. 147.

[41] December 9, 1923, Statute, art. 32, *League of Nations Treaty Series*, vol. 47, p. 55.

[42] *Ibid.*, Statute, art. 18, *ibid.*, vol. 58, p. 285.

[43] *Ibid.*, art. ix, vol. 36, p. 76.

[44] *Ibid.*, art. xi, vol. 58, p. 315.

either as belligerents or as neutrals ",[45] and the same provision appears in the Pan-American Convention on Commercial Aviation.[46] The provision was held by the Judicial Subcommittee of the 1919 conference to mean that the parties to the convention " regained their independence of action in order to assure the protection and safeguard of their interests and their rights, without being restrained in any manner by any of the dispositions of the Convention." [47] Broad as this statement appears, it does not justify complete suspension of the convention, unless the parties take the protection of their rights and interests to involve such a complete suspension. The delegates to the conference apparently acquiesced in the subcommission's interpretation, as there was no further discussion.

The most specific explanation of the method by which a neutral is released from his obligations in wartime occurs in the Washington naval treaty. In case a belligerent suspends the convention:

> The remaining Contracting Powers shall in such case consult together. . . . Should such consultation not produce agreement . . . any one of said Contracting Powers may, by giving notice to the other Contracting Powers, suspend for the period of hostilities its obligations under the present Treaty. . . .[48]

But this convention stands alone; no such exact interpretation appears to have been made elsewhere.[49] In the dis-

[45] October 13, 1919, art. 38, *ibid.*, vol. xi, p. 174.

[46] February 20, 1928, art. xxix, *U. S. Treaty Series*, no. 840.

[47] Roper, *Convention aérienne internationale du 13 octobre, 1919* (Paris, 1930), p. 187.

[48] Art. 22.

[49] *Cf.* art. 18 of the convention establishing a régime for the Straits (July 24, 1923, Hudson, *International Legislation* (Washington, 1931-32), vol. ii, p. 1038). This clause does not, however, authorize suspension

cussions of the various communications and transit conventions the only suggested basis for suspension by neutrals was that mentioned above, namely, nearness to the theater of war.

The following conclusions may be drawn from the provisions and discussions above; first, that States have frequently claimed the right to suspend the execution of treaty provisions in the name of self-defence, though the other parties to such a treaty are rarely disposed to grant such a right; second, that the rights and duties of belligerents and neutrals may warrant suspension, and in some cases it is definitely provided that they shall do so; third, that in the majority of cases there is little agreement among States as to the extent of the rights and duties of either belligerents or neutrals which would warrant suspension; fourth, that there is hesitancy in committing a definition of such rights and duties to paper in the form of treaty stipulations; and fifth, that in the absence of treaty provision to that effect the outbreak of war does not *ipso facto* terminate or even suspend treaties.

TREATIES OF PEACE

It has frequently been held that a subsequent war between the parties to a treaty of peace terminated the executory provisions of such a treaty. In the main such provisions in bipartite instruments have not been considered in force, but such a statement is subject to much more general exception in connection with multipartite conventions.

There are several reasons for this. In the first place multipartite peace treaties are not homogeneous; they almost uniformly have a great variety of questions to settle. Some of these questions are settled by provisions involving a bargain

by any of the parties, but gives the Council the right to decide upon means to combat a violation, attack or other act of war or threat of war, which might involve suspension of the convention in whole or in part.

between the parties, and such provisions may be terminated by a war in which all the parties involved in the settlement are belligerents. Other provisions set up regulations which bind all the signatories alike; such provisions may not even be suspended.[50] A multipartite peace treaty may be bilateral, as was the treaty of Versailles; in such a case a war between two of the obligee States would probably have no effect on the reciprocal rights and obligations of either with the obligor state. Subsequent wars between the parties to a peace treaty frequently arise from questions concerning its provisions, and if such are executory, execution is generally at least suspended.

It is thus difficult to discover any general rule which may be applied to the status of peace-treaty provisions in wartime, even as between belligerents. Such provisions must be considered separately, according to their nature, and according to the effect of wars of differing extent and duration.

BOUNDARY TREATIES

There appears to be unanimous opinion that war has no effect on boundary provisions either during or subsequent to hostilities. Text writers are practically unanimous on this point;[51] the character of boundary provisions would appear to prevent any other conception.[52] When a treaty specifies the line a boundary is to follow and that line has been determined by surveyors the power of the treaty in that connection

[50] *Cf.* treaty between Louis XIV and the Great Elector, 1679, in section concerning the Public Law of Europe, *infra.* p. 52.

[51] Halleck, *International Law,* Baker's ed. (London, 1908), p. 307, quoted in Moore, *Digest,* vol. v, p. 382. *Cf.* also von Martens, *A compendium of the law of nations,* Cobbett's ed. (London, 1802), p. 56.

[52] But see Bathurst's statement, 1815, *supra,* note 17. Territorial provisions were to suffer the same fate as the others; the reason for inserting new provisions in the treaty of Ghent was that the whole 1783 treaty had been terminated. Adams, however, refuted this claim.

has been exhausted, and whatever the subsequent fate of the treaty the boundary line is thenceforth independent of it.[53]

This conception appears to have received uniform acceptance by States as well as by text writers. There has been no claim seriously made by any State in modern times, either during the course of a war or thereafter, that the outbreak of war operated to cancel an antecedent treaty provision establishing a boundary. Even where territory has been conquered and occupied, no state appears to have considered that such occupation affected treaty provisions concerning the frontiers of such territory, until such time as the conquest was confirmed by subsequent treaty.[54]

This rule appears to be independent of the number of states indicating their acceptance of a frontier by treaty. The fact that the frontier between France and Germany was established in 1871 by those two Powers alone would not seem to have made the frontier provision of the treaty of Frankfort any less binding during the war than for example the frontier provisions in the 1878 treaty which drew the frontier lines of the Ottoman Empire, and to which all the Great Powers were parties. In neither case was there any official claim that war had any effect on the treaty provision for drawing the line, nor on the line itself.

[53] During the war of 1914-18 certain irresponsible French writers and speakers claimed that the outbreak of war had annulled the treaty of Frankfort, and that Alsace-Lorraine thus automatically returned to France. But the French Government and the French courts appear to have given no countenance to such a thesis. *Cf.* Miller, *Diary*, vol. iii, pp. 39-40.

[54] During the course of the war Belgium demanded a return of the territory of Luxemburg and Limburg taken away from her in 1839, but this claim was based on Germany's violation of the 1839 treaties, and not on the outbreak of war between the parties to them, an event which had taken place in 1866 and in 1870 without giving rise to such a claim.

TREATIES INVOLVING THE PUBLIC LAW OF EUROPE

The concept of a Public Law of Europe, though perhaps not consciously entertained by those who first expressed it, appears to have its foundation in the general settlement of Westphalia, though it was not then mentioned by name. This treaty between the Emperor, the states of the Empire and the King of France provided that the religious and territorial settlement should " serve as perpetual law, and as Pragmatic Sanction in the Empire, and obligate those absent no less than those present, ecclesiastics as well as seculars, whether states of the Empire or not." [55] That this settlement continued in force in wartime as in peacetime was made clear in the treaty of 1679 between Louis XIV and the Elector of Brandenburg, in which the former declared that "as the treaties of Westphalia should always be regarded as the most solid and assured basis of peace and tranquility in the Empire ", his intention was " to maintain them in all their force, even in wartime ", and the King of Sweden and the Elector testified to the same intent.[56]

The development of the idea of the Public Law of Europe became more tangible during the nineteenth century. The coalition which overthrew Napoleon was faced with the task of setting up a new order in Europe, which it accomplished by the General Act of the Conference of Vienna, with the Annexes attached. With the addition of France after 1818, assured by the treaty of Aix-la-Chapelle,[57] the five Powers, Great Britain, France, Prussia, Austria and Russia, continued to preside over Europe's destinies, and with the addi-

[55] October 24, 1648, treaty of Münster; Dumont, *Corps diplomatique universel,* vol. vi, pt. i, p. 450.

[56] June 29, 1679, art. iv, Dumont, *op. cit.,* vol. vii, pt. i, p. 408.

[57] October 9, 1818, Hertslet, *Map of Europe by Treaty* (London, 1875-91), vol. i, p. 557.

tion of Italy from 1856[58] maintained their control of the affairs of the continent until the war of 1914-18. These Powers took part in all the general settlements made during this period, even, as in 1856, when they were on opposing sides in a war, constituting themselves a sort of legislative body for Europe during the period in question.[58a]

They used various means for assuring the continuing validity of these arrangements. Sometimes the treaty arrived at contained no special provision testifying to the particular interest of the signatories. Sometimes a guaranty was attached to the entire treaty, as that of the five Powers to the 1839 settlement of the Belgian question,[59] or that of France, Great Britain and Austria to the 1856 treaty at the end of the Crimean war.[60] Sometimes certain provisions only were put under guaranty. In the case of the Danube navigation provisions of the treaty of Paris in 1856, it was indicated that these formed "part of the public law of Europe."[61] In general, the purpose of these provisions was to serve as a mutual assurance that the clauses in question would be respected, and as a warning to other states that any violation would involve the concerted action of the Great Powers.

Specific use of the term "Public Law of Europe" in treaties appears to be confined to the treaty of Paris of 1856. Here it was applied in Article XV to the provision which extended to the Danube and its mouths the arrangements of the General Act of Vienna concerning rivers which traverse

[58] The kingdom of Sardinia, Italy's predecessor, participated in the general settlement at the close of the Crimean war.

[58a] See *Fontes juris gentium*, ser. b, sec. i, pp. 970-5.

[59] Treaties between the five Powers and Belgium and Holland respectively, *Brit. & For. State Papers*, vol. 27, pp. 990, 1000.

[60] April 15, 1856, Hertslet, *op. cit.*, vol. ii, p. 1280.

[61] March 30, 1856, art. xv, *Brit. & For. State Papers*, vol. 46, p. 8.

or separate two or more states. The contracting Powers stated that this extension of the principle " henceforth forms part of the Public Law of Europe " and took it under their guaranty. It will be noted that the idea of a general guaranty and that of the Public Law of Europe are here tied together. But in the Treaty of Berlin of 1878, the Powers, in drawing up new regulations for navigation on the Danube, stated that their purpose was " to increase the guarantees which assure the freedom of navigation on the Danube which is recognized as of European interest ",[62] without using the term " Public Law of Europe " but approximating it to provisions which were of European interest, and again bringing in the idea of a guaranty.

Article VII of the 1856 treaty connects even more closely the idea of the Public Law of Europe and a guaranty. It states that Great Britain, France, Austria, Prussia and Sardinia " declare the Sublime Porte admitted to participate in the advantages of the Public Law and System (*Concert*) of Europe. Their Majesties engage, each on his part, to respect the Independence and the Territorial Integrity of the Ottoman Empire; Guarantee in common the strict observance of that engagement; and will, in consequence, consider any act tending to its violation as a question of general interest." It would appear then to indicate that the significance of the phrases was the body of principles by which the Great Powers proposed to be bound in the conduct of the general affairs of Europe. The observance of these principles they appear to have intended to guarantee to each other.

During the peace conference in 1919, Clemenceau threw additional light on what the Public Law of Europe signified, again tying it up with the idea of a European guaranty. The occasion for this explanation was a letter written to Paderewski regarding the minorities provisions in the treaty estab-

[62] July 13, 1878, Hertslet, *op. cit.*, vol. iv, p. 2759, art. 52.

lishing the Polish state. It had been "the established procedure of the public law of Europe", he said, that recognition of new states, or large acquisition of territory by an established state, should be accompanied by a convention between the state affected and the Great Powers, stipulating that the former should undertake to comply with certain principles of government. He admitted that such conventions contained the dangerous possibility of giving the Great Powers the right to interfere in the internal affairs of the state concerned, and recognized that the guaranty of such principles in future would be entrusted to the League of Nations.[63]

We arrive again at the close connection between the concept of the Public Law of Europe and the idea of an international guaranty, whether the provisions which are supposed to form part of that law involve territorial settlements, recognition of new states, principles governing the control of international rivers, or the revision of treaties. It would appear to be essential, therefore, to determine the significance of such international guaranties in order to appreciate correctly the scope of the phrase, and thus to determine whether those treaty stipulations covered by such an expression have any added validity beyond those not protected by its use.

TREATIES OF GUARANTY

While the designation "treaty of guaranty" has been common enough during the past three centuries, its significance has not always been clear. Usually such a treaty has consisted of clauses dealing with a variety of subjects, but containing somewhere in its provisions a guaranty of some or all of the treaty's stipulations or else of a dynasty, a title to territory or something else with which the treaty itself

[63] Miller, *Diary of the Peace Conference*, vol. xiii, p. 215.

does not deal. The treaty containing merely a guaranty and dealing with no other subject is very rare.

The seventeenth-century guaranty was generally specific in its nature. Its most frequent use was to insure the terms of a treaty between a weak and a strong state against breach by the latter, in the interest of general peace. There was usually an explicit statement of just what the obligation of the guarantor was in case of violation, sometimes even a stipulation as to the exact number of foot and horse he was to provide.[64]

During the eighteenth century the character of treaties of guaranty changed. The old definiteness of obligation disappeared and the variety of objects and provisions to which the guaranty applied was greatly increased. It is frequently difficult to differentiate between a guaranty and an alliance in these treaties, due to the fact that a mutual guaranty as between allies was included as part of the terms of the treaty creating the alliance.[65] The guaranties during this century covered such varied objects as part or all of the dispositions of treaties, dynasties, religious rights, cession, liberty and tranquillity, security, neutrality, and a variety of other matters as indefinite in character as some of the above.

In the nineteenth-century guaranties the indefiniteness of obligation noted in the preceding century is equally marked, as is the wide variety of objects of guaranty. The number of guaranteeing Powers increased, however, as the Concert of Europe took more definite form, and the frequency with which guaranties were resorted to appears to have diminished, due perhaps to the fact that all the Great Powers were gen-

[64] *Cf.* League of Augsburg, July 9, 1686, Dumont, *op. cit.*, vol. vii, pt. ii, p. 131.

[65] *Cf.* treaty between France, Great Britain, and Prussia, of September 3, 1725, art. v; *ibid.*, vol. viii, pt. ii, p. 127, containing a promise of mutual aid of an unspecified kind, to maintain the treaties of Westphalia and others.

erally parties to the important settlements of European affairs, and there was therefore less need to set up guaranties against any one of these Powers.

Since 1919, where guaranties have been resorted to, there has been much more detail both as to the nature and extent of the guaranty and the provision for means to carry it into effect, apparently a wholesome return to the custom of the seventeenth century. There is also an evident attempt to avoid the former habit of guaranteeing all the terms of a treaty, and to confine the guaranty to that of the inviolability of territory or frontiers, thus avoiding one of the main difficulties of the past century,—namely, of determining what constituted a violation of the guaranty.

In considering the effect of war on so-called treaties of guaranty it must be kept in mind, as indicated above that the usual form of a guaranty is one or more stipulations in a treaty involving other matters, and that it is only the question of the effect of war on the guaranty stipulated in the treaty which is of interest here, and not the fate of the rest of the treaty. Where the guaranty protects merely other treaty provisions, this will necessitate a distinction between the effect of war on the guaranty as distinct from its effect on the provisions guaranteed. It is also necessary to determine to whom the parties intended the guaranty to be given, and whether they intended either the treaty or the guaranty to continue in effect during wartime.

In general the status of the seventeenth- and many of the eighteenth-century guaranty treaties in wartime presents no difficult problem. They were generally directed against a specific Power, and called for common action in view of a prospective aggression which usually took place before the lapse of any very long period. The succeeding treaty of peace generally involved a new grouping of forces, in which the earlier guaranty found no place. Marked exception to these rules were the guaranties of the Westphalia and Utrecht arrangements. It appears to have been the general intent to maintain these two treaties as bases of each new peace settlement of the succeeding century, except as modified in the new settlements themselves.[66] But the guaranties included in the new settlements are new guaranties, the old apparently having been considered to require renewal after the war.

In only one case apparently was provision made that a guaranty was to survive a war between the parties, and that occurred in the guaranty of the Pacification of Geneva, by Berne, France and Sardinia in 1782,[67] in which it was specifically provided that war between two or all three of the guarantors was not to affect the obligations under the guaranty, which were to be carried out under rules carefully set forth in the treaty. The guaranty of any such arrangement or object outside of the territory or jurisdiction of the guarantors is capable of surviving an armed combat between the guarantors, and, as will be seen in the case of the nineteenth century guaranties, frequently did survive. The often expressed view that a treaty of guaranty could not survive such a struggle appears to have been based on the treaties of mutual guaranty of territory or dynasty, which partake more of the nature of alliance than of guaranty, and which, being incompatible with the prosecution of the war, did not survive. This criterion, compatibility with the prosecution of the war, while capable of wide differences of interpretation, is nevertheless useful.

The most common type of guaranty during the past century has been that of the neutralized status of certain states. It has been given in various forms, sometimes, as in the case

[66] *Cf.* art. ii of the treaty of Peace of February 10, 1763; Wenck, *Codex iuris gentium* (Leipzig, 1795), vol. iii, p. 329.

[67] Treaty of November 12, 1782, art. ii, Martens, *Recueil de traités*, vol. ii, p. 303.

of Belgium in 1839, as part of a guaranty of all the terms of a treaty containing the neutralization provision; sometimes specifically, as in the case of Luxemburg, in 1867, but without any clear indication of what action it was necessary to take; sometimes as in the case of the Aaland Islands, in 1921, with a definite statement of just what action was to be undertaken in case of violation. As the principal value of a guaranty of neutrality is its ability to survive in wartime, it is worth noting the effect of war on such instruments.

The guaranty of Belgium, as mentioned above, was part of a guaranty of all the terms of a treaty containing provisions also for demilitarization of Antwerp, a régime for the Scheldt River navigation, and a variety of territorial arrangements. The purpose of the guaranty was implied to be the assurance to Belgium of her independence and future existence, the protection of England against having a strong Power across the Channel, and the prevention of any French expansion in Belgium's direction.[68] Presumably because an explanation of what action would be required to maintain the treaty in force under the guaranty would have involved great political difficulties, no attempt was made to settle this question when the treaty was drawn up. In the Crimean and Austro-Prussian Wars, guarantors of the treaty were opposing belligerents, but in both cases the seat of the war was far from Belgium, and apparently the question of the status of the guaranty did not arise. But with the threat to the guaranty involved in the Franco-Prussian War, Great Britain took steps to discover, if possible, the in-

[68] January 27, 1831, Protocol of conference, *Brit. & For. State Papers*, vol. 18, p. 765. The early protocols of the 1831 conference which established the guaranty were quite specific. They stated it to be a guaranty of perpetual neutrality, integrity and inviolability. (*Cf.* protocols of January 20, February 19, and April 17.) In the final text the words "integrity and inviolability" do not appear, and the guaranty is extended to cover all the terms of the treaty.

terpretation of her co-signatories as to the extent of their obligation, confining her interest, however, to that under the neutralization provision. France and Prussia thereupon each entered into a treaty with Great Britain, providing for respect for Belgium's neutrality on a basis of reciprocity, and indicating clearly that they considered the guaranty in force throughout the war.[69] In 1914, in response to a similar query, Great Britain failed to obtain a definite interpretation of her obligation from Germany, though France gave the same interpretation she had given in 1870.[70] During the course of the war, in 1916, the ministers to Belgium of France, Great Britain and Russia, as representatives of the guaranteeing governments, assured Belgium of their intent to restore her to her old boundaries, an act which apparently was intended to constitute a recognition that the guaranty was still in existence during the war.[71]

It is evident that this guaranty was not even suspended by the wars to which it was subjected. Although one of the original purposes of the guaranty, namely, to prevent French aggression toward the north, appeared to have lost some of its significance, its principal aim, that of preventing an upset of the balance of power in this region, had not changed, and the British purpose of preventing the access of a strong Power to the Channel opposite Great Britain, and the assurance to Belgium of her future existence, were no less important ninety years after they were announced than at that time. The consent to the termination of the old guaranty appears to have been obtained only when the assurance under the old treaties was no longer sufficient to satisfy either Belgium or her former guarantors, and when a more

[69] Hansard, *Parliamentary Debates*, Commons, vol. lxv, col. 1818. Also *Brit. & For. State Papers*, vol. 60, pp. 10, 13.

[70] Cmd. paper, 7627: Misc. no. 12 (1914).

[71] *Revue générale de droit international public*, 1916 Docs., p. 126.

satisfactory guaranty had been substituted in the Locarno agreements.[72]

The guaranty of Luxemburg's neutrality, in 1867, appears to have been given by the Great Powers to induce Prussia's withdrawal of her garrisons from that territory and to end the possibility of France's acquiring possession of it.[73] There was a definite statement in this case that the guaranty was one of respect, and it was not tied up with any other provisions, as in the case of Belgium. Its history is similar to that of Belgium's guaranty; it was not affected by wars between its guarantors, but was terminated only when the events of the period of 1914-18 showed that it was no longer effective as an instrument to carry out the aim of the parties.

The third type of neutrality guaranty is that which describes in detail the nature of the guaranty and the means for applying it. An example of this sort is the Aaland Islands convention of 1921.[74] In 1856 Russia agreed, in a treaty signed also by France and Great Britain, that no military or naval establishment should be created or maintained on these islands,[75] but no direct guaranty of this undertaking was given by the other signatories. (There existed, however, a roundabout guaranty; this treaty was made part of the peace treaty of the same date,[76] all the terms of which were guaranteed by France, Great Britain and Austria.)[77] The 1856 convention was violated, however, by Russia dur-

[72] Treaty of Mutual Guaranty, October 16, 1925, preamble, *Brit. & For. State Papers*, vol. 121, p. 923.

[73] Putnam, *Luxemburg and her Neighbors*, p. 351 *et seq.*

[74] Non-fortification and Neutralization of the Aaland Islands, October 20, 1921, *League of Nations Treaty Series*, vol. ix, p. 211.

[75] Treaty of March 30, 1856, Hertslet, *Map of Europe by Treaty*, vol. ii, p. 1272, art. i.

[76] Treaty of Peace, same date, art. xxxiii, *ibid.*, p. 1250.

[77] Treaty concerning the Independence and Integrity of the Ottoman Empire, April 15, 1856, art. ii, *ibid.*, p. 1280.

ing the war of 1914-18, though the fortifications she then erected were later destroyed. There was a question whether Russia's obligations passed to Finland, the new owner under the peace treaties,[78] and in order to clarify the situation a new convention was drawn up in 1921, signed by the " interested Powers ", namely, the Baltic states (except Lithuania and Russia) and Great Britain, France and Italy. The aim of the new convention was to remove the obscurities of the 1856 agreement mentioned above, " without prejudice thereto." [79] It provides for non-fortification of the islands no matter in whom title rests, and stipulates that it shall remain in force in wartime, the Council of the League to decide upon the measures to be taken in case of violation.

It is clear from this Aaland Islands Convention that it is to be neither suspended nor terminated in time of war, and the course which the guarantors are to pursue is stipulated in case the guaranty is threatened. A treaty as meticulously drawn as this obviates most of the difficulties inherent in the other two types, but due to the fact that in this case there was practical unanimity as to the course to be pursued and as to the need of pursuing it, there was less difficulty in being specific. The more delicate political situations involved in the cases of Belgium and Luxemburg rendered such exactitude much more difficult.

Guaranties of independence and territorial integrity have been set up usually by strong states for the benefit of a weak one, in order to prevent control or absorption of the latter by one of their own number. The most frequent occasion for such guaranties has been when the Ottoman Empire or some of the states broken off from it have been threatened. Dur-

[78] Report of Committee of Jurists, *League of Nations Official Journal*, 1920, *Special Supplement No. 3*, p. 17.

[79] October 20, 1921, Preamble, *League of Nations Treaty Series*, vol. ix, p. 212.

ing the forties and fifties of the last century France, Austria and Great Britain were constantly preoccupied with the fear of the possible dismemberment of the Ottoman Empire by Russia, and when the Crimean War broke out over this question they determined that the integrity of that empire should be one of the bases of peace.[80] The Treaty of Paris therefore contained a common guaranty to respect the independence and territorial integrity of the Ottoman Empire, and it was declared that any violation of such guaranty would be a matter of common interest.[81] It is probable that this guaranty was not affected by the wars of 1859, 1866 and 1870 between the guarantors, chiefly because the theater of the war in each case was far from the Ottoman Empire, and Near Eastern politics were not an issue in these wars. The interest of the guarantors in the maintenance of the guaranty appears to have waned during the seventies, since Russia was able to obtain their consent to a new war, which, it was plain to see, was bound to affect at least the territorial integrity of the Empire.[82] Though when the full extent of her intended impairment became evident there was protest and even a threat of war, there was no appeal to the guaranty, but only to the treaty, and in any case by 1877 when the war broke out, the guaranty had lost its value, as indicated above.

The guaranty of Greece by the Powers was more durable. It resulted from a treaty signed in 1827 by Great Britain, France and Russia,[83] providing for joint measures to end the Greco-Turkish war. This treaty provided that any of the

[80] April 9, 1854, Protocol of Conference, including declaration of war, Hertslet, *op. cit.*, vol. ii, p. 1191.

[81] Art. vii.

[82] Phillipson and Buxton, *Question of Bosphorus and Dardanelles* (London, 1917), p. 132 *et seq.* Also Debidour, *Histoire diplomatique de l'Europe* (Paris, 1891), vol. ii, p. 500 *et seq.*

[83] July 6, 1827, Hertslet, *op. cit.*, vol. i, p. 769.

three Powers might if they chose guarantee any of the stipulations of the treaty which should eventually be drawn up at the end of the conflict. In 1832 this provision was carried out in the form of a new treaty guaranteeing Greece as a monarchical and independent state under the sovereignty of Prince Otho of Bavaria.[84] The guaranty apparently survived the Crimean War without being questioned, as it was subsequently appealed to by King Otho without having been confirmed after the war, and was replaced in 1863 by a similar guaranty, the old one being specifically mentioned.[85]

The new treaty substituted Prince William of Denmark for Otho of Bavaria. The succeeding year a new treaty guaranteed Greece, including the newly annexed territory of the Ionian Islands, as a constitutional as well as a monarchical and independent state.[86] This new guaranty was never subjected to a war between the guarantors, but was not suspended by the war of 1914-18 when the guarantors were co-belligerents. In 1916 the French, Russian and British Governments, as the " guaranteeing Powers of Greece ", sent a joint note to the Greek Government, protesting against the actions of that Government on the grounds that they were a menace to the constitutional nature of the Government, guaranteed by the protecting Powers.[87]

It is questionable whether the guarantor Powers intended the guaranty to survive beyond the period when Greece's existence and political stability were still insecure. It is probable, however, that the early guaranty remained in force during war between the guarantors when the guaranty was not one of the issues of the war, and the later guaranty during a war of a general character when the guarantors were co-belligerents.

[84] May 7, 1832, *op. cit.*, vol. ii, p. 895.

[85] July 13, 1863, *ibid.*, p. 1545.

[86] March 29, 1864, *ibid.*, vol. iii, p. 1589.

[87] June 21-23, 1916, *Brit. & For. State Papers*, vol. 110, p. 890.

A less common type of guaranty in modern times is that of all the terms of a treaty. In the seventeenth century, as has been indicated, it was more common. An early instance of this type of guaranty appeared in 1608 when Great Britain, France and the States-General entered into a treaty by which Great Britain guaranteed the observance of the terms of a projected treaty of peace between the States-General and Spain.[88] The purpose was to prevent evasion or violation of the treaty by Spain, a Great Power. The treaties of Westphalia contain similar guaranties by Sweden and France of the terms of the agreement between the Emperor and the Protestant princes.[89] The treaty of Ryswick of 1697 between France and Holland contains a guaranty of the terms of the treaty by the King of Sweden "and all other Princes and Potentates who have a mind to come into the same engagement",[90] and the treaty between France and Spain of the same date contains the same guaranty.[91] The purpose of these guaranties was to protect the weaker of the parties against a possible evasion or violation of the treaty's terms by the stronger. In the first of these mentioned, there was also a provision for the nature and the extent of the aid which Great Britain was to render in case of violation.[92] More commonly the guaranty served as a warning to the stronger state that the guarantors would have to be dealt with in case of violation.

This type of guaranty is rarer in modern times. An instance is the 1839 settlement concerning Belgium, already

[88] Headlam-Morley, *Studies in Diplomatic History* (London, 1930), p. 107 (art. ii of treaty).

[89] Dumont, *Corps diplomatique universel*, vol. vi, pt. i, pp. 450, 495, 562; Koch, *Table des traités*, vol. i, p. 175.

[90] Sept. 20, 1697, Dumont, *op. cit.*, vol. vii, pt. ii, p. 381, art. 20.

[91] Dumont, *op. cit.*, vol. vii, pt. ii, p. 408.

[92] Art. iii.

mentioned. The guaranteed treaty was drawn up between Belgium and Holland, and then all its provisions were guaranteed to each of these states by the five Great Powers. The exact nature and extent of the guaranty was not specified, consisting merely of the statement that the treaty's terms were "placed under the guarantee of Their Said Majesties." [93]

Another example of a blanket guaranty of all the provisions of a treaty appears in an agreement between France, Great Britain and Austria guaranteeing all the provisions of the treaty of peace of 1856 at the end of the Crimean War, and agreeing that any violation should constitute a *casus belli*. A guaranty of the same type was that given by Austria, Prussia and Russia to Great Britain, covering all the terms of the treaty which set up the British protectorate over the Ionian Islands in 1815.[94]

It is difficult to determine the effect of war on modern treaties of this type. It is evident in the case of the Belgian guaranty that the parties to the treaties of guaranty intended that war between the parties need not affect the guaranty. Though there was no such clear explanation of the will of the parties to the Treaty of Paris and Ionian Islands guaranties as occurred in the case of Belgium in 1870, there is no reason to suppose that war between the parties to the latter guaranties was intended to affect the guaranty any more than in the former case. It would have been impossible for Austria, in a war with France for instance, to terminate her guaranty of the Ionian Islands treaty in regard to France without affecting also her obligation toward England, a result to which England would be almost certain to object. But as there was no attempt on the part of any of the guarantors to take such action it is impossible to state what the result of such action would have been. It is plain, however, that it

[93] Art. ii.

[94] Hertslet, *op. cit.*, vol. i, p. 337, art. ii.

in spite of the guaranty of the Treaty of Paris, Russia had ceased to grant most favored nation treatment to either Austria or France while they were at war with each other, the other might have considered its guaranty of that provision at least as suspended or terminated without affecting its obligations to Great Britain, the other guarantor. Such an instance merely makes plain the varying value of a guaranty of an entire treaty, and the wisdom of clear definition of just what a guaranty involves.

A guaranty of respect for a principle, such as that which forbade the entrance of foreign ships of war into the Dardanelles or Bosphorus when the Porte was at peace, is more definite and less open to ambiguous interpretation than those of all the terms of a treaty, as described above. This principle was announced in its definite form in 1840, the Great Powers engaging to respect it.[95] The question of the status of the guaranty appears not to have been raised during the Austro-Prussian and Franco-Prussian Wars, nor in 1859 when Austria was at war with France and Sardinia, the seat of these wars being distant from the areas affected by the guaranty elsewhere. Inasmuch as Turkey was a belligerent in the other major European conflicts since 1841 there was no other occasion for the operation of the guaranty. It was still in effect in 1904 during the Russo-Japanese conflict, having survived the three wars mentioned, and occasioned great embarrassment to Russia.[96] The guaranty as worded makes it appear that the obligation lies only between the individual guarantors and the Porte, that is: (the signatories) "engage to respect this determination of the Sultan, and to conform themselves to the principle above declared." It is probable, however, that their understanding of the engagement was that

95 Treaty for the Pacification of the Levant, July 15, 1840, Hertslet, *op. cit.*, vol. ii, p. 1008, art. iv.

96 Graves, *Question of the Straits* (London, 1931), p. 137.

they should not only themselves conform to the principle, but should guarantee to each other its observance. For example, had Turkey been the only force with which Russia had to deal in 1904, it is likely that Russia's engagement to respect the principle would have been violated or denounced. It is clear that throughout all the period during which the guaranty was in force there was little, if any, weakening of the determination both of Turkey and England, at least, that the principle should be observed, and it is unlikely that the existence of a state of war when Turkey was not a party would have influenced that determination to any great extent. It is probable then that the guaranty remained in full force in wartime.

It is evident that war, even between guarantors, does not necessarily terminate nor even suspend guaranties. Both the nature and purpose of the guaranty and the nature and extent of the war must first be determined. It appears reasonable to conclude that the parties to a guaranty the object of which is to maintain a given region free from war or from annexation, or to set forth a given course of action in wartime, intend that such a guaranty should remain in force in wartime. But the non-specific guaranty of all the provisions of a settlement may be subject to varying conceptions in wartime. The intent of the parties generally being to give a greater solemnity to the provisions of the treaty than a mere signature would give, a violation of such provisions would obviously be more serious than if no guaranty existed, and any question involving them would be more apt to be the subject of an international understanding before any action was taken to modify them. But in the absence of express provision, there would appear to be as much difficulty in determining the status of a blanket guaranty of this sort in wartime as in determining that of the individual treaty provisions thus guaranteed. It is also probable that guarantors of a given régime or condition consider that when such a régime or condition ceases to exist through causes for which the guarantors are not responsible, and which are not provided against in the guaranty, the obligation ceases. If war be among such causes, then it may be said to have terminated the guaranty.

TREATIES OF ALLIANCE

There appears to be almost unanimous acceptance among writers, both early and modern, of the theory that war terminates alliances as between opposing belligerents. Primarily, however, this view appears to have been based on a consideration of bipartite treaties of alliance which do not survive such a conflict. The same rule does not necessarily apply to multipartite treaties, though, as with most treaty classifications, the rules governing bipartite conventions partially apply. The basis for determination of the possibility of survival of such multipartite conventions is found to be that which held in regard to guaranties—namely, did the allied states have in mind that the treaty should subsist in wartime, and if so did they intend it to subsist no matter what the nature of the war, or only when the survival of the treaty was compatible with the wartime operations? In a few cases among the seventeenth- and eighteenth-century treaties we have an indication of what the will of the parties was, but in most instances such indication is unfortunately lacking.

For the most part up until the Napoleonic era the shifts in alliances were very frequent, and although many of the treaties on which such alliances were based were characterized as perpetual, they were drawn up generally on the basis of an approaching or existing war to prevent excessive aggrandizement of any one state, and when the danger from such a state was past and the purpose of the alliance accomplished, the treaty is no more heard of. The precise time of its termination is generally not made clear, but in numerous cases it was not until after a war between the parties was over, and therefore the war could not have been the cause.

Most of the seventeenth- and eighteenth-century alliances were characterized as defensive in purpose. Frequently the purpose was stated to be the maintenance of the terms of a given treaty,[97] the alliance therefore including a guaranty,—but more often the purpose was armed defense against attack, and careful provision was made as to the exact number of soldiers and the amount of money which was to be furnished,[98] and under what conditions. During the seventeenth century the period during which such alliances were to subsist was generally specified, and ran from three to fifteen years;[99] during the eighteenth century, along with greater looseness in the terms generally, the provision for perpetual alliance became the rule rather than the exception. It was frequently specified that the new alliance was not to affect others already existing,[1] though frequently a proviso was included that no conflicting alliances were to be contracted.[2]

Due to the fact that the obligations of such states as Brandenburg and Hannover as members of the Holy Roman Empire might be contrary to their own interests, we find a specific arrangement, in an early treaty, concerning these conflicting interests in the event of war. In the 1725 alliance between France, Great Britain and Prussia, it was provided

[97] *Cf.* League of the Rhine, August 15, 1658, art. iv, Dumont, *op. cit.*, vol. vi, pt. ii, p. 239.

[98] *Ibid.*, arts. vii-ix.

[99] *Cf.* Quadruple Alliance of October 25, 1666, art. iv, *ibid.*, pt. iii, p. 122.

[1] *Cf.* Alliance of August 4, 1717, between France, Prussia and Russia; *ibid.*, vol. viii, pt. i, p. 490.

[2] *Cf.* Treaty of Alliance and Guaranty of May 26, 1732, art. iii; Dumont, *op. cit.*, supplement, vol. ii, pt. ii, p. 334.

that if the Emperor should make war on France because of aid given to the other two states under the alliance, Great Britain and Prussia should not furnish the contingents due the Empire, but if the attack on France was for a cause other than the treaty provisions, the furnishing of such contingents should not involve hostilities between France and her allies.[3] This is not, of course, a provision that war between the parties shall not affect a treaty of alliance, but rather an indication that a possible conflict between the troops of the allied states over a matter outside the sphere of the treaty of alliance shall not be called war. The important point in this arrangement, however, is the indication that only such conflicts as interfere with the aims and purposes of the alliance should affect the validity of the treaty, a theory which we find carried out in practice in more modern alliances.

A similar indication that allied states might engage in military operations against each other without affecting their treaty of alliance appears in a treaty between France, England and the United Provinces in 1659, in the form of an Alliance to Compel the Kings of the North to Make Peace. Here it is provided that if in the course of their efforts the allied states should disagree as to the equities involved, to the point where aid was given by one or another of the Allies to different sides, such action was not to be considered as involving a rupture between them, and the alliance and other treaties between them were to subsist in full force.[4]

In such treaties as provide that the new alliance is not to affect those already existing, there is generally no mention made of what course is to be followed if the two alliances should conflict. An exception occurs in the case of the 1667 treaty between the states of the Empire, where a provision is inserted to the effect that in case of conflict the state con-

[3] Separate articles ii and iii, Dumont, *op. cit.*, vol. viii, pt. ii, p. 127.

[4] Treaty of May 21, 1659, art. iv, Dumont, *op. cit.*, vol. vi, pt. ii, p. 252.

cerned must choose between the two alliances.[5] The term of this alliance was but three years, however, and as it was directed against France, from whom an attack threatened, the prospect of having to make a choice was not great.

In spite of the frequency with which long periods of time for the duration of these alliances were provided, they were intended, generally speaking, to meet an imminent danger, and when that danger had disappeared the usefulness of the treaty became questionable. Specific termination appears not to have taken place, but it seems safe to say that unless the maintenance of the treaty was incompatible with the conduct of the war the alliance was not necessarily terminated.

During the nineteenth century alliances became much less frequent, as the Concert of Europe, involving as it did the understanding that no state should be allowed to increase its proportionate strength at the expense of the others, acted as a continuous alliance between the Great Powers, which accomplished the aim attained in the preceding centuries only through specific agreements. The Quadruple Alliance between Austria, Great Britain, Prussia and Russia at the end of the Napoleonic wars,[6] which established the Concert of Europe along the lines which it followed through the century, was the most important during that period. As a treaty of alliance it was never subjected to a war between the parties, inasmuch as England withdrew from active participation when the other members authorized France's invasion of Spain, and France herself did the same when she gave up the old monarchy in 1830. As a joint policy, however, the Concert of Europe survived numerous wars between the participating states.

A treaty of alliance was drawn up among a number of the

[5] Treaty of August 22, 1667, art. xiii, *ibid.*, vol. vii, pt. i, p. 57.

[6] November 20, 1815, *Brit. & For. State Papers*, vol. iii, p. 273.

South American states in 1865, for the purposes of thwarting an attempt on the part of Spain to recover control of her former possessions. This treaty contained a provision to the effect that if any of the parties made war against any other the former should be proceeded against as if he were a non-signatory.[7] It is clear that this alliance was intended to survive in case of a war between the parties. It appears never to have actually been put to the test of such a war, however.

One of the most recent of these alliances made public was that of 1882 between Austria-Hungary, Germany and Italy, to which Roumania adhered.[8] It was never subjected to the test of war between the parties, inasmuch as Italy denounced it before entering the war, as did Roumania.[9] Due to the fact that it was chiefly concerned with joint action in case of war in which the signatories should be co-belligerents, it is difficult to see how it could have survived a war between them.

As in the case of guaranties, the nature of the alliance and the nature of the war must be taken into account in determining whether or not war operates to terminate or suspend alliances. The smaller the number of states which are parties the less likelihood there is that an alliance can survive the shock of war between them. In the case of a large number of states allied against a common external foe, or for the preservation of a common institution not affected by a local war between them, there would seem to be no reason why such an alliance might not continue in effect. The evidence of the intent of parties to such alliances that these arrangements should survive has been sufficient to indicate that no general rule of termination can be upheld. On the other

[7] Treaty of January 23, 1865, art. viii, *Brit. & For. State Papers*, vol. 58, p. 420.

[8] May 20, 1882, *ibid.*, vol. 121, p. 1018.

[9] May 23, 1915, *ibid.*, vol. 109, p. 963.

hand where the design is to provide for a common line of conduct over a given period, warfare if contrary to such common conduct would seem to suspend the alliance, at least while the war continued.

TREATIES CONCERNING INTERNATIONAL UNIONS AND BUREAUS

The determination of the status during wartime of those conventions which establish or regulate international unions whose functioning is at least partially independent of the states which brought them into being involves a consideration of the peculiar nature of such conventions. They ordinarily provide for the setting up of an international bureau or commission or both, the former made up of a personnel selected independently of their nationality, and the latter composed of delegates appointed by the member states and responsible to a greater or less degree to their states. This type of convention involves two sets of relationships between the member states of the union, the first, that directly between the states, and the second, those which are carried on or controlled through the commission or the bureau, and involving no such direct relations.

One of the earliest of these conventions was that which established the Universal Postal Union. This was drawn up in 1874,[10] and revised, without changing its essential character, several times since.[11] It established uniform rates for the carrying of mails, arranged for congresses to revise its own stipulations, and set up an international bureau at Berne to handle its international accounts and take care of its business. The commencement of hostilities in 1914 immediately involved the cessation of direct communication between the belligerents, badly dislocated the routing of mail, and due to

[10] October 9, 1874, *Brit. & For. State Papers*, vol. 65, p. 13.

[11] In 1878, in 1885, in 1891, in 1897.

the blockade policies of the various belligerents, seriously affected the service even between neutrals. But in spite of difficulties the Berne bureau continued in operation and published its journal, and contributions continued to come in for its support, from belligerent as well as from neutral members.[12] After the Armistice, when the blockade of Germany was partially lifted, mail service between the belligerents was resumed, and in general the parties appear to have again given effect to the convention without any agreement to resume.

In this case it may be said that the operation of some of the provisions of this convention was suspended, between opposing belligerents, and even between neutrals, but that the state of war as it existed from the date of the Armistice until the peace treaty went into effect failed to interrupt the execution of these provisions. The revisory congress called for by the convention [13] was not held during the war, but it was already overdue when the war broke out, so the war was not solely responsible for the failure to carry out that provision of the convention. The provisions relating to the central bureau of the union remained in effect through the entire period.

The international railway goods traffic in Europe was regulated before the war by a series of conventions based on an original treaty signed in 1890 by a majority of the continental States.[14] These conventions provided for international bills of lading, the distribution of statistics, the liquidation of accounts between railway administrations and for a

[12] *L'Union postale*, 1914, pp. 183-5. *Cf. ibid., passim*, through 1914-18; also Bühler, "der Weltpostverein", in *Volkerrechtsfragen*, 29 Heft, (Berlin, 1930), pp. 172-3.

[13] Convention of June 15, 1897, art. 25, *Brit. & For. State Papers*, vol. 89, p. 65.

[14] October 14, 1890, *ibid.*, vol. 82, p. 771.

central office. From 1914 to 1918 all direct communication by rail between the opposing belligerents was stopped, and thereby operation of most of the convention's provisions was interrupted. The effect of the war was not confined to that which it had on the communication between opposing belligerents, but in such neutral countries as Switzerland the international traffic dropped almost to nothing, due partly to the cessation of travel, but also to various prohibitions instituted by belligerents, which affected their traffic with neutrals to a great degree.[15] In spite of these conditions, however, most of the member states continued their contributions to the central office, which continued to function in the limited field which was left.[16] As indicated elsewhere, the French and German courts held that the treaty was not in effect between opposing belligerents, but France apparently considered that she still had obligations to the parties to it which were not her enemies, since she took pains in December 1918 to notify to them her denunciation of the conventions. Italy, Serbia, Bulgaria and Rumania apparently held the same view, as they followed suit the succeeding March, while the peace conference was still in session.[17] The limited traffic of the period was still carried on under the old conventional arrangements, and as no new treaty had been drawn up by the time the denunciations were to have gone into effect, they were withdrawn and the old convention was prorogued for three months' periods.[18]

The concept of the parties to the railroad conventions

[15] *Railway Age Gazette*, vol. 57, p. 850; vol. 62, p. 1454.

[16] Slavko, *Régime international des voies ferrées et la Société des Nations* (Paris, 1925), p. 59.

[17] Stieler, "Der internationale Eisenbahnverband," *Völkerrechtsfragen*, 11. Heft (Berlin, 1926), pp. 6-7.

[18] *League of Nations Treaty Series*, vol. ii, pp. 184, 302; vol. vi, p. 48; vol. vii, p. 248; vol. xii, pp. 214, 220.

appears to have been; first, that the provisions affecting interstate traffic were suspended as between opposing belligerents during the period of hostilities; second, that so much of the convention as concerned the central office remained in force; third, that where the conduct of the war involved interference with the traffic with neutrals the provisions of the conventions did not stand in the way of measures destined to further success of war operations.

The interpretation of the telephone and wireless conventions by the belligerents resembled that discussed in connection with the railroads. The rules governing international transmission of telegraphic messages were set up by the convention of 1865, which also created an information bureau.[19] In 1906 a convention concerning wireless transmission was drawn up, and the old bureau was given similar functions concerning the new method of transmission.[20] During the war direct communication between the opposing belligerents ceased, but as in the case of the railroads the central bureau remained open and active during the war, and contributions from the member states continued to come in. Direct application of the convention was suspended only as between opposing belligerents; the convention remained in force as between belligerents and neutrals, and between the neutrals themselves; and even as between opposing belligerents the provisions concerning the central bureau received full application.[21]

Under the conventions which established the Industrial Property and Literary and Artistic Property Unions in 1883 and 1886 respectively, two bureaus were set up working in conjunction with each other. In 1914 these bureaus recom-

[19] May 17, 1865, *Brit. & For. State Papers*, vol. 56, p. 294.

[20] November 3, 1906, Malloy, *Treaties, etc. of the U. S.*, vol. iii, p. 2889.

[21] Otto Kunz, "Die internationalen Telegrafen-Unionen," *Tübinger Abhandlungen zum Öffentliches Recht* (Stuttgart, 1924), p. 133.

mended to the members of the unions that the conventions be observed during the war, even in the relations between opposing belligerents, and to a limited extent the suggestion was followed.[21a] In both of these cases the bureau continued in operation, the Industrial Property Bureau continuing its registration of trademarks and patents and the publication of the official journal, and the Literary and Artistic Property Bureau continuing its services connected with international copyright in so far as possible under the restrictions imposed by the belligerents.

In the case of the conventions dealing with these two types of property, suspension even between belligerents was less complete than in the case of the other conventions noted, due to the greater hesitancy of belligerent states in suspending the private rights involved. The attitude toward the central bureaus was the same here as in the case of the other unions discussed, that is, that the war should be no bar to their functioning. Although certain of the provisions of these conventions were partially or totally suspended between the opposing belligerents, the conventions otherwise remained in force both as between opposing belligerents and in their relations with neutrals, and those provisions concerning the central bureaus remained in full effect.

An International Institute of Agriculture was set up at Rome by a convention signed in 1905,[22] to disseminate information and submit suggestions for agrarian legislation, and a central bureau was set up to carry out these duties. Although its work was greatly curtailed during the war, the bureau was maintained throughout that period, it published its *Annuaire*, and the member states continued to appoint their delegates to the Permanent Commission. As there was

[21a] See these conventions under "Individual Rights", *infra*, pp. 98-119.

[22] June 7, 1905, Malloy, *Treaties, etc. of the U. S.*, vol. ii, p. 2140.

no action under this convention calling for direct relations between the states parties to it, and as all the parties apparently gave effect even if somewhat reluctantly and in a dilatory fashion to its provisions, there is no indication that it was completely suspended even as between opposing belligerents.[23]

By a treaty signed in 1907, an International Office of Public Health was established at Paris, pursuant to a recommendation contained in the International Sanitary Convention of 1903.[24] This office, under the control of an executive committee, was to gather statistics, publish laws concerning health, and describe methods of combating disease. It happened that none of the Central Powers in the war of 1914-18 was represented on this committee, but in spite of that fact the committee failed to continue its sessions through the period of the war, and the office was occupied by the Allied sanitary service. The office did, however, continue to publish its Monthly Bulletin throughout the war, containing such information as it could gather, using unofficial channels when the official ones were closed. But even before the peace treaty had been signed, and with no preliminary agreement between the parties to the convention regarding renewal of the old convention, the sessions of the committee were resumed.[25]

This convention, although the parties to it were all neutrals or co-belligerents, was partially suspended during the period of active hostilities. It was put back into full force at the close of hostilities, without waiting for the signing or rati-

[23] *Annuaire de législation agricole*, vols. for 1915-18, *passim*; Hobson, *International Institute of Agriculture* (Berkeley, 1931), p. 73. In 1918 the reports from Austria-Hungary and Germany do not appear in the *Annuaire*.

[24] December 9, 1907, Malloy, *op. cit.*, vol. ii, p. 2214.

[25] *Bulletin de l'office international d'hygiène publique*, vols. for 1914-18, *passim*.

fication of the peace treaty, and without any formal agreement on the part of the parties.[26] It is not clear that war was deemed to be the cause of the cessation of the meetings of the committee, or if it was so considered, why the chief function of the office, the collection and dissemination of facts relating to public health, should have been continued while the meetings of the committee controlling the office should have been discontinued. It is plain, at any rate, that whatever the cause may have been for the interruption, it ceased with the end of active hostilities, and resumption was not dependent on a technical return to a peace basis.

Latin Monetary Union

In 1865 a monetary union was formed by France, Belgium, Italy and Switzerland, providing for the exchange of their metal currencies.[27] The Union was later joined by Greece.[28] It survived a series of wars to which one only of the signatories was a party, and was not affected until the war of 1914-18. The currency difficulties of the belligerent states and the resulting change in the comparative value of their metal moneys resulted in a flood of such money coming into Switzerland. That country demanded a new agreement, which was made in 1920 and further modified the following year.[29] At no time, however, in spite of the difficulties connected with the maintenance in force, was the prewar arrangement considered as terminated. The problem of opposing belligerents among the parties, however, did not arise in this case, as the belligerent signatories were all allied.

Because of the strain put upon her resources by the flood

[26] U. S. Treasury, *Weekly Public Health Report*, vol. 40, pt. ii, pp. 1728-30.

[27] December 23, 1865, *Brit. & For. State Papers*, vol. 56, p. 207.

[28] In 1868.

[29] March 25, 1920, *ibid.*, vol. 113, p. 944.

of depreciated metal currency coming into Switzerland during the war, that country suspended the convention in 1920 by restricting the free exchange of metal money.[80] This suspension did not, however, serve to terminate the convention in the view of the other signatories, nor did they use Switzerland's act as an occasion to denounce the convention. It thus survived the war, the intent of the parties apparently being to maintain it in force so long as their national economy made it at all possible, considering the existence of a state of war. It is interesting to note, however, that a convention between co-belligerents and neutrals was suspended, not by an ex-belligerent, but by a neutral, by reason of disorders arising from the war.

Conclusions

It appears, from the experience of the period from 1914 to 1920, that the effect of war on treaties setting up international unions varies considerably, not alone as between treaties but as between different parts of the same treaty. Such parts of these conventions as regulated direct relations between governments were generally suspended between belligerents. Such parts as deal with individual personal or property rights were apt to receive a more or less limited application even as between opposing belligerents. Those provisions dealing with the setting up and subsequent activities of an international bureau received practically full application. Such action was no doubt facilitated by the fact that most of these bureaus were located in neutral territory, though the bureau of the Institute of Agriculture is a striking exception. Where the successful conduct of the war appeared to be affected detrimentally by the observance of any provision, its application was apt to be suspended. On the

[80] Nolde, "La Monnaie en droit international," Académie de droit international de la Haye, *Recueil des Cours*, vol. 27, pp. 380-1.

other hand, there was a marked tendency gradually to resume complete observance of these conventions from the time hostilities had ceased, regardless of the fact that an interval of more than a year elapsed before the first of the peace treaties went into effect. It is notable that none of these conventions contained provisions as to their wartime status, and that belligerent governments appeared to be very chary of giving an opinion as to how far they considered themselves bound during this period. It is not established that the parties to these conventions intended to express such an opinion either when the conventions were drawn up or later, and in view of the divergency of opinion expressed on the subject in post-war discussions it is by no means certain that states are yet prepared to commit themselves on the question of the binding character of such conventions in wartime.

TREATIES OF COMMERCE AND COMMUNICATION

Commerce

There has been no unanimity of opinion regarding the status of commercial treaties in wartime.[81] Among those contending that commercial treaties are terminated the principle on which their belief is based appears to be that commerce between the belligerents is necessarily at an end, and therefore treaties regulating such commerce must be at an end also. Actually, however, commerce is not necessarily completely interrupted, and therefore commercial treaties are not necessarily terminated on that ground. The state of war would presumably operate, however, to deprive a belligerent of the right to demand fulfilment by an enemy of his obligations under a commercial treaty, but this condition would

[81] *Cf.* Fauchille, *Traité de droit international public* (Paris, 1921), vol. ii, p. 55, and Oppenheim, *International Law*, McNair's edition (London, 1926), vol. ii, sec. 99, for conflicting interpretations.

disappear with the close of hostilities, and there would thus be suspension rather than termination.

In practice, nevertheless, states themselves have frequently accepted the doctrine of uniform termination of commercial treaties during the past century. In 1856, during the negotiations at the end of the Crimean War, Russia acknowledged that her prewar commercial treaties with Turkey had been terminated.[32] Russia and Japan approved the doctrine in their treaty of peace at the close of the war of 1904-5.[33] Similar views were expressed by Italy,[34] Germany,[35] Greece [36] and Serbia [37] during the war of 1914-18.

The basis on which rests the argument that such treaties are terminated by the outbreak of war is that the stipulations of such treaties are not of a permanent character, and do not purport to manifest a design on the part of the contracting states to establish rights which should survive a war.[38] But an examination of the particular conventions used as the basis for such a statement indicate that the classification "commercial treaty" is used in a narrow sense, and if all conventions dealing with commercial matters were included, the rule indicated would apply only partially.

The type of convention usually indicated either by text writers or in treaty negotiations as having been terminated

[32] Session of March 25, 1856, Protocol No. 14, *Brit. & For. State Papers*, vol. 46, p. 97.

[33] August 23, 1905, Treaty of Peace, art. xii, *Brit. & For. State Papers*, vol. 98, p. 735.

[34] Decree of May 31, 1915, *Brit. & For. State Papers*, vol. 109, p. 964.

[35] *Reichsanzeiger*, August 8, 1914, no. 187; Clunet, *Journal de Droit International*, 1916, p. 331.

[36] Denunciation of Commercial Treaty of October 27, 1852, with Sweden, *Brit. & For. State Papers*, vol. 12, p. 1109.

[37] December 24, 1914, Treaties with Turkey, *ibid.*, vol. 109, p. 1016.

[38] *Cf.* Hyde, *International Law Chiefly as Interpreted and Applied by the United States* (Boston, 1922), vol. ii, § 550.

between belligerents by the outbreak of war, is bilateral and governs reciprocity of treatment, usually with special favors attached. In practice, commerce between belligerent states being almost completely interrupted, it is impossible to carry out the provisions of such treaties. The war over, it has generally been found advisable to put the commercial relations between the ex-belligerents on a new footing, and as the old treaty was thus replaced by a new, the former's last date of effectiveness was that of the outbreak of the war.

There are then three reasons for considering such treaties terminated by the outbreak of war, first: impossibility of performance due to prohibition of commerce between belligerents, second: the treaty, consisting of an exchange of advantages, is unsatisfactory to the parties under postwar conditions, when their bargaining position may be greatly changed, and third: the intent of the parties is usually to provide arrangements for peacetime commerce only.[39] So far as treaties conform to the type indicated above they are almost uniformly suspended at least during hostilities. It frequently happens, moreover, that a conflict is so widespread in its consequences, that all commerce, that of neutrals as well as of belligerents, is gravely affected. During the period from 1914 to 1920 this was the case, and a number of states availed themselves of the right of denunciation usually granted in bipartite commercial treaties, to denounce all those to which they were parties, whether with belligerent or with neutral states.[40] It has not been maintained, however, that war *ipso facto* had any effect on these treaties, and a local war of short duration might very well have none on those to which non-belligerents were parties.

[39] But see argument against considering United States–Germany commercial treaties as terminated; Miller, *Diary*, vol. viii, p. 322.

[40] Greece, Russia, Italy, Spain and France all took such action; *Brit. & For. State Papers*, Denunciations, *passim*, vols. 111 and 112.

But neither bipartite nor multipartite commercial treaties are invariably as homogeneous as those on which the generally accepted rules for termination are based. Among the former, we frequently find provisions concerning navigation and consular rights included, the latter of which at least are much more apt to be suitable to postwar conditions than are provisions regulating tariff preferences, for example. Commercial treaties from the fifteenth century on frequently provide that in the event of war sufficient warning should be given to allow the nationals of each party within the territory of the other to return home, a provision indicating clearly that the parties contemplated a future war and intended that at least so much of the treaty should be neither suspended nor terminated by its outbreak. Among multipartite conventions, the Treaty Revising the Berlin and Brussels Acts, signed in 1919, although dealing to some extent with commercial matters, contains subjects as varied as commercial equality, rules for the acquisition of property, the conservation of natural resources, navigation on the Niger River, suppression of slavery, and arbitration. The provisions regarding navigation on the Niger would hardly be seriously affected by a war between non-riparian signatories, even as between themselves, but the provisions concerning commercial equality would certainly be at least suspended between them.

The subject matter of multipartite commercial conventions differs from that of the ordinary bipartite commercial treaty. It has generally been the setting up of regulations for the international community as a whole, and for this reason such conventions are less likely, even as between the belligerents, to be affected by war. Of this type are such conventions as that drawn up in 1923 between the American States providing for uniformity of customs nomenclature, and that concerning the publicity of customs documents. Other conventions have provided for mutual protection of the rights of the nationals of the signatory Powers, and so involve the question whether treaties providing for private rights are terminated by war, which will be considered later. Of this group are the numerous conventions providing for the international protection of patents and trademarks. Conventions dealing with the regulation of trade and traffic on international rivers also present special problems apart from the question of exchange of advantage between the signatory Powers. Where multipartite conventions call for the setting up of an international commission or union, such as the river commissions and the copyright and industrial property unions, it is difficult to apply a theory of exchange of advantages which is intended to fit the case of a treaty involving a simple bargain between two states.

The criterion adopted by the United States courts after the war for solving the question of the termination of commercial treaties, points the way to a partial solution of the problem. In a number of postwar decisions it was held that the standard of survival was the compatibility of the provision in question with the conduct of the war. It will be noted that this was a frank abandonment of the idea of the unified character of a commercial treaty, and weakened the theory that these arrangements consist of a closely interdependent exchange of rights and obligations.[41]

The view that the stipulations of commercial treaties do not manifest a design on the part of the contracting states to establish rights which should survive a war, if applied to the provisions of the multipartite treaties mentioned, serves as a sound basis for determining the fate of commercial treaties. While it may be assumed that it was frequently not the design of the parties to a bipartite commercial treaty granting special favors to each other that the stipulations of such a treaty

[41] *Techt v. Hughes* (1920), 229 N. Y. 222, at 241-7. Also *Rickmers Rhederei Aktiengesellschaft v. U. S.* (1930), 45 Fed. (2nd) 413, 421.

should survive in wartime,[42] such is not necessarily the case in dealing with the multipartite treaties mentioned above. The double obligation of a multipartite treaty, that between any two of the signatories between themselves, and that of each to the group as a whole, must be considered. Commercial advantages given by each of the parties to each of the others may properly be considered as subject to suspension at least between belligerents, but it is difficult to see why war between two of the parties should be considered as resulting in automatic withdrawal from a union, or abandonment of a uniform customs nomenclature. As will be seen elsewhere in considering various categories of treaties containing commercial clauses, the tendency is to consider that technical provisions were intended to remain in force, while provisions with a political aspect are judged according to their subject matter which, if it involves other questions besides commerce, may be considered as intended to survive also. In general the multipartite commercial treaty is concerned with regulations of a technical nature suitable for the international community as a whole, and insofar as this is true the design of the parties, either expressed or implied, appears to be that it should survive in wartime even as between belligerents, except in so far as incompatible with the conduct of the war.

Air Navigation

Inasmuch as air navigation conventions are a postwar growth, it has been impossible to determine as yet to what extent they will be affected by a state of war. The multipartite agreements governing aerial navigation in 1932 are the convention of Paris of 1919,[43] with its amendments of

[42] *Cf.* the interpretation of the intent of the parties in *Flensburger Dampfer Compagnie v. U. S.*, 73 U. S. Court of Claims, 646 (1932).

[43] October 13, 1919, *League of Nations Treaty Series*, vol. xi, p. 174.

1920,[44] 1922,[45] and 1923,[46] the air mail conventions of 1927[47] and 1929,[48] the customs convention of 1926,[49] the Spanish-American convention of 1926,[50] and the Pan-American Convention of 1928.[51]

The first of these may be deemed the charter of air navigation, and stipulates that its provisions shall not affect the freedom of action in wartime of either belligerents or neutrals.[52] As a large part of this convention has to do with aerial commerce, it will of necessity be suspended between belligerents in wartime, but those provisions concerning the work of the International Commission of Air Navigation, if the experience of other similar international commissions may serve as a guide, will receive at least partial application even as between belligerents. The Spanish-American Convention, copied in large measure from the 1919 convention, and setting up an Ibero-American Commission similar to the International Commission of the earlier convention, contains a similar provision concerning the rights and duties of belligerents and neutrals.[53]

The air mail conventions form part of the group of general postal conventions, and are subject to the same rules; they need not concern us here. The customs convention is a tripartite arrangement between Great Britain, France and Belgium, and contains no provision either for denunciation

[44] May 1, 1920, *ibid.*, p. 307.

[45] October 27, 1922, *ibid.*, vol. 78, p. 438.

[46] June 30, 1923, *ibid.*, p. 441.

[47] September 10, 1927, *ibid.*, vol. 75, p. 7.

[48] June 28, 1929, *ibid.*, vol. 103, p. 221.

[49] May 5, 1926, Hudson, *International Legislation*, vol. iii, p. 1878.

[50] November 1, 1926, *ibid.*, p. 2019.

[51] February 20, 1928, *U. S. Treaty Series*, no. 840.

[52] Art. 38.

[53] Art. 38.

or suspension. It would of course be suspended between belligerents in wartime, but there appears no reason for its termination as between the belligerents and the neutral party.

There appears to be no marked difference between these conventions and those regulating similar traffic on the ground. Commercial traffic between opposing belligerents during war is prohibited in any case, which eliminates the usefulness of customs conventions, and international bureaus and commissions should remain unaffected to the degree that their existence does not interfere with war operations. That the general convention of 1919 and the Spanish-American Convention are to remain at least partially in force during the war period is evident from their own provisions; that the postal conventions will do the same appears likely from the experience of other postal conventions in past wars, even in the absence of provision in the treaties.

International Waterways

General

The general problems to be dealt with in this connection are the preservation of the right of individual citizens, both of belligerent and of neutral states, as well as of their governments, to use these streams for pacific purposes, so far as this is compatible with the prosecution of the war, and the maintenance of the navigability of the streams as provided in treaties, both for present and for future use, during the period of hostilities.

Rhine

During the period of 1914-1918, the convention of 1868, which regulated this traffic before the conflict, appears to have been considered in force by the states previously bound by it.[54] It is clear, however, that the rights and duties of

[54] Convention of Mannheim, October 17, 1868, *Brit. & For. State Papers*, vol. 59, p. 470.

neutrals and belligerents, where conflicting with the provisions of the convention, were given precedence over the latter. A lengthy discussion and correspondence between the British and Dutch Governments and between the latter and the German Government, regarding the use of the river for the shipment of German supplies, involved frequent invocations by Holland of her rights and duties under the 1868 convention, with apparently no disposition on the part of either Germany or England to question its existence.[55] Great Britain discovered in Holland's stand that the latter was determined to uphold the convention's provisions regarding commerce except where in conflict with her duties as a neutral, and expressed great satisfaction with this interpretation.[56]

The French prize courts recognized the existence of the 1868 convention during the war period, confiscating conditional contraband as destined to Germany when it was destined for ports from which shipment up the Rhine to Germany was likely, and when by the terms of the convention the goods were suitable for such shipment.[57]

After the Armistice, an Interallied Military Commission regulated navigation on the upper river, but this was recognized of course as a temporary measure, and appears not to have changed the attitude of the parties to the 1868 convention that it was and must be continued in force until replaced by another more suitable convention.[58]

[55] *Cf.* Dutch memorandum to British Government, October 9, 1917, *ibid.*, vol. III, p. 414 and October 26, *ibid.*, p. 434.

[56] *Cf.* Cmd. paper 8915: Misc. 2 (1918); *ibid.*, 8693: Misc. 17 (1917). See also Chamberlain, *Regime of International Rivers, Rhine and Danube* (New York, 1923), pp. 271-5.

[57] August 12, 1915, Conseil des Prises, *Journal officiel*, September 8, 1915, p. 6210.

[58] March 28, 1919; Miller, *Diary*, vol. XV, p. 525.

Elbe

The 1922 treaty regarding navigation on the Elbe[59] provides that in time of war, so far as compatible with the rights and duties of belligerents, the provisions of the convention shall subsist.[60] Specific arrangement was made also for the provision by Germany for free navigation on the river for Czechoslovakia, should the former be at war and the latter at peace.[61] It is evident that the existence of war is to have no effect *ipso facto* on the validity of the treaty, but may serve to suspend its operation under certain conditions, and may bring the provision concerning Czechoslovakia's special position into effect.

Scheldt

Navigation on the Scheldt has been conducted under the rules laid down in the three treaties of 1839 between Holland and Belgium and between each of them and the Great Powers in identical terms,[62] coupled with the general rules laid down in the General Act of the Congress of Vienna.[63] In 1866 the Austro-Prussian war, and in 1870 the Franco-Prussian War, although fought between parties to these treaties, did not involve the region of the Scheldt, and so apparently the treaty arrangements were not called in question. In 1914, however, the situation was different. Holland, as sole riparian of the lower river, promptly closed it to use by the armed forces of the belligerents, and changed certain of the navigation provisions by unilateral act in the interest of neutral navigation, which meant practically exclusively her own. The result was the inability of Great Britain to bring

59 February 22, 1922, *Brit. & For. State Papers*, vol. 116, p. 598.

60 Art. xlix.

61 *Ibid.*

62 *Ibid.*, vol. 27, pp. 990, 1000 (secs. 1-8).

63 Annex xvi, *ibid.*, vol. ii, p. 178.

forces to assist in the defense of Antwerp, which facilitated its conquest by the Germans.[64]

Due to the fact that a considerable part of the river was in the theater of war in 1914-18 there was practically complete suspension of the provisions of the convention concerning navigation. This fact did not, however, result in its termination, since the prewar regime was put in effect after the war without any arrangement for its renewed application.

Danube

Twice since it was first internationalized the Danube has been in the direct path of hostilities. The first time, in 1877-78, both Russia and Turkey took measures against navigation which eventually resulted in its complete cessation, and the European Commission, charged with the control and maintenance of navigation at the mouth, and dependent on tolls for the maintenance of its work, had to suspend operations.[65] The neutral Powers protested against the acts of the belligerents, who issued orders to respect the rights of neutral shipping, but took military action which rendered any navigation on the river practically impossible.[66] There was no claim made, however, that the provisions of the conventions of 1856[67] and of 1871,[68] which regulated international navigation on the river, were terminated or even suspended, and the Treaty of Berlin at the end of the war made provision

[64] Temperley, *History of the Peace Conference*, vol. ii, p. 194.

[65] *La Commission européenne du Danube et son oeuvre de 1856 à 1931* (Paris, 1931), pp. 27, 28.

[66] Russia defended her acts regarding neutral shipping on the basis that these acts were permissible in dealing with neutrals on the high seas, but failed to explain the basis on which the internationalized Danube was to be considered as part of the high seas.

[67] March 30, 1856, arts. xv-xix, Hertslet, *Map of Europe by Treaty*, vol. ii, p. 1257.

[68] March 13, 1871, *ibid.*, vol. iii, p. 1919.

against a repetition in wartime of several of the acts committed during hostilities.[69]

The Italo-Turk war of 1911 and the Balkan wars of 1912-13, resulting in the closing of the Straits, paralyzed navigation on the river, and the Rumanian mobilization resulted in practically complete cessation,[70] but no military operations would appear to have been directly responsible for violation of treaty stipulations.

During the early part of the war of 1914-18 navigation continued, though in diminished volume, and the European Commission held its regular sessions. But the entry of Turkey into the war closed the Straits, and practically put a stop to navigation, and there were no more regular sessions of the Commission after Bulgaria became a belligerent. The commissioners remained on Rumanian soil, however, until the entry of that country into the war. At that juncture Rumania expelled the delegates from the enemy states and interned the agents of the Commission from those states. Meanwhile the Commission asked for and received contributions from the states represented on the Commission, and continued the execution of navigation works on the river.

With the invasion of Rumania the Rumanian and Russian delegates left for Odessa, but the French and British remained at Galatz until recalled by their Governments. But even while represented only by the Rumanian and Russian delegates, the Commission was able to obtain new advances from the British and French Governments. Early in 1918 these two delegates returned to Galatz. By the peace of Bucharest the old Commission was replaced by a new, on which for the moment only the representatives of the Central Powers were represented, but with the Armistice the new delegates left Rumania, and a Rumanian delegate alone administered the

[69] July 13, 1878, arts. lii-lvii, *Brit. & For. State Papers*, vol. 69, p. 749.

[70] *La Commission européene du Danube, op. cit.*, p. 38.

affairs of the Commission, with some financial help from the Rumanian Government. After the peace treaty had been signed, and before it had gone into effect, a meeting of French, British and Italian delegates voted measures to re-establish the Commission on a working basis, pending the drawing up of a new arrangement.

Throughout the entire period from the outbreak of the war until the treaty of peace went into effect in January, 1920, with the exception of the short period from May to November 1918, when the provisions of the treaty of Bucharest were in effect, the European Commission carried on its work. For a large part of this period it received aid and contributions from belligerents of both camps.[71] There appears never to have been a claim that the war released any of the parties to the conventions of 1856, 1871 and 1878 from their obligations, and even after the conquest of Rumania by the Central Powers a new regime was not set up until provided for by treaty. Though no opinion was expressed that the stipulations of these conventions continued in force, they were given effect by all the belligerents, with rare exceptions, so far as operations incident to the war would allow, even to the point of allowing delegates of enemy states to remain at their places until recalled by their governments. During the period between the close of hostilities and the coming into effect of the peace treaty there was a gradual resumption of functions by the commission, indicating, as we have seen elsewhere, that it is the operations of the war, and not the mere existence of a state of war, which induce the parties to suspend the enforcement of treaty stipulations of this sort.

The conventions setting up an international régime for the control of navigation during the war were plainly not completely suspended by the advent of war. It appears that provisions allowing freedom of navigation were suspended as

[71] *Ibid.*, pp. 37-9.

between belligerent riparians and their enemies, as they naturally did not allow the rivers within their boundaries to be used by enemy vessels. But so far as circumstances permitted, the river commissions continued their work, and neutral riparians observed the conventions' provisions. The difficulties in the way of such observance have been recognized in the postwar Elbe convention,[72] and in the statute attached to the convention of 1921 for Freedom of Transit[73] and the 1923 convention dealing with the International Regime of Maritime Ports,[74] all of which contain provisions maintaining the conventions in force so far as compatible with the rights and duties of belligerents.

As was the case with most other conventions regulating commercial intercourse, the suspension of those provisions affected by the war did not continue as fully during the period between the end of hostilities and the date when the peace treaties went into effect. So far as the disorganized conditions permitted, traffic was resumed subject to the old regulations and such new rules as the military commissions in charge considered necessary. There appeared to be no attempt to determine the status of the conventions during this intervening period, but pending a definite solution by the peace conference the old regulations appear to have been considered as a *modus vivendi,* if not permanently reestablished.

Railways

This group includes a number of conventions regulating the international transport of goods by rail, the sealing of railroad cars through the customs and the technical unity of

[72] February 22, 1922, art. xlix, *Brit. & For. State Papers,* vol. 116, p. 598.

[73] April 20, 1921, art. 8, *League of Nations Treaty Series,* vol. vii, p. 12.

[74] December 9, 1923, Statute, art. 18, *ibid.,* vol. 58, p. 285.

railways. The most important of these was the 1890 Convention regulating the Transport of Goods by Rail, with its additions and modifications.[75]

The universal stoppage of commercial intercourse and the closing of frontiers between belligerents naturally rendered the provisions regulating such intercourse valueless during the war. Traffic between belligerents and neutrals was also seriously affected, and of course the frontier customs régimes were greatly modified, often with little regard to the requirements of the neutrals.[76] But the convention was not denounced during the period of hostilities.

Both France[77] and Germany[78] considered the treaty as no longer in force between them while the war was in progress, a position maintained by the courts of both countries when the war was over in dealing with affairs taking place during the war period. But they and the other signatories appear to have considered it in effect as between belligerents and neutrals. France announced her denunciation of the convention after the Armistice, but before the peace treaty was signed. Serbia, Bulgaria and Rumania, all of whom had adhered, and Belgium and Italy, of the original signatories, all denounced it in 1919, while the war period technically existed, giving the notice required by the convention.[79]

[75] October 14, 1890, Convention and Protocol, *Brit. & For. State Papers*, vol. 82, p. 771; September 20, 1893, Additional Declaration, *ibid.*, vol. 85, p. 750; July 16, 1895, Additional Agreement and Protocol, *ibid.*, vol. 87, p. 806; June 16, 1898, Additional Convention, *ibid.*, vol. 92, p. 433. September 19, 1906, Additional Convention, Martens, *Nouveau recueil général des traités, etc., 3me série*, vol. iii, p. 920.

[76] Slavko, *Régime international des voies ferrées et la Société des Nations* (Paris, 1925), p. 59.

[77] December 21, 1922, *Société des anciens établissements Wenger c. C. F. P. L. M.*, Sirey, *Recueil*, vol. ii, p. 112.

[78] Stieler, "Der internationale Eisenbahnverband", in *Völkerrechtsfragen*, 11. Heft, (Berlin, 1926), pp. 6-7.

[79] *Cf.* correspondence, September–October, 1920, *League of Nations Treaty Series*, vol. 18, p. 247; vol. 2, pp. 184, 302.

Meanwhile the Central Bureau established under the treaty continued to function, and the states' contributions continued to be paid.

In practice, then, this convention was suspended between belligerents during the period of hostilities, the suspension becoming less complete in the post-Armistice period. It was not suspended between belligerents and neutrals, though the observance of its provisions was far from exact. The provisions concerning the Central Bureau were not suspended, but remained in force through the war.

St. Gothard Railway

In 1870, following a bipartite arrangement between Italy and Switzerland the preceding year,[80] these two Powers and Germany drew up an agreement concerning the route through the St. Gothard tunnel, by which Germany agreed to pay a subsidy for construction and maintenance.[81] This convention was followed by several others, all of which were replaced in 1909 by an agreement between these same three states,[82] followed by a procès-verbal.[83] During the war, of course, through traffic was stopped, and a new arrangement was necessary.[84] It was entered into between Italy and Switzerland in 1918, before the Armistice, and provided that it should " modify partially and temporarily " the 1909 agreement, and the new measures were characterized as of an " exceptional and temporary character." [85] This 1918 agreement was prorogued in 1920 for another two years, again " exceptionally and temporarily." [86] The succeeding year,

[80] October 15, 1869.

[81] June 20, 1870, Martens, *Nouveau recueil général*, vol. 19, p. 99. October 28, 1871, *op. cit.*, p. 103.

[82] October 13, 1909, *Brit. & For. State Papers*, vol. 105, p. 639.

[84] *Railway Age Gazette*, vol. 57, p. 850.

[85] July 1, 1918, Martens, *op. cit., 3me série*, vol. xii, p. 310.

[86] July 21, 1920, *ibid.*, vol. xv, p. 69.

however, a further indefinite prolongation took place, with no mention of the exceptional or temporary character of its provisions.[87]

It seems definitely established that the parties did not consider the prewar conventions terminated by the war. By a series of bilateral agreements, Switzerland and Italy modified the earlier conventions without Germany's consent, though they took pains at first to specify that the modifications were tentative only. This appears to be an example of the frequent practice of extra-legal treaty modification to meet a pressing situation.

TREATIES CONCERNING INDIVIDUAL RIGHTS

As has been indicated above in the introduction, the theory that war does not affect the rights of individuals, or affects them only in so far as essential to the success of the war, is of old standing, and, on the continent at least, of general acceptance. To apply this doctrine to treaties, however, is possible only where the provisions of treaties may be considered separately, as those conventions dealing with private rights with rare exceptions deal with governmental affairs outside that sphere as well. Treaties of guaranty and alliance rarely involve individual rights, and private law conventions deal with such rights to the practical exclusion of governmental rights. But practically all other conventions deal with both, and in practice the provisions of the two kinds have been considered separately, though existing in the same treaties.

On the continent the traditional acceptance of the theory that war is a matter between states has resulted in a liberal construction of the possibility of survival of treaty provisions protecting such rights. In Great Britain, on the contrary, they were more strictly construed. The United States has occupied a middle ground, perhaps closer to the British than

[87] September 24, 1921, *League of Nations Treaty Series*, vol. xii, p. 369.

to the continental view. In practice, however, the British Government made numerous exceptions to the common law rule of the absolute termination of such rights where opposing belligerents were concerned, both regarding British rights in enemy countries, and the rights of enemy aliens in Great Britain. The constantly increasing network of international private relations makes reciprocal curtailment of the rights of alien enemies a progressively costly matter to all belligerents, and in the last war consideration appears to have been given to this fact.

A review of the multipartite conventions dealing with private law, patents, copyrights and trademarks, will serve to show the careful consideration given to the subject of these rights by the belligerents in the last war.

Industrial Property

The group of conventions in question comprises the Industrial Property Convention of 1883,[88] which established the Union for the Protection of Industrial Property, with its final protocol, the conventions of 1891 providing for the expenses of the Central Bureau of the Union and containing an interpretation and application of the 1883 conventions,[89] the Additional Act modifying it,[90] and its 1911 revisions;[91] also the corresponding Trade Mark Conventions of 1891,[92] 1900[93] and 1911,[94] and the 1891[95] and 1911[96] agreements

[88] March 20, 1883, Malloy, *Treaties, etc. of the United States*, vol. ii, p. 1935.

[89] April 15, 1891, *ibid.*, p. 1943.

[90] December 14, 1900, *ibid.*, p. 1945.

[91] June 2, 1911, *ibid.*, vol. iii, p. 2953.

[92] April 14, 1891, *Brit. & For. State Papers*, vol. 96, p. 839.

[93] December 14, 1900, *ibid.*, p. 848.

[94] June 2, 1911, *ibid.*, vol. 108, p. 404.

[95] April 14, 1891, Martens, *op. cit.*, *2nd série*, vol. xviii, p. 842.

[96] June 2, 1911, *ibid.*, vol. 104, p. 137.

for the Prevention of False Indications of Origin.[97] The position of these conventions was of more than ordinary importance during the war, as the question of the status of the patent and trademark rights of enemy aliens had to be dealt with, and both the Courts and the legislatures of most of the states which were parties concerned themselves with the question. None of the treaties contained any provision for its own status during wartime, so the matter was left to interpretation.

Shortly after the war's outbreak, the International Bureau of the Union for the Protection of Industrial Property, established under the 1883 convention, maintained that the conventions should be respected and applied so far as possible, for the benefit of the private rights of the citizens and subjects of all the belligerent states. The suggestion was received with varying degrees of support, but in no case was cooperation refused outright.[98]

In Great Britain, by an act of August 7, 1914, amended August 28th, 1914, the Board of Trade was given power to avoid or suspend the registration of any trade mark which was the property of an enemy alien, as well as any proceedings on an application for a new trade mark. The act was to remain in force for the duration of the war and for six months thereafter. Similar measures were taken in the British dominions and colonies.[99]

[97] The conventions of 1900 and 1911 replaced the earlier ones as between the parties to the later, but in each case there were some parties which failed to ratify the later convention, leaving the earlier binding as between themselves or between them and the parties to the later convention. Only seven of the parties to these conventions remained neutral during the war. (Basdevant, *Traités de la France*, vol. iv, p. 228).

[98] Ladas, *The International Protection of Industrial Property* (Cambridge, 1930), p. 723 *et seq.*

[99] Patents, Designs and Trademarks, 4 and 5 Geo. V, c. 27 and c. 73; Chitty, *Statutes* (6th), '14-'16, pp. 289, 291.

The common law theory was that all commercial intercourse with the enemy or with persons residing in enemy territory became illegal with the outbreak of war, except in so far as authorized by municipal legislation.[1] The British Government in practice modified this rule to the extent that persons of enemy nationality were deprived of such right to whatever extent the national interest required during the war. The British did, however, extend to all persons the benefit of protective legislative measures taken during the war, whereas most other belligerent states confined these benefits to states according reciprocity to their own subjects.[2] Prohibition of trade with enemies had the effect here, as elsewhere, of preventing the use of a patent or trademark by a national of an enemy state.

That France conceived of these conventions as in force during the war is proved by the adhesion of French Morocco to the 1911 convention in 1917.[3] In the interest of national defense, however, she forbade the exploitation of any patent or the use of any trademark to subjects or *ressortissants* of Germany or Austria-Hungary, though she allowed the obtaining and conservation of industrial rights subject to a delay in the delivery of certificates until the end of the war.[4] Delays of priority fixed by the Convention were suspended from the beginning of the war, and benefit of the delay was not available except on condition of reciprocity, except for those alien enemies or *ressortissants* who had rendered signal service to France.

Early in the war the German Reichsgericht held that the binding force of the convention ceased as between the opposing belligerents as from the outbreak of the war, but that the

1 Chitty, *Law of Nations* (Boston, 1812), p. 1.

2 Ladas, *op. cit.*, p. 731.

3 *Brit. & For. State Papers*, vol. 111, p. 591.

4 May 27, 1915, *Journal officiel*, May 29, 1915, p. 3414.

convention was nevertheless binding on the courts inasmuch as there was a statute, putting the treaty into force in German municipal law, which had not been repealed and was therefore still binding.[5] In 1915, however, Germany issued an ordinance resembling the British statute mentioned above, which gave to the Chancellor the right to limit or suppress, in the public interest, the industrial property rights of *ressortissants* of enemy countries.[6]

Austria took the same stand as Germany in regarding the conventions as part of her municipal law and therefore binding until contrary action by the political branch of the government. In 1915 such action was taken.[7] The right of filing patent and trademark applications was granted to French and British citizens and *ressortissants* only so long as reciprocity was observed. In 1916 the delivery of patents and the registration of designs and trademarks by alien enemies was suspended.

The Japanese position was explained in a decision of the Court of Cassation in 1915. It was held that the 1883 Convention supposed the existence of friendly relations between the countries of the Union, but that the convention might be suspended unilaterally, and Japan considered it suspended between herself and Germany during the entire duration of the war.[8]

[5] *S. H. H. v. Ch. in Paris*, Reichsgericht in Zivilsachen, vol. 85, p. 374.

[6] July 1, 1915, Clunet, *op. cit.*, vol. 42, p. 963.

In retaliation for Russia's measures, Germany declared void all applications made subsequent to Russia's termination of the same privilege. The Russian action which was the occasion of the retaliatory measures was a ukase providing that all patents important to the defense of the Empire and belonging to enemy aliens should be transferred to the State without compensation, and all others annulled. Russia was not a party to the conventions, however, and so her action and the retaliatory measures were not contrary to their provisions. (Garner, *International Law and the World War*, vol. i, p. 111.)

[7] August 26, 1916, Clunet, *op. cit.*, vol. 42, p. 968.

[8] Nakamatsu, *Propriété industrielle* (Berne, 1915), p. 109.

The United States, which had acceded to the 1883 convention and was a party to the others, took action suspending several provisions of the conventions in her relations with Germany and Austria. In 1917 the right of alien enemies or their allies to protection of patents or trade marks was suspended in case an American should apply for permission to use them and the President consider it a matter of public welfare to grant a license to that effect. The enemy owner was given the right to file a bill in equity after the war for the recovery from the licensee for his use and enjoyment of the property.[9] In 1918 an order of the President stopped the issuing of patents and copyrights to enemy subjects, and permission for Americans to apply for patents in enemy countries was revoked.[10] Just before the end of the war the enemy-owned patents for which licenses had not been issued were transferred to the Alien Property Custodian, and no provision was made for their return.[11]

Those not so seized, however, remained the property of their German owners. The seized patents were sold at private sale to the Chemical Foundation, a corporation which thereupon issued licenses to operate these patents to United States citizens or corporations. The proceeds, amounting to about $250,000, were turned into the United States Treasury. In 1928 an Act was passed by Congress setting aside the sum of $100,000,000, to be prorated among the German owners of the seized patents and other German claimants. The money was to be paid on the basis of what the Government would have paid for such patents had they

[9] October 6, 1917, Trading with the Enemy Act, *U. S. Statutes at Large*, 65th Cong., vol. 40, p. 411 (H. R. 4960).

[10] April 16, 1918; Garner, *op. cit.*, vol. i, p. 112.

[11] November 4, 1918, Act Making Appropriations to Supply Deficiencies in Appropriations for the Fiscal Year ending June 30, 1919; *U. S. Statutes at Large*, 65th Cong., vol. 40, pt. i, p. 1020 (H. R. 13086).

been disposed of to the Government by United States citizens.[12]

There was no recognition in this Act that the action of the Government in seizing and using the patents during the war was contrary to international law, or any treaty obligation. During the war period the design of the government had been to inflict economic as well as military damage on the enemy, and the 1928 Act may be conceived of as an equitable measure intended merely to limit the effect of that damage on enemy individuals.

Italy suspended the delivery of patents and the registration of trade marks on application filed by enemies. It was provided that the state might use any patent in the interest of national defense, but this applied to patents owned by nationals of allied as well as of enemy states, and to Italy's own nationals as well.[13]

Portugal, Hungary and Tunis [14] also suspended the issuing of patents and the registration of trade marks to enemy nationals or *ressortissants*.

But in spite of the action of the individual states members of the Union, contrary to the provisions of the conventions to which they were parties, they also took measures to preserve rights guaranteed under the conventions which would otherwise have lapsed due to the war. The principal measures taken contrary to the conventions were the refusal to issue licenses for patents or trade marks to enemy nationals or *ressortissants* and the prohibition to work those already issued, coupled sometimes with action by the state either to work them itself or to give its own nationals that right where public interest in working the patent was shown.

[12] Settlement of War Claims Act, 1928, *U. S. Statutes at Large*, 70th Cong., vol. 45, pt. i, p. 255 (H. R. 7201), sec. 3 (b) (3).

[13] Ladas, *op. cit.*, pp. 728-9 (footnotes).

[14] *Ibid.*, p. 727.

On the other hand the right to apply for such patents and trademarks was rarely denied,[15] and the United States allowed the prosecution of the application up to the point of issuance.[16] The periods of priority for the filing of an application for a patent or registration of a trademark, which would have almost inevitably been insufficient for such action between enemy states, were extended by most states, at the suggestion of the International Bureau, until a given period after the conclusion of peace.[17] The periods within which a patent must be worked were also extended for periods of varying length after the war.[18] The only reservation in connection with these provisions was reciprocity on the part of the enemy states, only the British Empire, among the belligerents, not requiring it.[19] Most of the states, in spite of their decrees prohibiting trading with the enemy, allowed payments necessary to keep alive patent and trademark rights in enemy countries.

So far as the neutral countries were concerned there seems to have been no disposition to have considered the conventions as other than in full force and effect. Sweden adhered to the 1911 convention in 1916. Denmark, Norway, Spain, Switzerland and the Netherlands extended indefinitely the periods of priority under the convention and several of the neutrals did the same for the period for the working of

[15] Ladas, *op. cit.*, p. 726. In July, 1918, however, the British Government, by Ordinance of the Controller General, put a stop to any proceedings regarding trade marks or patents deposited by enemy aliens (see Clunet, *op. cit.*, vol. 45, p. 1604).

[16] Ladas, *op. cit.*, p. 726.

[17] *Ibid.*, p. 729.

[18] *Ibid.*, p. 731.

[19] France, Law of May 27, 1915, *Journal Officiel*, May 29, 1915, p. 3414; Austria-Hungary, *Avis* of Mary 1, 1915, Clunet, *op. cit.*, vol. 42, p. 968; Great Britain, License of November 4, 1914, Pulling, *Manual of Emergency Legislation* (1915), p. 145.

patents. Both Denmark and Switzerland granted the benefit of the protective measures without demanding reciprocity. None of the neutrals suspended the acceptance of registration or the delivery of patents or registration certificates. Except, therefore, for the extension of time beyond that required by the conventions for the exercise of rights under them, the neutrals appear to have maintained them in full force so far as the disordered state of business in most of the states of the Union would permit.[20]

The International Bureau itself considered the conventions in effect, and as mentioned above urged the member states at the beginning of the war to observe them. The contributions of the member states continued to come in, and the international registration of patents and trademarks was kept up throughout the conflict, though the number was greatly diminished. These registrations were generally accepted as valid by the member states, even when registered by the citizens or *ressortissants* of enemy states.[21]

A consideration of the action of the leading states which were parties to the conventions would lead to the conclusion that they conceived that the provisions which appeared inimical to the successful prosecution of the war might be suspended. It does not appear that political departments of the states concerned considered that such suspension was automatic, inasmuch as the individual rights guaranteed by the conventions were allowed to subsist until contrary legislation was passed. It appears also that in many cases the courts, in the absence of any positive action by the legislative or executive branches of the government, considered the conventions automatically suspended as between opposing bellig-

[20] Ladas, *op. cit.*, pp. 723-27.

[21] *Ibid.*, p. 727; *cf.* Act of July 3, 1918, making appropriations for the fiscal year ending June 30, 1919, *Statutes at Large*, 65th Cong., vol. 40, p. 757 (H. R. 13086).

erents, but their view is not sustained by the action of the lawmaking division of the governments. There was unfortunately no mention of the conventions in the legislation concerning the rights specified in them; the courts on the other hand considered the problem as a treaty problem and expressed themselves quite definitely on the status of the treaties as a whole. But their opinions were based largely on the writings of jurists of a period before the type of union such as that set up by the 1883 treaty had been subjected to the test of a general war, and who had therefore had no occasion to see what the actual effects of such a conflict would be. The legislators, on the other hand, having no precedents to guide them, appear to have dealt with the subject on a pragmatic basis, with a result which has strengthened the probability of enforcement of international agreements of this sort in wartime.

There were several reasons why it was a practical policy to allow at least parts of these conventions to remain in effect even as between opposing belligerents. To begin with, the arguments in favor of suspending conventions granting reciprocal advantages to states carry little weight here. The interests are those of private individuals in the main, and where belligerents have anything approaching equality of numbers the disadvantage of the loss of the future market of the opposing state roughly offsets the advantage of depriving that state of the local market, except where such an act is important to the successful conduct of the war.

It is to be supposed therefore, that the states which are parties to the conventions did not presume a state of peace for their execution. As further evidence there is the fact that war, except where it results in the annihilation of one of the states, does not result in making the convention inapplicable thereafter. Defeat does not make recognition of patents and trademarks by the defeated state a consideration of doubtful value.

Literary and Artistic Property

The conventions concerned here are that of 1886,[22] generally known as the Berne Convention, which created the International Union for the Protection of Literary and Artistic Property with its central bureau, the Additional Act of 1896,[23] and the revisory Act of 1908.[24] None of these conventions contains any provision in regard to its status during wartime; the only method of termination provided in the treaties is by the unanimous withdrawal of the parties upon notice, or by unanimous revision. Where a revised treaty was drawn up without unanimous consent, the old convention was to be binding in relations with the states not ratifying the new.[25]

It so happened that in three of the important wars between the founding of the union and 1914 only one of the belligerents was a party to any of the conventions. In 1898 Spain was a member and the United States was not; in 1900 Great Britain was bound while the Boer republics were not; in 1911 it was Italy who belonged to the Union, and Turkey which was not a member. In the Balkan wars none of the belligerents was bound. In none of the conflicts mentioned was there a denunciation or suspension of the convention by those belligerent states which were parties.[26] It was not until the war of 1914-18 that the conventions were put to a severe test of their ability to survive a general war.

To understand the significance of the action of the different states members, differing often from that in regard to

[22] September 9, 1886, *Brit. & For. State Papers*, vol. 77, p. 22.

[23] May 4, 1896, *ibid.*, vol. 88, p. 36.

[24] November 13, 1908, *ibid.*, vol. 102, p. 619.

[25] *Cf.* arts. xvii and xx of 1886 convention.

[26] Ruffini, *Oeuvres littéraires et artistiques*, Académie de droit international de La Haye, *Recueil des Cours*, vol. xii, pp. 464-470.

industrial property, the distinction between the two types of property must be understood. Intellectual property, as the term is here used, is peculiarly closely connected with its creator. The possibility of unconscious infringement is less than in the case of industrial designs and models. Also there is less chance that protecting the originator of the work will be prejudicial to the national interest. For these reasons the intellectual property conventions have not provided that recurring steps be taken to protect such works. For the same reasons the danger of such works in the exclusive possession of enemy aliens is less pressing.[27]

As a matter of fact, during the last war the distinction indicated above appears to have been overlooked, and literary and artistic property were quite generally lumped together with industrial property, apparently on the general theory that war legitimized any measures designed to injure the rights of enemy aliens or *ressortissants*. As will be seen, this theory was not applied to its full extent by any of the states members, and the extent of its application differed widely. There seems to have been no attempt to apply any judicial conception of the effect of war on treaties by any of the states concerned; the action of the states appeared to be more in the nature of individual measures taken as particular difficulties arose, with reference alone to those difficulties.[28]

At the outbreak of the war the International Bureau invited the members of the Union to protect the individual rights guaranteed by the convention,[29] but the results of the appeal were limited. Whether as a result of the appeal or from other causes, the convention was not denounced, and

[27] Ladas, *op. cit.*, p. 723.

[28] Chabaud, *La propriété industrielle, littéraire et artistique* (Nancy, 1921), p. 5.

[29] *Droit d'auteur*, 1914, pp. 118-9.

Morocco[31] registered her adhesion to the 1914 convention as a French Protectorate during the course of hostilities.[32]

The Association of Editors and the Society of Authors of Great Britain early in the war came strongly to the support of the Berne convention.[33] The former held that "to profit from the state of war to appropriate the property of others would constitute not only a rupture of the Berne convention, but would throw discredit on a nation which was struggling for the maintenance of honorable obligations."

The government, however, looked at things in a different light, and invested a public curator with the copyright on all works appearing for the first time in an enemy country during the war.[34] The justification for this measure was the necessity of avoiding the effects of the common law, which would have denied the right to enemy aliens in wartime, and thus left the originators of the work without any protection. It cannot be said, therefore, that the government's measure involved recognition of even the suspension of the convention, in spite of the fact that such a suspension by England was stated by the German courts to be the case.[35]

In Germany the Circle of Booksellers, the Society of Music Sellers and the Society of Music Publishers all went on record

[31] June 16, 1917, *Brit. & For. State Papers*, vol. 113, p. 781.

[32] An example of the attitude of a great state at an early date is that of France during the Thirty Years' War, when Rubens, a native of the Austrian Netherlands, was a painter in Paris. An attempt was made to withdraw his monopoly of reproducing his own works "in the public interest", but the Parlement of Paris in three decrees held that the existence of a state of war between France and Austria was insufficient to warrant the withdrawal of the monopoly, which was held not to be prejudicial to the interest of the State. Ruffini, *op. cit.*, p. 462.

[33] *Ibid.*, p. 459.

[34] August 10, 1916, *ibid.*, p. 462; see also *Droit d'auteur*, 1916, pp. 109, 119.

[35] *Cf. Ricordi c. Benjamin*, July 14, 1917, Oberlandesgericht Hamburg, Clunet, *op. cit.*, vol. 45, p. 301.

to the effect that Germany still considered herself bound by the Berne convention.[36] These associations in all countries appear to have universally taken the same point of view, realizing the common advantage of such a stand.[37] The governments, however, had other interests to consider, which apparently prevented such a liberal attitude.

The status of the Berne convention came up in the German courts in 1917, and although there was no direct statement that the convention was unaffected by the war, it was held that war between some of the parties to a convention was insufficient in itself to terminate that convention.[38] The opinion was held, however, that a bipartite convention on the same topic between opposing belligerents had ceased to be effective. The statement was also made that private rights regularly acquired under a convention would not be put aside as a result of war. Reciprocity in this respect between the belligerents was not considered essential.

As in Germany and Great Britain, the French societies concerned with literary and artistic property were strongly in favor of continuing the convention in force. The " Syndicat " for the Protection of Intellectual Property at Paris, and the " Cercle " of Booksellers of Paris both went on record for the maintenance in force of intellectual property rights as defined in the Berne convention. A French publisher who attempted to put out unauthorized copies of the works of Grieg found himself immediately in difficulties with the Chambre syndicale des éditeurs de musique of Paris. This body called on the Civil Tribunal of the Seine under the

[36] *Droit d'auteur*, 1916, pp. 111-12.

[37] *Cf. Chronique*, Cercle de la librairie de Paris, July 30, 1915, Clunet, *op. cit.*, vol. 42, p. 569.

Italian Assn. of Printers and Booksellers, *Droit d'auteur*, Mar. 15, 1917.
Association of British Editors, *ibid.*, 1916, p. 114.

[38] *Ricordi c. Benjamin*, *supra*, note 35.

Berne convention, and the court authorized the government's "Séquestre", who was in control of the rights of the German owner of the copyright, to proceed to bring suit.[39] Before the case was brought, however, the infringer voluntarily desisted from his project.

It was also during the course of the war that France, Japan and Luxemburg, among the belligerents, and Great Britain for Canada and South Africa, adhered to the 1914 additional protocol, signed in March 1914.[40] Italy adhered, but in 1914, before she became a belligerent. Switzerland, Denmark, Spain and the Netherlands adhered also during the course of the war.[41]

The Italian Association of Printers and Booksellers took the position that the convention was "suspended during the war, but continues in full force", leaving its exact position in some doubt. The government, though it denounced its 1907 convention with Germany, failed to take similar action regarding the Berne convention, even in regard to enemy states.[42] Further, the denunciation of the German convention was made in accord with the provisions of the convention itself, and was so accepted by Germany, indicating a belief that even such a bipartite convention did not terminate automatically with the outbreak of war.

Private International Law

This is a group of three conventions signed in 1902, concerning Conflicts of Laws in the Matter of Marriage,[43] in matters of Divorce and Separation,[44] and regulating the

[39] Johannes Platt case, *Droit d'auteur*, 1916, p. 11.

[40] March 20, 1914, *League of Nations Treaty Series*, vol. i, p. 243.

[41] *Droit d'auteur*, 1915, p. xi; 1915, January 26, Switzerland; March 19, Denmark; April 20, Spain; April 7, Netherlands

[42] *Brit. & For. State Papers*, vol. 110, p. 911.

[43] June 12, 1902, *Brit. & For. State Papers*, vol. 95, p. 411.

[44] *Ibid.*, p. 416.

Guardianship of Minors,[45] and three signed in 1905, concerning Conflict of Laws regarding the Effects of Marriage on the Rights and Duties of Married Persons in their Personal and Property Relations,[46] the Deprivation of Civil Rights and Analogous Measures of Protection,[47] and regarding Civil Procedure.[48] None of these conventions contained any provision for their wartime and postwar status. All contained provision for denunciation unilaterally without effect on the validity of the convention among the remaining signatories.

All during the war the conventions were invoked, the most frequent point at issue being whether enemy aliens from states parties to the Civil Procedure convention were dispensed from depositing the *cautio judicatum solvi,* as provided in the convention, or whether the war had terminated or suspended the convention and therefore the dispensation no longer held. Generally speaking, the treaties were considered as being subject to one general rule, the separate articles and separate conventions being conceived as standing or falling together, but in the case of the dispensation from the *cautio* the German courts considered this clause separately.

In 1914 the Landgericht in Berlin held that all clauses whose fulfilment was contrary to the purposes of the war were "at least temporarily not in force", as well as those which strengthened the position of the nationals of the enemy state in relation to those of the home state. Such was held to be the result in this case, inasmuch as it would have been impossible to prosecute successfully a claim for costs in Russia, the state of the plaintiff, if the latter should lose the

[45] *Ibid.,* p. 421.

[46] July 17, 1905, Martens, *Nouveau recueil général, 3me série,* vol. vi, p. 480.

[47] *Brit. & For. State Papers,* vol. 116, p. 770.

[48] *Ibid.,* vol. 99, p. 990.

case.[49] The succeeding year the same provision of the treaty was held to be no longer in force between France and Germany because of lack of reciprocity.[50]

A decision by the Kammergericht the following year appears to modify unfavorably the leniency of the German courts in dealing with suits brought under these treaties. It was held that the entire Civil Procedure convention was no longer in force between belligerents as a result of the declaration of war, " like all treaties between belligerents which do not have war as an object." The fact that the treaty had been published in the Reichsgesetzblatt, and might therefore be considered as part of the law of the land, was not important, as this type of treaty was only in force internally so long as it was maintained in force internationally.[51]

At about the same time the Kammergericht held that the civil procedure convention was not in effect between belligerents because during wartime a state was free even to intern or expel enemy aliens, and therefore could not be held to be obliged to afford them an equality of treatment with nationals in the courts of justice. The court repeated the argument given above also, to the effect that in this case the plaintiff's state, Russia, was not allowing reciprocity, which fact automatically released Germany.[52]

In 1915, also, the Oberlandesgericht of Hamburg held that the convention was not binding between belligerents, on

[49] November 6, 1914, *Markenschutz und Wettbewerb*, 1915, p. 156; October 16, 1914, Landgericht Köln, same decision. For further cases see Kosters-Bellemans, *Les Conventions de la Haye de 1902 et 1905 sur le droit international privé* (Hague, 1921) *passim*.

[50] July 5, 1915, *Boutiflat case*, Tribunal de Sarreguemines, 2me ch. civ., "X", "Annulation des traités ... par la Guerre", *Revue de droit international privé*, vol. 11-12, p. 5.

[51] January 28, 1915, Kosters-Bellemans, *op. cit.*, p. 1157; see also Oberlandesgericht Dresden, June 8, 1916, *ibid.*, p. 1176.

[52] February 26, 1915, *ibid.*, p. 1159.

the ground that its effectiveness depended on the maintenance of regular relations between the states concerned.[53] This point of view was maintained by the German courts from then until the end of the war.

The Hamm Oberlandesgericht repeated the arguments already given for suspension between belligerents, and added that even though the absence of regular relations might not affect certain provisions of the convention, the convention must be considered as a homogeneous whole, of which part might not remain in force while the rest was suspended.[54]

The Belgian courts conceived that the convention concerning the Conflict of Laws regarding Divorce and Separation remained in force even as between opposing belligerents until denounced according to the terms of the convention itself.[55] A post-war decision, however, held that this, like all multilateral treaties was abrogated in the relations between opposing belligerents.[56] As the statement in the latter case was dictum while in the former it was vital to the decision, the former is probably the more reasoned opinion.

The Russian Government at the very outbreak of the war issued a decree stating that the Civil Procedure convention had lost its force as far as the nationals of enemy states were concerned, and that the latter specifically lost the rights to appear in court as plaintiffs.[57]

The French courts were concerned only with the 1905 conventions, France having denounced those of 1902 just before the outbreak of the war.[58] In 1916 she also

[53] June 11, 1915, *ibid.*, p. 1173.

[54] May 12, 1915, Kosters-Bellemans, *op. cit.*, p. 1167.

[55] December 31, 1920, *W. c. T. et Baltus "Qualitate Qua", Séquestre W.*, Cour d'appel de Bruxelles, 3me, *Pasicrisie belge*, 1921, vol. ii, p. 21.

[56] *Berthe Auslander case*, March 30, 1930, Cassation, 2me chambre; *ibid.*, 1930, vol. i, p. 137.

[57] July 28, 1914, *Juristische Wochenschrift*, 1915, p. 418.

[58] November 12, 1913, Kosters-Bellemans, *op. cit.*, p. 22.

denounced the conventions on the Effects of Marriage and the Deprivation of Civil Rights,[59] so that by 1917 she was bound only by the Civil Procedure convention. During the war the French courts had occasion to apply only the 1902 convention regulating Conflicts in matter of Divorce and Separation in dealing with enemy aliens but in the case concerned the action was commenced before the outbreak of the war and while France was still bound by its provisions. No mention was made of the status of the convention during the war period.[60]

In a case arising some time after the war, in 1925,[61] it was held that the Civil Procedure convention was "suspended by the fact of war" as between the belligerents. No distinction was made between different parts of the convention, though the case concerned the dispensation from the *cautio judicatum solvi*.

The Italian courts assumed a more liberal attitude. In 1915, 1917 and in 1918 the convention regarding Divorce and Separation was applied between an Italian and a Hungarian with no mention of the effect of war on its provisions.[62] A decree published in 1915 however deprived Austro-Hungarian subjects of the right to sue in Italian courts, and the same restriction was later extended to Ottoman subjects.[63] It was not however extended to German subjects.

59 December 5, 1916, *ibid.*, p. 819.

60 January 1, 1915, *Bonneboit c. Durig*, Cour d'appel de Pau, *ibid.*, p. 293.

61 July 29, 1925, *Etablissements Coullerez c. Maison Stein*, Colmar, 1st civ. ch., Clunet, *op. cit.*, vol. 53, p. 604.

62 February 18, 1915, Cour d'appel de Venise, Kosters-Bellemans, *op. cit.*, p. 484; April 12, 1917, Cour d'appel de Cagliari, *ibid.*, p. 490; April 2, 1918, Cour d'appel de Rome, *ibid.*, p. 504. *Cf.* also Cour de Venise, October 9, 1917, Clunet, *op. cit.*, vol. 46, p. 418.

63 October 9, 1917, *Domini c. Kenk*, Cour d'appel de Venise, *ibid.*, p. 493.

The criterion established by the Italian courts as to whether treaties were suspended or not between belligerents in wartime was whether such treaties by their nature might be considered incompatible with the state of war. The convention regulating Conflicts of Law regarding Divorce and Separation was held to be among those the execution of whose provisions encountered no obstacle arising from the state of war. It would be only in the nature of a reprisal if a party to such a convention refused to apply it during wartime, and such a reprisal would require the evidence of an express denunciation or some official act, which in the case of Italy was still lacking.

There appears to have been no other occasion in any of the belligerent countries for an appeal under any of these conventions during the war period by a national of an opposing belligerent state. Both belligerents and neutrals allowed the conventions to be invoked freely by the nationals of neutral states during this period. Belgium denounced one of the conventions during the war,[64] and France another,[65] but in neither case was the war the cause of the denunciation, it being due rather to the unsatisfactory results from contradictory interpretations by the different parties. It would appear from these acts that as between belligerents and neutrals or between co-belligerents or between neutrals the conventions were conceived as remaining in full force unless denounced.

As between opposing belligerents the consensus of opinion appears to have been that at least some of the provisions of these conventions might remain in force provided there was reciprocity, that no advantage was given to enemy nationals,

[64] October 30, 1918, Conflict of Laws in the Matter of Marriage, Kosters-Bellemans, *op. cit.*, p. 22.

[65] Effective June 24, 1917, Conflict of Laws concerning the Effects of Marriage, *Brit. & For. State Papers*, vol. 116, p. 666.

or that the political branch of the government did not take definite action to suspend their application.

Labor

At the outbreak of war in 1914 two multipartite conventions concerning conditions of labor in industry, drawn up at Basle in 1906, were in force. These were the conventions concerning the Prohibition of Night Work for Women in Industrial Employment,[66] and the Prohibition of the Use of White Phosphorus in the Match Industry.[67] Both call upon the parties for internal enabling legislation to put into effect the principles laid down in the conventions, and a number of states had set up such legislation before the war.

Neither of these conventions was denounced by any of the parties during the war, yet neither received full application. The convention concerning Night Work for Women contained a clause permitting suspension in case of *force majeure*,[68] when production in the factory concerned is interrupted in a manner impossible to foresee and not having a periodic character. Though there was no special mention of the status of the conventions in wartime, the parties almost uniformly suspended their enabling legislation during that period.[69] At the Washington conference of the International Labor Organization in 1919, when the subject matter of the convention was under discussion, nothing was said concerning this wartime action, its justifiability being apparently accepted.

The convention concerning the Use of White Phosphorus appears to have been treated in much the same fashion,

[66] September 26, 1906, *Brit. & For. State Papers*, vol. 100, p. 794.

[67] *Ibid.*, vol. 99, p. 986.

[68] Art. iii.

[69] Bureau International de Travail, *Etudes et documents*, Série I, no. 2 (Genève, 1931), p. 111.

though it contained no suspensory clause. This convention provided for its own entry into force for adhering states or colonies five years after such adhesion,[70] and in the case of several of such states and colonies this date arrived during the course of the war.[71] Very little enabling legislation was passed however, until the close of the war, and none apparently by these latter states and colonies. Italy announced that " owing to the war the measures for bringing the [enabling] law into force have been deferred until the sixtieth day after the conclusion of peace ",[72] and her action appears to have aroused no comment among the other parties.

In both cases it appears that the parties felt that they were free to suspend the application of these conventions during the war, even without the formality of a preliminary announcement. This view of the nature of their obligations appears to be confirmed by postwar discussions of the subject.

When the matter was discussed in the International Labor Conference in Washington in 1919, mentioned above, it resulted in no general agreement on the subject. A provision for suspension contained in the draft convention concerning the Hours of Work in Industrial Undertakings[73] " in the event of war or other national emergency " was objected to by a Swiss delegate on the ground that the convention probably would be suspended under these circumstances without such a provision, but that the Labor Conference was not in a position to say whether or not it should be suspended. A French delegate indicated his belief that if the words " event of war " were eliminated there might be a dangerous extension of the scope of the term " or other emergency endan-

[70] Art. v.

[71] *Report on the Employment of Women and Children and the Berne Conventions of 1906* (London, 1919), p. 63.

[72] *Ibid.*

[73] November 28, 1919, Hudson, *International Legislation*, vol. i, p. 392.

gering national safety." In the end, in view of the fact that in several states national legislation embodying the eight hour day advocated by the convention provided for suspension of this limitation in the event of war, the clause was left in.[74]

The attempt to include a similar clause in the draft convention concerning the Age of Children Admitted to Industrial Employment[75] was defeated by a large majority. There was no internal legislation to be considered in this case, but it is not clear whether the intent back of the omission was to indicate that such conventions were considered as automatically suspended by war or whether they automatically remained in force in spite of it. The convention concerning Night Work for Young Persons in Industry[76] contained only the " national emergency " clause,[77] but in this case the convention was based on the 1906 agreement controlling Night Work for Women in Industry,[78] which contained merely a provision for suspension in case of an emergency not periodic in character, and it was felt undesirable to make any change in adapting the provision to the new convention.

The labor conventions signed between 1919 and 1930 contain no provision for suspension either by war or by other national emergency. But in 1930 the question of such suspension came up for discussion again in connection with the convention concerning the Regulation of Hours of Work in Commerce and in Offices,[79] the original draft of which contained the clause permitting suspension in case of war or other emergency endangering national safety. Its inclusion

[74] Art. xiv.

[75] *Ibid.*, p. 417.

[76] *Ibid.*, p. 421.

[77] November 28, 1919, art. vii, *ibid.*, p. 421.

[78] September 26, 1906, *Brit. & For. State Papers*, vol. 100, p. 794.

[79] June 28, 1930, *International Labor Conference*, vol. i, pt. iii, p. 877.

in this convention [80] was successfully sponsored by Belgium on the same grounds as in 1919, that is, in order to harmonize this convention with that of 1919 concerning the Hours of Work in Industrial Undertakings and with national legislation providing for such suspension. The draft convention concerning Hours of Work in Coal Mines,[81] signed at the same time, omitted this clause, as it was felt that the purpose was accomplished by the words "emergency endangering national safety." [82] It will be recalled, however, that in 1919 the two phrases were considered as supplementary, helping to define each other.

Neither in the 1919 nor in the 1930 conferences was there a discussion of the effect of war on those conventions from the point of view of international law.[83] Where the war clause appears it apparently was included primarily to harmonize the conventions with national legislation; where this is not necessary it is omitted. There appears to be no theory generally accepted by states concerning the status of these conventions in wartime. It is doubtful whether states would consider suspension automatic in such an event; however, the experience with labor in past wars indicates that states would not hesitate to suspend provisions concerning hours of labor if such suspension were important for successful conduct of the war.

CONCLUSIONS

From the foregoing discussion a number of rules governing the status of multipartite treaties in wartime may be suggested:

[80] Art. ix.

[81] *Ibid.*, p. 842.

[82] It was inserted, however, in the final draft, art. xiii.

[83] See *International Labor Conference*, Washington, pp. 128, 154, 247 *et seq.*; also *ibid.*, 1930, vol. i, pp. 456, 781.

1. Subject to numerous exceptions to be mentioned later, multipartite conventions may be said to be generally suspended so far as they concern direct relations between belligerents, but to remain unaffected where neutrals are involved. They are rarely terminated.

2. Apart from this generalization, such treaties may be split into clauses, and the effect of war on each clause considered separately.

3. The nature and extent of the war may determine whether a clause is suspended or not. If the clause is involved in the causes of the war, or if it concerns a region in the path of hostilities and is of an executory nature, it may be suspended. If the war is intense and general and of long duration the suspension is apt to be more general than if the war is localized and short.

4. If the clause deals with a matter of technical regulation rather than with a political question, or if it imposes an equal obligation on all the parties rather than forming part of an exchange of advantages of different sorts, it is less apt to be affected.

5. If the clause involves the establishment of a common standard of measurement or conduct within the limits of each state, it generally remains in full force.

6. If it deals with private real or personal rights it is less apt to be suspended than if it deals with the rights of states.

7. War may operate to suspend treaty provisions in the relations between neutrals and belligerents or even between neutrals. This is particularly true in conventions dealing with communications or with financial matters and involving both belligerents and neutrals in the course of a severe or prolonged general war or one occurring in a region affecting the communications involved, or upsetting the financial stability of one of the parties whether a belligerent or neutral.

The old categories have only a limited usefulness. It was

customary, for example, to consider treaties of commerce, alliance and guaranty as among those terminated by war, yet we have seen that if the first is regulatory it may not even be suspended between belligerents, that if the object of the alliance is not involved and the number of parties is large it may be merely suspended between the belligerents, and that inasmuch as guaranties cover practically the entire field of treaty relations there is no general rule which can be applied. However, the rule that treaties providing for the conduct of war come into force with such an event appears sound.

There are several categories of treaties that are found only in multipartite form; such are those setting up the public law of Europe, those establishing international unions, and the great peace treaties at the close of general wars. It has been found that the first were a species of guaranty, and might be considered with that category; that the second were suspended between belligerents so far as direct relations between them were concerned, but generally remained in effect where they provided for relations with a central body, or rules for the operation of that body; and that the third, the general peace treaties, had to be considered piecemeal, there being no possible generalization concerning the effect of war.

It has been noted that there is a growing tendency to make provision, in treaties dealing with communication and transit, that they should survive in wartime so far as the rights and duties of neutrals and belligerents would permit. In other conventions it appears to be the intent of the parties to await the event, inasmuch as war brings in its train so many unforeseen consequences that it appears better to allow complete freedom to the parties to deal with the situation. In spite of this absence of provision for survival of treaties in wartime, suspension among multipartite treaties is by no means a general rule. As this type of treaty concerns itself more and more with international regulation and less with contractual relationships with differing obligations for the different parties, the probability of suspension becomes less.

The difficulty of the task of defining the rights and duties of belligerents and neutrals under such treaties as have mentioned them appears to have been sufficient to deter the parties from attempting such a definition, and no new one has been attempted since 1907. The extremely varied history of the conventions described indicates the enormity of the task involved.

As has been noted, only a small number of conventions state specifically what their wartime status shall be. The reason for this is to be sought in the varied and uncertain effect which the operations of war have upon treaties. It is essential to recall in this connection that war *ipso facto* has no effect upon the great majority of treaties. In those setting up rules for the conduct of hostilities, the effect of war is to bring them at once into operation. In the case of the few treaties where a war might destroy the subject matter, (as it might in the case of the convention for the maintenance of the Cape Spartel light, for example), the convention presumably would be terminated, and would require a new arrangement of the parties to rebuild the lighthouse. But in the case of most other treaties there need be no effect of war beyond making performance of certain obligations temporarily impossible. Outside of the limited categories mentioned, if it were the intent of the parties to maintain the conventions in force there would be no bar to their doing so.

But it is extremely difficult in most cases to determine what that intent was, as the conditions which war produces can not often be foreseen. We have in such cases a determination by each state of its own intent, and thus the great differences of opinion concerning the status of these conventions in wartime, and the consequent disagreement as to whether a new act of the parties is essential for their survival thereafter.

Experience indicates however that states are inclined to interpret liberally their obligation to maintain treaties dealing with purely technical matters or those involving private rights, and to interpret strictly such obligation in regard to arrangements concerning political matters. But as war must by its nature remain uncertain in its effects on the objects which treaties are intended to accomplish, there is little prospect that states will be generally inclined to register in the terms of a treaty their intent regarding such effects.

CHAPTER II

Termination at the Close of Hostilities

INTRODUCTION

There are two different phases of a treaty's postwar history which must be discussed here. The first phase, that between the cessation of hostilities and the coming into effect of the peace treaty, may be very short, in fact so short as to be of minor consequence in connection with the status of treaties. It may on the other hand be of considerable duration. After the war of 1914-18 the period from the time of the Armistice on November 11, 1918, to the date when the Treaty of Versailles went into effect on January 10, 1920, was fifteen months. In the cases of the Austrian and Hungarian treaties it was longer, and the time from the Armistice of Mudros when Turkey capitulated, until the treaty of Lausanne went into effect, was over five years. During such periods the state of war legally continues, but it is obviously possible to resume peace-time relations to some extent, and it will be observed to what extent this is done in practice.

There has seldom been occasion to consider in detail the status of treaties in such an intermediate period as occurred between the various armistices and the dates when the peace treaties went into effect between 1920 and 1923. The parties to these treaties almost uniformly considered this interval officially as part of the war period, yet in practice there was a much greater degree of observance of many of the provisions of prewar conventions during his time than while hostilities were actually in progress. The chief value of a consideration of this period is in showing that though states officially are inclined to take the view that the period of war legally extends from the date of its declaration until the date when the treaty of peace enters into effect, actually they are disposed to permit a resumption of observance of prewar treaties during such a period to the extent that it does not prejudice the peace negotiations. There appears to be only a limited concern over a possible upset of the contractual balance involved in giving effect to only a part of a treaty's provisions. Particularly the desire to reestablish the lines of commercial intercourse operates to bring about a resumption of activity, with old treaties as a convenient basis, except where states present active opposition.

The comparison between the attitude of states concerning their treaty obligations while hostilities are in progress and in the intermediate period under discussion, serves as guidance in determining the actual effect of war on treaties. During the war there is a limited field where all inter-state activity ceases and therefore treaty relations are suspended within that field. There is another limited field in which states have determined that whatever the immediate advantage may appear to be, it is ultimately wise to allow treaty relationships to subsist in full force. There is a large intermediate field in which treaty relationships are suspended in so far as the conduct of the war appears to make it essential.

But with the cessation of active hostilities the guiding principles are somewhat changed. In so far as hostile operations have ceased a large resumption of interstate activity theretofore prohibited becomes possible, and, in so far as it conduces to rehabilitation of the belligerent state, desirable. Such renewed activity calls for regulation, and pending new arrangements the old can usually be made to serve. So in spite of the fact that such arrangements are frequently held not to be binding if they have been considered as suspended during hostilities, the exigencies of the situation have often given them a quasi-validity, and in some cases national courts have considered them as in force. Both the field in which treaty relationship had ceased and that in which it had been partially suspended are in practice therefore considerably reduced. To justify such a resumption of old relations it must take place in accordance with the aims of states in resorting to war, a question considered in dealing with the postwar status of international agreements.

It is not clear, however, until the peace treaty has been ratified what the postwar status of prewar conventions is to be, and it is chiefly what has been provided, or what the negotiators failed to provide, in such instruments which will concern us here. Where part of a treaty has been maintained in effect and part suspended during war—a course of action which may upset the contractual balance established by the treaty—the agreement reestablishing peace furnishes the evidence of how that balance was reestablished. It sometimes indicates in general the estimate of the parties of the binding character of their engagements in wartime, and whether the conventions of the prewar period were intended to survive such an event. Where the peace treaty makes no mention of old conventions, an attempt will be made to determine the significance of the omission—whether the parties intended thereby that the old convention was to be considered as terminated, whether it required no action by the parties to retain its force, or whether they intended to leave the matter in abeyance.

TREATIES REGULATING THE CONDUCT OF HOSTILITIES

Conventions for the purpose of regulating the conduct of war may be considered as expressions of the ripened thought of the signatory states regarding established principles, generally combined with the detailed provisions necessary to carry these principles into effect. In so far as these conventions express such principles their existence is not dependent on conventional statement. This is evidenced by the attitude of the signatories of the Declaration of London of 1909,[1] a declaration having no binding force as a convention, but which nevertheless was considered binding as a statement of principles by some of the belligerents at the outbreak of the war.

On the other hand the detailed provisions, though comprised in the same convention, would seem to have less of an immutable character, being administrative rather than declaratory. For example, the Hague convention for the Adaptation to Naval Warefare of the Principles of the Geneva Convention[2] provides that military hospital ships cannot be captured while hostilities last,[3] and that these ships shall be distinguished by being painted white outside with a horizontal band of red;[4] the latter provision might be changed in favor of a more easily distinguished mark purely as a matter of expediency, without affecting the principle on which the entire convention is based.

In practice, however, such a distinction appears not to have been made. Such conventions have been regarded apparently as an indissoluble whole, and although violations of the administrative provisions have not been considered as serious as violations of the principle, war appears to have affected both types of provisions in the same way where it has affected them at all.

[1] February 26, 1909, Martens, *Nouveau recueil général des traités, etc., 3me série*, vol. vii, p. 39.

[2] October 18, 1907, Malloy, *Treaties, etc. of the United States*, vol. ii, p. 2326.

[3] Art. iii.

[4] Art. v.

1904 Conventions Concerning the Exemption of Hospital Ships in Time of War from the Payment of Dues and Taxes for the Benefit of the State.

The 1899 convention applying the rules of the Red Cross Convention of 1864 to naval warfare,[5] contained provisions concerning hospital ships in its first three articles, and the 1904 [6] convention amplified the principles there enunciated. As distinct from the conventions already considered, it was mentioned in the Treaty of Versailles as one of the conventions which was to be applied as between Germany and the Allied and Associated Powers.[7]

The reason for this is not clear. In character the treaty appears to resemble the Hague conventions, from which it derives. It apparently was considered as binding during hostilities, and would therefore seem not to require mention in a peace treaty more than other conventions of the sort. Its wide acceptance by states would indicate too that its provisions were held to have binding force apart from the convention which first declared them. If an act of the signatories was necessary to restore the convention to binding force, we are faced with the situation of a long list of conventions, including those of the Hague, which remain suspended in view of the absence of such an act of the parties. One is forced to the conclusion that the differential treatment was not due to any design of the parties at the Peace Conference to distinguish between these conventions, but that the convention under discussion belongs in the general category of the Hague conventions and the others discussed.

[5] July 29, 1899, Malloy, *Treaties, etc. of the United States*, vol. ii, p. 2035. Spain, Persia, China, Mexico, the Netherlands, Peru, the United States and Switzerland were parties to this convention though not to the peace treaties. Presumably they are all still bound.

[6] December 21, 1904, Malloy, *Treaties, etc. of the United States*, vol. ii, p. 2135.

[7] Art. 282.

Hague Conventions, 1899 and 1907.

The 1899 group of agreements was confined to measures for the settlement of international disputes and for ameliorating the horrors of war. Three conventions, that regarding the Pacific Settlement of International Disputes,[8] that With Respect to the Laws and Customs of War on Land,[9] and that concerning the Adaptation to Maritime Warfare of the Principles of the Geneva Convention,[10] were replaced by conventions of similar title in 1907, as between the parties to the latter group. The convention concerning the Pacific Settlement of International Disputes does not concern us here.

There were a number of belligerents bound only by the earlier conventions when war broke out in 1914.[11] As has been observed, however, both sets of conventions lost their binding force due to the presence of non-signatories among the belligerents, yet both were given effect by many of the belligerents. Neither set was mentioned in the treaty of peace, yet postwar adhesions to the 1907 conventions indicate that they are considered as still in force.[12] There is, however, no reason to suppose that those states formerly bound only by the 1899 conventions are no longer bound, even in the absence of such definite evidence as adhesion by a non-signatory state.

The reason for this lack of mention of the Hague conventions in the peace treaties is not made clear. If it is due to

[8] See art. xci of 1907 convention.

[9] See art. iv of 1907 convention.

[10] See art. xxv of 1907 convention, *Treaties, etc., of the United States*, vol. iii, p. 2220.

[11] Bulgaria, Greece, Italy, Montenegro, Serbia, Turkey.

[12] Finland adhered to all the 1907 conventions, and Latvia only to the convention concerning the Adaptation to Naval Warfare of the Principles of the Geneva Convention.

the fact that most of them deal with the conduct of the war and are therefore unaffected in their validity by war that would account for all but two, those which deal with the Pacific Settlement of International Disputes and the Employment of Force for the Recovery of Contract Debts. If they are all conceived of as expressions of international law, then there was no need of any statement in the peace treaties concerning their binding force. The fact of their frequent violation seems to indicate that revision might be advisable; this need has indeed been recognized in a convention concerning the Treatment of War Prisoners, signed in 1929.[13] It is doubtful whether, without revision, they would find as general acceptance in another war of the duration, intensity and widespread character of the last.

Amelioration of the Condition of the Wounded in Armies in the Field.

This convention, signed in 1864,[14] was adhered to by most of the states of the world. In 1868 a new agreement containing several additional articles, and laying down rules for the application of some of the articles of the original convention to similar situations in naval war, was signed but not ratified.[15] In spite of this, France and Prussia announced their intention to observe the rules of the 1868 additional convention during the Franco-Prussian War.[16] These are two additional instances of general conventions which would seem to be expressions of current standards of behavior on the part of states, and which they informally agree to observe in the absence of a binding convention.

[13] July 27, 1929, *U. S. Treaty Series*, no. 846.

[14] August 22, 1864, Malloy, *Treaties, etc. of the United States*, vol. ii, p. 1903.

[15] *Ibid.*, p. 1907.

[16] Renault, *Les deux conférences de la paix 1899 et 1907* (Paris, 1909), p. 179.

In 1906 the 1864 convention was superseded among the parties to the earlier convention [17] by a convention bearing the same title. The later convention was not mentioned in the Peace Treaties, but in view of a number of adhesions since 1920 [18] may be presumed to be in effect. In view of the absence of any agreement between the parties since the war, it may be conceived of as having survived the war.

Declaration of Paris, 1856.

Although at the time the Declaration of Paris concerning Maritime Law was drawn up in 1856,[19] only the signatories of the Peace Treaty of the same date had signed, the declaration itself provided that it should remain open for accession, and by 1914 it had been accepted by almost all states, including all the belligerents at that time.[20] The United States, though it had refused to adhere to the Declaration, had not done so through unwillingness to accept the principles involved, and had in fact both in 1861 and 1898 announced its intention to respect that one which forbade privateering.[21]

Since 1856 the principles involved in the Declaration have not been confirmed in any treaty of peace, nor has the Declaration itself received mention. There has apparently been no question, however, of their binding character. It has presumably therefore been unnecessary for the parties to the Declaration to take any formal action, even after a general war, to maintain it in force.[22]

17 July 6, 1906, Malloy, *Treaties, etc. of the United States*, vol. ii, p. 2183.

18 Dominican Republic, Ecuador, Greece.

19 April 16, 1886, *Brit. & For. State Papers*, vol. 46, p. 26.

20 Garner, *International Law and the World War*, vol. i, p. 13.

21 Higgins, *The Hague Peace Conference* (Cambridge, 1909), p. 3.

22 The freedom of principles of international conduct once enunciated, from dependence on a specific convention is nowhere better shown than

HAGUE CONVENTIONS I AND II OF 1907

The theory that the Hague Conventions, as agreements establishing rules for the conduct of war, cannot be suspended by such an event, does not apply to the First Convention dealing with the Pacific Settlement of International Disputes,[23] and the Second Convention of 1907, Limiting the Employment of Force for the Recovery of Contract Debts,[24] as neither is concerned with the conduct of war. Both contain statements of principle which might be said to have binding force apart from the convention in which they are stated, and neither contains any provision for its own status in wartime. Both prescribe procedure for the peaceful settlement of disputes which would necessarily be suspended between opposing belligerents.

As a matter of fact, proceedings begun under the former were partially suspended during the war even between co-belligerents and between belligerents and neutrals. When war broke out in 1914, a compromis had been agreed to by Peru and France for submission to the Court of Arbitration set up under the convention, but with the outbreak of hostilities pro-

in the history of the Declaration of London. When this was drawn up in 1909 it was provided that unanimous and complete ratification was necessary to bring the agreement into operation, a condition not yet attained at the outbreak of the war in 1914. An inquiry sent out by the United States Government at that time, brought responses indicating partial or conditional acceptance of the Declaration from all the European Great Powers. Germany, morever, incorporated the Declaration's rules regarding contraband in her prize code. There were extensive modifications during the course of the war, but no complete abandonment. The Declaration, like that of Paris, had never been mentioned in a treaty of peace, and of course has no binding force as a treaty; on the other hand it would probably be inaccurate to say that Governments have felt justified in ignoring its provisions for that reason.

[23] October 18, 1907, Malloy, *Treaties, etc. of the United States*, vol. ii, p. 2220.

[24] *Ibid.*, p. 2248.

cedure under it was suspended by agreement of the parties. A second case, between France, England, Spain and Portugal, begun before the war, suffered a similar interruption.[25] No new cases were submitted during the period from 1914 to 1921. There is no indication, however, that the convention itself was considered by the parties to have been suspended.

The proceedings of the League of Nations Committee of the Peace Conference of 1919 indicated the belief of some of the members of that committee that the first convention was considered to be in force. Both of the French members, Larnaude and Bourgeois, were anxious for specific mention of the work of the Hague Conference in the preamble to the League Covenant. President Wilson and Lord Cecil, on the other hand, professed to see no need for any specific reference, but avoided making any definite statement concerning the status of any of the Hague conventions. Bourgeois expressed the opinion that the trial of those responsible for the war should take place according to the Hague procedure, but again the English and American representatives avoided any expression concerning the status of the convention or its suitability in the instance under discussion.[26]

Although all mention of the convention was eliminated from the preamble to the Covenant by vote of the Committee, House and Cecil took pains to explain that such action was not to be considered as indicating that the convention was without force, but merely that mention in the preamble would be unwise.[27] The matter of the Hague conventions was not brought up again, and they were not mentioned in the peace

[25] Scott, *Hague Court Reports*, Second Series (New York, 1932), p. 199.

[26] Miller, *My Diary of the Peace Conference*, vol. v, pp. 326-8, 365-8, 396. But see German and Italian draft proposals, *ibid.*, vol. iii, p. 86, iv, p. 286, v, p. 78.

[27] *Ibid.*, pp. 434-5, 449-50.

treaties at all.[28] But in 1921 the Court resumed procedure on the two cases mentioned, in accordance with the agreement of the parties concerned.[29] Presumably the parties to the convention considered that no action was necessary to continue it in force. Czechoslovakia, Finland and Poland have adhered to the First Convention since the war.[30]

The second of these conventions, dealing with the Recovery of Contract Debts, calls for abstention from an action classed as illegal rather than for positive action. There appears to have been no attempt to collect contract debts by force during the war period, so the question of its status during that time was not raised. No state indicated, however, that it ceased to consider itself bound. As with the First Convention, there was no mention of its status in the peace treaties. Finland has adhered to this convention since the war, indicating that it has continued in force with no new act of the parties.

It would appear that these two conventions have survived the war on the basis of general acceptance by civilized states. The procedure set up by the First Convention has diminished in importance through the creation of other machinery, though the convention appears to be accepted as in force. The principle embodied in the Second Convention appears to have attained sufficiently general acceptance so that the convention embodying it is considered to be in force without postwar action by the parties concerned.

[28] See amendment proposed by Vesnitch, *ibid.*, pp. 217-18, 233-4.

[29] *Expropriated Religious Properties Case*, Scott, *op. cit.*, pp. 153, 199; *French Claims against Peru*, *ibid.*, pp. 202, 206. The Statute of the Permanent Court of International Justice (December 16, 1920, art. 1; Publications of the Court, series D, no. 1) testified to the existence of the 1907 court at the time of its signature.

[30] Hudson, *American Journal of International Law* (1931), p. 114.

TREATIES OF GENERAL SETTLEMENT

The multipartite treaty of general settlement is ordinarily much more than the settlement of the causes of the war preceding it. It has constituted usually either a new charter or a series of amendments to an old one. For the purposes of this discussion we will commence with the treaties of Westphalia,[31] which, taken as a whole, constitute the first great European charter. This settlement was made at the end of a general European War, commenced as a religious struggle with political aspects, and finished with the political aspect the dominant one. The settlement at the end reflected the complicated issues of the war; the treaties set up a religious settlement, established rules for diplomatic intercourse between states, and made a territorial settlement for Germany. The latter provisions were involved in a long succession of wars running through the eighteenth century, and were changed by treaty at the end of these wars. In each case, however, the treaty of peace confirmed such parts of the settlement of Westphalia as had not been changed, as well as such parts of the succeeding modifying treaties.[32] Thus we find in the treaty of peace of 1763 after the Seven Years' War that, beginning with Westphalia, no less than sixteen treaties were " renewed and confirmed in all their points from which there is no derogation in the present treaty." [33] To have attempted to draw up in one agreement just what provisions of Westphalia were still left intact would have been a task of great difficulty, if possible at all; in any case it was not attempted.

[31] Dumont, *Corps diplomatique universel,* vol. vi, pt. ii, pp. 403, 429, 445, 450, 469, 495, 562; Koch, *Recueil de traités,* vol. i, p. 75.

[32] *Cf.* art. iii of the Treaty of Peace of Aix-la-Chapelle of October 18, 1748; *Traités publics de la royale maison de Savoie* (Turin, 1836-61), vol. iii, p. 51.

[33] February 10, 1763, Martens, *Recueil des traités,* vol. i, p. 33.

After the Napoleonic wars a new charter was drawn up, in which no mention of the prewar treaties occurs. Again a great variety of questions was settled, many of which were unconnected with the succession of wars preceding the treaty. The General Act of the Congress of Vienna [34] set up provisions which have since been reflected in customary international law, such as those concerning diplomatic rank [35] and the abolition of the slave trade.[36] It included territorial settlements which remade the map of Europe.[37] It included a constitution for the German Confederation in one of its Annexes.[38] It made several dynastic settlements.[39] As in the case of the settlement of Westphalia, there was no clear indication which provisions were considered as declaratory of general international principles and which were part of the price for obtaining the consent of any of the parties. In the course of the century following, this settlement was broken down, sometimes by unilateral act, as when Polish autonomy was terminated by Russia,[40] sometimes as a result of war.[41]

The need of an examination of the entire arrangement of 1815, in order to settle a number of questions then threatening the peace of Europe and to gather together such parts of the original arrangement as were still valid, was recog-

June 9, 1815, *Brit. & For. State Papers*, vol. ii, p. 7.

[35] Annex xvii.

[36] Annex xv.

[37] Annexes i-viii.

[38] Annex ix.

[39] Annex viii, concerning the House of Orange-Nassau; annex v concerning the House of Schönburg, and others.

[40] For the circumstances, see Hertslet, *Map of Europe by Treaty*, vol. ii, p. 875 *et seq.*

[41] Annex vi, concerning territorial arrangements between Prussia and Hannover. The war of 1866 resulted in the annexation of Hannover.

nized by Napoleon III in 1863. He attempted to call a general conference to make such a revision, but Great Britain discouraged it, fearful that the delicate questions involved might hasten a war if an attempt was made to settle them in general conference.[42] Among the questions proposed, two [43] resulted in war within a few years, and the other three [44] were settled as a result of other wars. It is in this field of treaties forming charters for parts of Europe that amendment by peaceful means has been most difficult; in general it is only after a military struggle that a new settlement has been reached.

The third general settlement acting as a new charter was that comprised in the peace treaties of 1919-23. A new method of attacking the problem of how to preserve the old arrangements was here employed, consisting of an enumeration of those treaties or parts of treaties which were to be preserved, and in most cases indicating that the remaining treaties or parts were to be considered abrogated. For the first time detailed provisions concerning prewar treaties were made, and as this procedure is probably an important precedent for future action it will be given close consideration.

PEACE TREATIES, 1919-1923

The first point which stands out from the peace treaties of 1919-23 is their avoidance of any indication of the status of prewar treaties during the period of the war. The peace conferences were faced with the primary problem of setting up a new charter for the control of international affairs, and they devoted themselves to this task without involving them-

[42] For discussion, see Hertslet, *op. cit.*, p. 1575 *et seq.*

[43] The question of the Danish Duchies, which brought on the war of 1864, and that of Venetia, which was settled by the war of 1866.

[44] Poland, Danubian Principalities, occupation of Rome by French troops.

selves with the problem of what the situation had been during the past war. A comparison of the texts of the various treaties in both the English and French versions and of the wording of the different articles dealing with prewar treaties indicates a careful avoidance of any statements which would indicate a definite stand on the question of the extent to which their validity was affected during the war.

The prewar economic and technical treaties still considered to be useful to the Allies, according to all the peace treaties except that with Turkey, were to be "applied";[45] in the latter treaty they were to "enter again into force."[46] On the other hand, in the English version, the parties to all the treaties were to "apply" the postal and telegraph conventions mentioned,[47] whereas according to the French version the expression used was "appliqueront de nouveau."[48] According to the Versailles treaty, Industrial and Literary and Artistic Property conventions were "again to come into effect",[49] but according to the St. Germain and Trianon treaties they were to be "applied",[50] and in the French version, "remis en vigueur." Germany's treaties with her allies signed since the beginning of the war "are and remain abrogated",[51] while Austria's and Hungary's "are of no effect."[52] The Allied and Associated Powers were to notify Germany and Bulgaria which bilateral treaties they wished

[45] Art. 282 of Versailles, 234 of St. Germain, 217 of Trianon, 162 of Neuilly.

[46] Art. 99 of Lausanne.

[47] Art. 283 of Versailles and corresponding articles of other treaties.

[48] For French version of Versailles treaty see Martens, *Nouveau recueil général, 3me série*, vol. xi, p. 323.

[49] Art. 286.

[50] Art. 237 of St. Germain, 220 of Trianon.

[51] Art. 290 of Versailles.

[52] Art. 242 of St. Germain, art. 225 of Trianon.

"to revive",[53] and to notify Austria and Hungary the same treaties which they wished "to be in force"; [54] on the other hand, in dealing with these treaties the French wording in the Versailles treaty approaches in meaning the English version of the Austrian and Hungarian treaties—namely, "remettre en vigeur."

There is thus no uniformity between the wording of the different treaties, nor an exact correspondence between the English and French versions. If, as would appear, the parties intended to avoid any commitment concerning the wartime status of these treaties and merely to indicate their postwar validity, then the ambiguity of these expressions is a matter of no moment. Under any other hypothesis the variations only lead to confusion.

In several cases, however, it was made clear that the termination of Germany's rights under prewar treaties was to be considered as dating from the outbreak of the war. This was the case with Germany's renunciation of her rights under the Moroccan [55] and Egyptian capitulations,[56] and in Samoa under the treaty of 1899.[57] It was true also of Germany's rights under her bilateral treaties with France concerning Morocco,[58] and of the Act of Algeciras.[59] These instances must be regarded as exceptions, however, as otherwise the transfer of rights was to take place as from the coming into force of the peace treaty.

There apparently was but one recognition of the peculiar

[53] Art. 289 of Versailles, 168 of Neuilly.

[54] Art. 241 of St. Germain, 224 of Trianon.

[55] Art. 142.

[56] Art. 147.

[57] Art. 288.

[58] Art. 141.

[59] *Ibid.*

status of the period between the Armistice and the entering into effect of the peace treaty; in the case of Alsace-Lorraine it was provided that restoration to France was to be considered as dating from November 11, 1918.[60] There is, however, no such provision concerning any of the other territorial arrangements, and this case must be considered rather an exception than a rule.[61]

Further evidence of the unwillingness of the parties to espouse any rule concerning wartime status is found in the provisions concerning bilateral treaties. In all except the Turkish treaty the Allied and Associated Powers were allowed the privilege of notifying the defeated state which bilateral agreements they wished to "revive" or "to be in force",[62] guided by the general principles or special provisions" of the peace treaty concerned.

An unusual provision in connection with bilateral treaties would appear to indicate an intent to approximate the effect of war on such treaties to the effect of breaking off diplomatic relations. It is provided that the rules concerning bilateral treaties as indicated should apply "even if the said Allied and Associated Powers have not been in a state of war" with the Power concerned.[63] Inasmuch as several states listed among the Allied and Associated Powers[64] had merely broken off diplomatic relations with one or more of the Cen-

[60] Art. 51.

[61] *Cf.* German view, expressed in the German Delegation's Observations on the Conditions of Peace, Official Summary, Senate Document 149, 66th Cong., 1st Sess., 1919, no. 7608, Sect. 4. This presumably explains the inclusion of the Armistice date in the provision concerning Alsace-Lorraine.

[62] Art. 289 of Versailles, art. 241 of St. Germain, etc., *ibid.*

[63] *Ibid.*

[64] E. g., Peru, Bolivia, Ecuador and Uruguay. *Cf.* protest in the German Delegation's Observations on the Conditions of Peace, Second Part. (See note 61, *supra.*)

tral Powers, the effect was to allow them the right of unilateral denunciation by virtue of breaking off such relations.

In many cases the peace treaties failed to indicate the fate of prewar treaties at all, and in others left it ambiguous. No prewar peace treaties were mentioned. A small number of economic or technical treaties, such as those controlling the International Sugar Union,[65] were left out. Of the treaties providing for the conduct of war, only one, that Exempting Hospital Ships from Dues in Time of War [66] was mentioned. In a number of cases the defeated state was forced merely to renounce its rights under a treaty, with no mention of the fate of the treaty as a whole.[67] In other instances provision was made for the temporary or permanent application of part of a prewar treaty's provisions with the proviso that a new convention was to be drawn up to replace the old.[68]

The usual saving clause to the effect that the conventions to be applied are "subject to the provisions . . . of the present Treaty" [69] occurs in all these peace treaties. But nothing is said of the right of non-belligerents to be consulted in making the modifications which the peace treaties involved, (with the exception of the provision for obtaining Holland's consent to the revision of the 1839 treaties concerning Belgium) [70] even where such modifications were considerable.

Several principles guiding the Allied and Associated Powers in dealing with the question of prewar treaties appear

[65] March 5, 1902, convention relative to Bounties on Sugar, and Protocol, *Brit. & For. State Papers*, vol. 95, p. 6; August 28, 1907, Additional Act and Declaration, *ibid.*, vol. 100, p. 482; March 17, 1912, Protocol Prolonging Union, *ibid.*, vol. 105, p. 392.

[66] Art. 282, Versailles.

[67] E. g., art. 141.

[68] Art. 345.

[69] Art. 282 of Versailles, and corresponding articles.

[70] Art. 354.

to stand out from the above. First: there was an evident design to avoid a commitment on the status of these treaties in wartime. Second: whatever that status was, it was considered to persist until the peace treaties went into effect, regardless of the fact that hostilities had ceased some time since.[71] Third: the rupture of diplomatic relations might have the same effect on treaties as the actual resort to hostilities. Fourth: a general congress such as that which assembled at Paris in 1919 may determine the status of prewar treaties, without necessarily consulting non-belligerent parties, where these are few, not of the first rank, and not vitally concerned in the matters dealt with in the treaties.

Of the three great European charters, those of 1648, 1815 and 1919, only the last was a settlement where the defeated parties were not represented during the negotiations. For this reason the latter arrangement is more an expression of the victors' will than a compromise between the extreme views of the ex-belligerents, except where there was a conflict of interests between two or more of the Allies; in such cases more dispassionate thought concerning the value of the provisions as equitable settlements was evident. But the Paris settlement was of great value as being the first detailed disposal of the question of the effect of a general war on precedent treaties, by any considerable part of the community of states.

BOUNDARY TREATIES

The rule that boundary provisions in treaties act as certificates of title, and are independent of conditions existing during or after a war, appears to be established beyond question. Peace treaties generally fail even to mention prewar

[71] But see *Sophie Rickmers* and *Flensburger* cases for attitude of United States courts (45 Fed (2nd), 413, and 73 Ct. of Claims, 646 (1932).

boundary lines between belligerents where such boundaries have been neither a cause of the war nor the scene of conflict. In practice the only means of altering boundaries once established appears to be by a new treaty between the parties concerned in such an alteration. This need not, however, include the same parties as those participating in the creation of the earlier line, except such states as have the new boundary as a frontier. Boundaries are however frequently a matter of general interest, and states geographically distant may have a direct interest in their maintenance.

An example of the situations described is offered by the boundary between France and Germany. This frontier was established in 1815 by a treaty to which Great Britain, Austria, Prussia, Russia and France were parties.[72] It was altered in 1871 by France and Germany alone,[73] and the other parties to the 1815 convention apparently conceived that they had no claim to participate in the change. It was altered again in 1919 by a treaty to which most of the civilized states of the world were parties, but in which Russia and Austria of the 1815 parties were not represented.[74] Due to the international guaranty of this frontier by Germany, Belgium, France, Great Britain and Italy, signed in October 1925,[75] these Powers would presumably have to participate in any change of the Versailles provision regarding this frontier, but this would be due to the guaranty treaty, and it is not believed that any of the other parties to any of the peace treaties would, under most circumstances, be deemed to have

[72] Treaty of Peace of November 20, 1815, Hertslet, *Map of Europe by Treaty*, vol. i, p. 342, art. i.

[73] February 26, 1871, Preliminary Treaty of Peace, *ibid.*, vol. iii, p. 1912, art. i.

[74] Art. 51 of Versailles.

[75] *Brit. & For. State Papers*, vol. 121, p. 923.

a right under these treaties to participate in the negotiations concerning any change in this boundary.

There appears to be no rule to determine whether any states other than those whose limits are directly affected have an interest in a change of boundary by treaty. In the instance just cited a multipartite arrangement was changed by a bipartite treaty, which in turn was revised by another multipartite arrangement. Where a change in frontier is included in the war aims of one of the belligerents, the status of the boundary is apt to be mentioned in the peace treaty, whether the boundary is changed or not, and all the belligerents thus become parties to the new arrangement. Should the same boundary be involved in a subsequent war the new group of belligerents will be parties to the new arrangement, by virtue of their participation in the peace settlement. This fact does not signify that other states with a special interest in the boundary, on a variety of grounds, may not also be parties to the new arrangement; it merely connotes that the status of belligerent almost invariably involves participation in the treaty settlement of boundary questions involved in a war, and lack of participation in a subsequent war concerned with the same boundary may serve to eliminate a state from participation in a change in that settlement. Such an elimination does not apply to a state whose territorial limits are affected by the new settlement.

TREATIES OF GUARANTY

The uncertain nature of many guaranties frequently makes difficult the determination of their status after a period of war has been brought to a close. A classification of the forms in which multipartite guaranties are given will help in determining whether such guaranties may be expected to survive a conflict in which the parties to the guaranty are belligerents.

These may be divided into three groups. The first of these is the simple statement of a guaranty only. An example of this type is the guaranty given to Belgium and the Netherlands by the Great Powers in 1839.[76] This type is of uncertain significance, as the obligation resting on the guarantors is not made clear. The second type of guaranty calls for consultation or common action by the guarantors in case of infraction of the treaty guaranteed, but still does not bind the parties to any given course of action beyond that.[77] The third, less common during the nineteenth century than earlier, provides for specific steps to be taken by each of the guarantors.[78] Any of these types might be included in the terms of the treaty guaranteed or be the subject of a separate instrument.

The seventeenth- and eighteenth-century guaranties were generally made to forestall a situation likely to arise within a limited number of years, such as an attempt to invade a given territory or to overthrow the provisions of a treaty. Rarely does one find mention of such guaranties in a peace treaty after the war against which the guaranty was to provide. The treaties guaranteed were generally those dealing with a specific situation, and a war resulting in the modification of that situation was sufficient to cancel a guaranty calling for a stated number of horse and foot to defend the stipulations of such treaties.

As has been indicated, the nineteenth-century guaranty was of a different character. It was rather a declaration by the guaranteeing Powers (usually the Great Powers) that certain

[76] April 19, 1839, *Brit. & For. State Papers*, vol. 27, pp. 990, 1000.

[77] Treaty relating to Insular Possessions and Insular Dominions in the Pacific Ocean, December 13, 1921, *League of Nations Treaty Series*, vol. 25, p. 183, art. i.

[78] *Cf.* League of Augsburg, July 9, 1686, Dumont, *Corps diplomatique universel*, vol. vii, pt. ii, p. 131, art. iii.

treaty provisions were considered of general interest and any attempt at violation would be a matter of general concern. Only in rare instances was it made clear what action the guarantors were to take in case of violation.

For such guaranties there was much less need of revision after a war, even a war between the guarantors. Unless through the events of the war the provisions under guaranty had ceased to be a matter of general interest, the guaranty might be presumed to continue in force. Unfortunately, however, it is not always clear when the guaranteed provisions cease to possess such an interest, and therefore the moment at which the guaranty has terminated is not always indicated. It is essential always to distinguish the provision guaranteed from the guaranty itself; a treaty of peace will frequently indicate that a treaty provision remains in force, but leave obscure the question whether the guaranty has subsisted or not.

Ionian Islands, 1815

In 1815, subsequent to the signing of the General Act of Vienna, England, France, Prussia and Russia joined in a treaty establishing an English protectorate over the Ionian Islands.[79] The latter three Powers "formally guaranteed all the dispositions"[80] of the treaty, and jointly with England attached it to the General Act of Vienna. The treaty, including the guaranty clause, apparently survived the Crimean War, in which three of the parties to the treaty were opposing belligerents, since with no intermediate act the same parties ratified a second treaty in 1863 revising the earlier treaty and terminating the protectorate.[81] It is to be sup-

[79] November 5, 1815, Hertslet, *op. cit.*, vol. i, p. 337.

[80] Arts. i and ii.

[81] November 14, 1863, Hertslet, *op. cit.*, vol. ii, p. 1569.

posed that the guaranty lasted as long as the treaty of which it formed a part.

Greece, 1832

In 1832, when the Greek Government was organized under Otho of Bavaria, Great Britain, France and Russia stipulated that "under the Guarantee of the 3 Courts" Greece should "form a monarchical and independent state" under his sovereignty.[82] It is to be presumed that this guaranty survived the Crimean War, in which all the guarantors were engaged, although with the abdication of Otho that part of the guaranty involving his personal sovereignty was obviously terminated. The balance of the guaranty, involving Greece's monarchical government and independence, apparently survived even the abdication, since with the repetition of the guaranty in 1863,[83] substituting the name of William of Denmark for Otho, occurred a discussion indicating that the guarantors considered that that much of the guaranty was still in force.[84]

In 1864, at the time of the union of the Ionian Islands to Greece, the guaranty of Greece as a monarchical, independent and constitutional state was repeated, this time without mention of the name of the ruler.[85] It was presumably this latter guaranty which survived down to 1914, and which was invoked by the Allied Powers in 1916 at the time of their landing in Saloniki. It is to be observed that the guaranty treaty has not been subjected to the test of war between the guarantors.

In view of the fact that the monarchical government no longer exists in Greece, and that none of the guarantor

[82] May 7, 1832, *ibid.*, p. 895.

[83] Treaty of July 13, 1863, art. iii, *ibid.*, p. 1545.

[84] Protocol of Conference, June 26, 1863, *ibid.*, p. 1544.

[85] Treaty of March 29, 1864, art. i, *ibid.*, vol. iii, p. 1589.

Powers took any decided steps to maintain it, that much of the guaranty at least would appear to have been terminated. There is nothing to indicate that the events of the war were specifically responsible, and the subject was not mentioned in any of the treaties of peace. That the guaranty survived at least until the last year of the war, in the opinion of the guarantors, is clear however from their action at Saloniki, described elsewhere. This would indicate that, having survived so much of the war, it was perhaps independent of the existence of a state of war, and was terminable only on other grounds. That the guaranty as a distinct part of the treaty survived is established by the fact that in the Saloniki incident it was invoked by name. There is seldom as clear an indication that the guarantors are acting under a guaranty where the obligations of the guarantors are left as obscure as in this case.[85a]

Norway, 1907

In 1907, after the separation of Norway from Sweden was completed, Germany, France, Great Britain and Russia "recognized and engaged to respect the integrity of Norway", by a treaty to which Norway also was a party.[86] The guaranty was made specific by the statement that "if the integrity of Norway was threatened or injured by any Power" these Governments "engaged, after a communication to this effect from the Norwegian Government, to lend their

[85a] The preamble to the treaty of Sèvres, August 10, 1920, between the Principal Allied and Associated Powers and Greece, provided that France and Great Britain "renounce the special rights of control and supervision devolving on them" from the treaties of 1832, 1863, and 1864, mentioned above. It would appear that the guaranty was considered by these powers to have subsisted through the period of hostilities, and was terminated only by the later treaty.

[86] Treaty of November 11, 1907, *Brit. & For. State Papers*, vol. 100, p. 536.

support to that Government in whatever way was most appropriate with the view of safeguarding the integrity of Norway." [87]

In 1924 Norway denounced the treaty in accordance with its terms, on the ground that the guaranty was contrary to the spirit of the Covenant of the League of Nations, and that a number of unforeseen circumstances such as the war, the Russian revolution and the treaty of Versailles had changed both the requirements of Norway and the value of the guaranty.[88] She announced therefore that she would no longer avail herself of the guaranty pending the two years' interval before her denunciation could take effect. The denunciation was immediately accepted by all the other signatories except Russia, which was not consulted.[89] It is clear from the above that this guaranty survived the war of 1914-18, in which all the guarantors were belligerents.

Luxemburg, 1867

The neutralization of the Grand Duchy of Luxemburg was guaranteed by the five Great Powers in 1867.[90] Three years later France and Prussia, two of the guarantors, were at war with each other, but though Germany protested alleged French violations,[91] each belligerent promised to respect the guaranty if respected by the other.[92] The guaranty was in force in 1914, when war broke out, and was the subject of discussion at the Peace Conference.[93] The treaties of Ver-

[87] Art. ii.

[88] January 8, 1924, *League of Nations Treaty Series*, vol. 23, p. 65.

[89] *Ibid.*, pp. 65-67.

[90] Treaty of May 11, 1867, Hertslet, *op. cit.*, vol. iii, p. 1801.

[91] December 3, 1870, Bismarck to Bernsdorff (ambassador to Great Britain), *ibid.*, p. 1901; Feb. 8, 1871, Bernsdorff's statement, *ibid.*

[92] July 17, 1870, Loftus to Granville, *ibid.*, p. 1877.

[93] April 4, 1919, bulletin no. 131, Miller, *Diary*, vol. xvii, p. 365; March 3, *ibid.*, p. 30; March 5, *ibid.*, vol. xv, p. 149 *et seq.*

sailles and of St. Germain provided that Germany and Austria "adhered to the termination of the régime of neutralization" of Luxemburg,[94] though there was no indication as to when and how this termination took place. A possible explanation of this question was given in the Assembly discussion in 1920 regarding Luxemburg's possible admission into the League of Nations, where it was stated that "the Powers signatory to the disarmed neutrality of Luxemburg decided its abrogation by the Treaty of Versailles."[95] If this is the correct interpretation, then the guaranty survived the war of 1914-18 also, and was terminated only by the Treaty of Peace.

In this case the neutrality, the subject of the guaranty, was specified in the same provision as the guaranty, and they stood and fell together. Though there was no indication of the nature of the obligation of the guarantors, it was clear that if the peace treaty terminated Luxemburg's neutrality it also terminated the guaranty of that neutrality. The peace treaty provision cited as terminating the disarmed neutrality of Luxemburg fails to do more than to state that Germany, one of the guarantors, adheres to the termination of the régime of neutrality, but Luxemburg and the other guarantors have proceeded as though specific provision for termination had been made, indicating that all the parties to the guaranty consider it as no longer in force.

Belgium, 1839

In 1839, as a result of negotiation begun in 1831, a treaty between Belgium and Holland was guaranteed separately to the two states by the five Great Powers.[96] In 1870, at the

[94] Art. 40 of Versailles, 84 of St. Germain, 68 of Trianon.

[95] December 16, 1920, Plenary meeting, *Records of Assembly*, Plenary Meetings, 1920, p. 585.

[96] Treaty of April 19, 1839, between Belgium and the Netherlands, *Brit. & For. State Papers*, vol. 27, p. 1000.

beginning of the Franco-Prussian war, the question of the nature of the obligation of the guarantors was discussed,[97] but there was no suggestion that the war between two of the guarantors had terminated the guaranty. The guaranty was considered by all the parties as being still in existence in 1914 at the outbreak of the war, though the guarantors appear since then to conceive that the neutralization guaranty at least has been terminated.[98] The peace treaty was far from clear on the status of the 1839 treaties,[99] due to a divergence of view as to what disposition should be made of them. Belgium sought to convince the peace conference that the treaties as a whole were terminated, which would automatically have included the guaranty, but failed.[1] Both she and the guarantors have indicated that both the neutralization provision and the guaranty of neutralized status are terminated. But the balance of the provisions are still considered to be in force, and there is no definite indication that the guaranty as applied to these provisions is not still in force. It has been argued that a neutralized status was not in harmony with the obligations of Article XVI of the Covenant of the League of Nations,[2] but none of the guarantors appears to have definitely espoused such a view in this case. Moreover, there is every reason to believe that provisions regarding Belgium's independence and frontiers are still matters of general Euro-

[97] *Ibid.*, vol. 60, pp. 10, 13; also Hansard, *Parliamentary Debates*, Commons, vol. lxv, col. 1818.

[98] *Cf.* writer's article in *American Journal of International Law*, July, 1932, vol. 26, no. 3, p. 514.

[99] *Cf.* art. 31 of Treaty of Versailles.

[1] *Cf.* Belgium's demand for revision of these treaties in 1917, Miller, *Diary*, vol. iv, p. 426.

[2] This is based on the obligation of art. 16, par. 3, of the Covenant of the League, requiring member States to permit the passage of troops across their territory.

pean interest, and their guaranty even if involving only respect, as interpreted by some of the parties, would still be of value.

It is possible that in view of the guaranty of Belgium's German frontier given at Locarno,[3] coupled with the statement in that agreement that the parties took note of the abrogation of the old treaties,[4] they may be considered as terminated, and therefore the guaranty is also terminated. But this can only be accepted on the basis that the executed provisions are not included, and that England's interest in guaranteeing the southern frontier against France or the northern frontier against the Netherlands no longer exists. In any case, it appears established that the parties to the guaranty conceived that the events of the war had brought about changes which resulted in the termination of the neutralization provision and of the guaranty which accompanied it.

Aaland Islands, 1856

In 1856 Russia declared, in a bilateral treaty with France and Great Britain, that in response to the desire expressed by those Powers she would not fortify the Aaland Islands, and that no military or naval establishment should be created or maintained there.[5] This treaty was attached to the general convention signed the same date by the same Powers plus Austria, Prussia, Sardinia and Turkey,[6] and which was guaranteed by a third convention signed by Austria, France and Great Britain.[7] It would thus appear that Russia was obligated by treaty to six Powers not to fortify the islands, and

[3] *Brit. & For. State Papers*, vol. 121, p. 923, art. i.

[4] *Ibid.*, preamble.

[5] March 30, 1856, Hertslet, *op. cit.*, vol. ii, p. 1272.

[6] Same date, art. xxxiii, *ibid.*, p. 1250.

[7] April 15, 1856, *ibid.*, p. 1280, art. ii.

that three of these had guaranteed Russian observance of the obligation.

In 1859 war broke out between two of the guarantors,[8] but as Russia made no attempt to fortify the islands at that time there was no occasion to determine whether the guaranty had survived the war. There was no further warfare between the guarantors until 1914, but this time Russia built fortifications. By the treaty of Brest-Litovsk, however, she agreed to demolish them.[9] When title passed to Finland, the latter state attempted to fortify the islands, justifying herself on the ground that the treaty of 1856 had been annulled by the war. When the case was brought before the Council of the League it was referred to a committee of jurists, who held that the treaty had not been annulled by the war, but did not mention the guaranty.[10]

There is no clear indication of the date when this guaranty ceased to be binding. In 1898 the British Government published a list of those guaranties to which it was a party, and that of the Aaland Islands was not included.[11] It was not made clear what event was the cause of the termination of the British obligation, however, nor whether her release was part of a general termination of the guaranty or merely unilateral. It is clear, however, that the guaranty was not related in its fate to the provisions guaranteed, which in this case have long survived the guaranty.[12]

[8] Between Austria, France and Sardinia, of which the former two were guarantors.

[9] March 3, 1918, Temperley, *History of the Peace Conference*, vol. iii, iii, p. 42, art. vi.

[10] League of Nations, *Official Journal*, 1920, Special Supplement, no. 3, p. 18.

[11] May 15, 1898, Cmd. paper 9088, Misc. no. 2, 1898.

[12] *Cf.* note 10, *supra*.

Bosphorus and Dardanelles, 1840

In 1840 the Sultan of Turkey announced the policy of non-admittance of foreign ships of war into the Straits while the Porte was at peace, and Great Britain, Austria, Prussia and Russia engaged to respect this principle.[13] This declaration was repeated in a convention the following year with France as an additional signatory.[14] At the close of the Crimean War, which involved three of the guarantors, a convention was signed by all the parties to the 1841 agreement " renewing " the old obligation to conform to the principle of the closed Straits.[15] Inasmuch as the respect for the principle was binding only while the Porte was at peace, and the Porte had been a party to the war, it would have seemed unnecessary to renew the engagement when the war was over. It appears that the principle was unchanged, as it was referred to in the treaty of peace as the " ancient principle "; the guaranty alone was renewed.

Nothing more is heard of the guaranty in peace treaties, either when Turkey is or is not a belligerent in the precedent war. In practice, however, the principle guaranteed was observed, and in the negotiations following the Russo-Turk War, Russia made clear her intent to abide by it.[16] The principle itself was modified in 1923, in the treaty of Lausanne.[17]

It is frequently difficult to determine the effect of war on guaranties, or to account for lack of their mention in treaties

[13] July 15, 1840, art. iv, Hertslet, *op. cit.*, vol. ii, p. 1008.

[14] July 13, 1841, art. i, *ibid.*, p. 1024.

[15] March 3, 1856, preamble, *ibid.*, p. 1266.

[16] Russian declaration, Berlin Congress, July 12, 1878, *ibid.*, vol. iv, p. 2727.

[17] July 24, 1923, Treaty concerning the Régime of the Straits, art. i, *British Treaty Series*, 1923, no. 16, p. 109.

of peace, in view of the fact that often this indefiniteness appears with a clear history of the provisions guaranteed. Frequently such a condition appears due to the fact that the guarantors intended to set up what is known as a " European principle " or " Public Law of Europe ". Once a guaranty has been given it appears to be deemed to have given the provisions guaranteed such a special character. The former guarantors thenceforward appear to consider that the subject matter of the guaranty had become of general interest, and does not require for its observance any further evidence of support from specific Powers.

This conception does not, however, aid us in discovering at what time and in what way the specific guaranty becomes merged in the general. Presumably there is no fixed date; all would depend on when there was sufficient evidence of general acceptance of the guaranteed arrangement to warrant the withdrawal of the specific guaranty. If war results in a change in the arrangement subject to guaranty then of course the guaranty falls with the arrangement. If the arrangement subsists without challenge, the guaranty will probably not be repeated in the peace treaty. If it is challenged, however, during the war or at the peace conference, the guaranty is apt to be repeated.

TREATIES CONCERNING INTERNATIONAL UNIONS AND BUREAUS [18]

The peace treaties of 1919-23 left little ambiguity concerning the postwar status of the international unions. All those unions actually in existence before the war whose membership included states among both sets of belligerents were

[18] For a discussion of the juridical nature of such unions and bureaus, see Ruffini, " La Protection internationale des droits sur les oeuvres littéraires et artistiques ", Académie de Droit International de la Haye, *Recueil des Cours*, vol. 12, p. 472 *et seq.*

provided for in these treaties, through stipulations that the conventions under which the unions were operating before the war should be again " applied ", " in force ", or otherwise binding on the parties.[19]

It is not to be supposed, however, that in the absence of a provision in a peace treaty these unions would not survive. In view of the fact that a number of the unions had almost completely resumed their prewar status before the peace treaties went into effect, it is probable that the parties to these treaties intended rather to indicate their recognition of the existing situation than to provide an essential treaty basis for the operation of such unions.[20]

Most of the international bureaus in existence in 1914 were set up in connection with a corresponding international union. Practically all of them functioned to some extent during hostilities, and had resumed a large part of their activities before the peace treaties went into effect. Apparently the only international bureau set up by treaty and in existence in 1914 which was not provided for in the peace treaties was that set up under the Hague convention for the Pacific Settlement of International Disputes. The reason for this is not clear; the activity of the Bureau was largely interrupted, and was resumed without any provision in the peace treaties. There was apparently no decision on the status of the bureau in the peace conference. It is nevertheless clear that no treaty

[19] E. g., art. 282 of Versailles contains provisions concerning the Institute of Agriculture, art. 283 concerning the Postal Union, art. 286 the Union for the Protection of Industrial Property, etc.

[20] It is interesting to note that the international union apparently most seriously affected by the war was the Latin Monetary Union. None of the Central Power belligerents were members, and it was not mentioned in the peace treaties in consequence. But the dislocation of the currencies of the member states due to wartime inflation brought about its termination soon after the war. This is another instance of the effect of war on treaties to which opposing belligerents were not parties.

provision was necessary to confirm the postwar existence of this bureau.

The status of the individual unions and bureaus will be considered under the subject matter of the conventions which established them, in the sections which follow.

TREATIES OF COMMERCE AND COMMUNICATIONS

As has been indicated above in dealing wtih commercial treaties in wartime, their status during hostilities depends on whether their stipulations are of a permanent character and whether they manifest a design to establish rights which should survive a war. As between belligerents the result has usually been to suspend all provisions dealing with an exchange of goods, inasmuch as such exchange has been forbidden and the regulations are therefore redundant. But provisions dealing with personal and real property rights generally have been given effect.[21] Such procedure, of course, is apt to change the contractual unity of the convention, and therefore has resulted in revision in the peace treaty or by separate agreement shortly after the war.

The situation regarding commercial treaties to which neutrals and belligerents are parties, or those between co-belligerents, is similar.[22] They are not necessarily suspended during the war, but are frequently denounced, not of course for the reason that commercial intercourse is forbidden, but because it is difficult or impossible. As in the conventions between opposing belligerents, the contractual balance between rights and obligations is broken, and postwar revision is usually resorted to. This was the case at the close of the

[21] *Champeaux-Grammont c. Cardon*, January 15, 1811, *Recueil général des lois et des traités, Collection nouvelle*, 3, 1, 377, Cassation; cited in Jacomet, *La Guerre et les traités*, p. 87.

[22] United States-Netherlands correspondence, 1873, *U. S. Foreign Relations*, p. 715 *et seq.*

last two general wars, in 1815 and in 1918, when there was a general clearing away of old commercial agreements with replacement by new.[23]

This does not, however, apply to broadly accepted multipartite agreements dealing with commercial matters. The reason for this is clear. As such agreements set up identical obligations of a technical nature for all the parties there is no upsetting of the balance between rights and obligations among them, and hence the conventions are as applicable after the war as before. This principle was recognized in the Treaty of Versailles, which, in Article 282, provided for the application of a long list of these agreements. Among these are the 1890 convention for the Publication of Customs Tariffs,[24] the 1913 convention regarding the Unification of Commercial Statistics,[25] the 1907 convention regarding the Raising of the Turkish Customs Tariff,[26] the conventions regulating the redemption of tolls on the Sound and Belts,[27] the Elbe[28] and the Scheldt,[29] the 1875 convention regarding the Unification of the Metric System,[30] and others.

On the other hand, where a multipartite convention consists of a bilateral arrangement between one state and a group of others, the question of the balance between rights and

[23] *Cf.* Fish to Westerberg, Aprii 9, 1873, *U. S. Foreign Relations*, 1873, p. 725, concerning status of commercial treaties in 1815 after the Napoleonic wars. For Italian denunciations during 1914-18 see *Brit. & For. State Papers*, vol. 111, p. 753; for French and Spanish, *ibid.*, pp. 834-9.

[24] July 5, 1890, Malloy, *op. cit.*, vol. ii, p. 1996.

[25] December 13, 1913, *Brit. & For. State Papers*, vol. 116, p. 575.

[26] April 25, 1907, *ibid.*, vol. 100, p. 575.

[27] March 14, 1857, *ibid.*, vol. 47, p. 24.

[28] June 22, 1861, Hertslet, *op. cit.*, vol. ii, p. 1471.

[29] July 16, 1863, *Brit. & For. State Papers*, vol. 53, p. 8.

[30] May 20, 1875, Malloy, *Treaties, etc. of the United States*, vol. ii, p. 1924.

obligations is a matter of concern at the end of a war, and at least some of the parties would probably attempt to bring about revision.[31] The nature of the obligation rather than the number of the parties is largely determinative of the postwar status of commercial conventions.

Waterways

The conventions concerning navigable waterways deal primarily with the control of navigation on these waterways through some international agency, and to that extent involve the possibility of maintaining such an agency in existence when its members are nationals of opposing belligerent states. A further question arises when the waterway is in the path of hostilities and navigation thereon is thereby disorganized. Much of the postwar discussion concerning the status of prewar conventions has hinged on the attempt to determine whether the parties intended such conventions to survive a situation involving one or both of these difficulties.

The Danube

Twice since the Danube was internationalized in 1856 it has been in the path of hostilities, once in 1877, during the Russo-Turk War, and again in 1914-18. In both instances there was a partial suspension of the conventional provisions governing navigation of the river,[32] but in neither case was there an indication that any of the belligerents considered the treaty stipulations as more than suspended, and in both there was partial resumption of navigation under the old treaty rules before the postwar arrangements went into effect.

In neither case was there a clear indication by the parties

[31] *Cf.* Lausanne treaty of Commerce, July 24, 1923, *Brit. & For. State Papers*, vol. 117, p. 612, art. xviii.

[32] *La Commission européenne du Danube et son oeuvre de 1856 à 1931* (Paris, 1931), pp. 27-8, 37-9.

to the peace treaties of their opinion regarding the status of the prewar treaties. The Berlin agreement in 1878 provided that the provisions of the 1856 convention which established the status of the Danube as an international river, and the agreement of 1871 modifying the 1856 agreement were "maintained in all those dispositions which are not abrogated or modified" by the new treaty.[33] The definitive statute of the Danube drawn up in 1921 pursuant to the provisions of the treaty of Versailles provided that "all the treaties, conventions, acts and arrangements relative to the regime of international rivers in general and to the Danube and its mouths in particular which are in force at the moment of signature of the present Convention are maintained in all their dispositions which are not abrogated or modified by the preceding stipulations."[34]

The question of the survival of the prewar arrangements came up in connection with the Fourteenth Advisory Opinion of the Permanent Court of International Justice, which was called on to determine the extent of the jurisdiction of the European Commission.[35] In the opinion itself, the Court speaks of the "reestablishment" of the situation existing before the war, and states that "the statute . . . now in force . . . was prepared under the provisions of the Treaty of Versailles and the corresponding provisions of the other Peace Treaties", without reference to any prewar conventions.[36] Judge Nyholm, in a concurring opinion, observes that "as regards treaties prior to the Treaty of Versailles, there seems to be no doubt that they have been abolished. In

[33] July 13, 1878, art. lxiii, *Brit. & For. State Papers*, vol. 69, p. 749.

[34] July 23, 1921, *ibid.*, vol. 114, p. 535, art. xli.

[35] Competence of the European Commission between Galatz and Braila, *Publications of the Permanent Court of International Justice*, series A/B. 25.

[36] *Ibid.*, p. 12.

fact at the moment when the Treaty of Versailles was drafted, the position was an entirely new one, all the past having been cleared away."[37] Judge Negulesco, the Rumanian dissenting judge, upheld the prewar treaties as strengthening Rumania's case, but failed to mention the effect of the war or its events on these engagements.[38]

Nyholm's opinion is, however, at variance with the facts. As has already been noted, navigation on the Danube was being carried on largely according to the prewar arrangements by the time the peace treaty went into effect, and the provision of the Definitive Statute quoted above took this situation into account. Nyholm appears to have adopted the old theory of the termination of all treaties by war, a theory scarcely applicable to a case such as this. The opinion of the court contained no definite statement because none was required in its solution of the question at issue.

That the treaties survived the wars in part seems established. It appears evident also that the peace conferences, faced with the task of providing at least a temporary régime, did so by leaving conditions as they existed, and postponing provision for a permanent settlement to a later conference.[39]

Congo and Niger

The Berlin General Act of 1885 [40] provided that commercial traffic on the Congo and Niger rivers should always be free,[41] and as a further safeguard stated that the provisions of the Act of Navigation, which formed part of the General Act, should remain in force in time of war.[42] The provi-

[37] *Ibid.*, p. 72.

[38] *Ibid.*, p. 95.

[39] Arts. 346-9, Treaty of Versailles.

[40] February 26, 1885, *Brit. & For. State Papers*, vol. 76, p. 4.

[41] Arts. xiii and xxvi.

[42] Arts xxv and xxxiii.

sions regarding freedom of traffic would appear to have been suspended only as between the opposing belligerents during the war. France and Great Britain were in complete control of the Niger, and Belgium, after the repulse of an initial German invasion, retained with France entire control of the Congo.[43]

The treaty of peace provided that " Germany undertakes to accept and observe the agreements made or to be made by the Allied and Associated Powers or some of them with any other Powers with regard to the . . . matters dealt with in the General Act of Berlin and . . . Brussels ",[44] leaving the field open for future agreements. Later in the year, at the time of the signing of the Austrian Peace Treaty, the projected new arrangement was made, reaffirming the principle of the freedom of commercial traffic, on the Niger only,[45] and abrogating the balance of the convention of 1885.[46]

It will be observed that the treaty of Versailles did not renew or apply the Berlin Act, but merely secured Germany's acquiescence to prospective new agreements. The status of this act at the time of the St. Germain agreement would thus appear to have been what it was at the close of the war. The St. Germain treaty dodged the question of the effect of war on the Berlin Act by abrogating it " so far as . . . binding between the Parties to the present Convention." [47]

There are two noteworthy changes in this later convention. The first is the withdrawal of the Congo from freedom of com-

[43] *Cf.* report submitted by Belgian Government, January 30, 1919, Miller, *Diary*, vol. xiv, pp. 114-20.

[44] Art. 126.

[45] Treaty Revising the General Acts of Berlin and Brussels, September 10, 1919, Malloy, *Treaties, etc. of the United States*, vol. iii, p. 3739, art. 5.

[46] *Ibid.*, art. 13.

[47] Art. 13.

mercial traffic, and the failure to replace the clause providing that such traffic should always be free in wartime as well as in peacetime. In view of the changed status of the Congo territory since the earlier convention a new statute for the Congo appeared necessary, and the experience with commercial traffic on international rivers during the last war indicated that national prohibitions went far to nullify the treaty arrangement for free navigation.

The Scheldt

As far back as 1648, the Scheldt was closed to international navigation by the treaty of Munster,[48] a condition unchanged until the action of the French Convention in 1792 in reopening it.[49] In 1814 one of the secret articles of the treaty between the four Allied Powers and France provided for the free navigation of the river,[50] on the same basis as that of the Rhine, stipulated in the same treaty.[51] The General Act of the Congress of Vienna provided that the Rules for the Navigation of Rivers,—Annex XVI to the Act,[52]—should have the same force and value as if part of the Act itself.[53] The Annex provided for liberty of navigation of several rivers, including the Scheldt,[54] made the riparians responsible for its maintenance,[55] and stated that future provisions must

[48] January 30–March 1, 1648, art. xiv; Abreu y Bertodano, *Collecion de los tratados de paz* (Madrid, 1740-1752), vol. vii, p. 322.

[49] November 16, 1792; Adanya, *Régime international de l'Escaut* (Paris, 1929), p. 41.

[50] May 30, 1814, art. iii, Hertslet, *op. cit.*, vol. i, p. 18.

[51] *Ibid.*, art. v, p. 8.

[52] *Brit. & For. State Papers*, vol. ii, p. 162.

[53] Art. 118.

[54] Special articles relating to the Neckar, Main, Moselle, Meuse and Scheldt, attached to annex XVI.

[55] Art. v.

be made on the basis of the greatest freedom of commerce and navigation.[56]

The statute in force in 1914 at the outbreak of the war was that included in the treaties of 1839 between the Great Powers and Belgium and Holland respectively.[57] The provisions regarding freedom of navigation specified in the General Act of Vienna [58] were renewed in this convention, and detailed regulations were included governing navigation,[59] demilitarizing Antwerp [60] and assuring the Netherlands control of both banks of the lower river,[61] a control which necessitated her refusal to allow the passage of belligerent vessels in wartime.

The great difficulties which these provisions caused the Allied Governments during the war,—the inability to provision Antwerp when the German occupation threatened, and the delays incident to getting supplies into Belgium early in the war through the small Channel ports which were not thus closed,[62] made the Allies willing to turn a friendly ear to Belgium's claim to a rectification of the situation. A strong effort was made to build up a case for revision of the 1839 treaties, but Belgium was also interested in other questions involving these treaties, such as boundary changes and the end of the régime of demilitarization of Antwerp, and attempted to have them all considered at the same time.[63]

All these attempts failed, however, in view of the refusal

[56] Art. vii.

[57] *Brit. & For. State Papers*, vol. 27, p. 992.

[58] Arts. cviii-cxv.

[59] Art. ix.

[60] Art. xiv.

[61] Art. i.

[62] Temperley, *History of the Peace Conference*, vol. ii, p. 194.

[63] Miller, *Diary*, vol. iv, p. 426.

of Holland to consider herself bound by the provisions of the Versailles treaty regarding the Scheldt, by the inability of Holland and Belgium to agree on any program, and by the unwillingness of the other states (due perhaps to the impossibility for them to reach an agreement) to force Holland to accept an imposed regime.[64] So in spite of the fact that Belgium's neutralization (provision for which was included in the same 1839 treaty) appears to have been terminated, the balance of the treaty, including the provisions regarding the Scheldt, was considered generally as in force when the war was over.[65]

The 1839 convention survived the Franco-Prussian and Austro-Prussian wars between its signatories, without any mention in the treaties of peace in either case. The same result, with the exception of the neutralization provision, appears to have occurred after the war of 1914-18, in spite of the Belgian effort to secure a recognition of the termination of the treaty, backed by the support of some of the American and French delegates.[66] The series of attempts by Holland and Belgium since then to come to an agreement for modification have made no mention of the termination of the old treaty by the war.[67]

Rhine

The General Act of the Congress of Vienna established international control of the Rhine,[68] and applied to it the prin-

[64] *Ibid.*, vol. x, p. 50.

[65] Navigation on the Scheldt has since been governed by the provisions of the 1839 treaties, and the territorial provisions still stand.

[66] Miller, *Diary*, vol. iv, p. 491, and vol. x, p. 50.

[67] *La Revision des traités de 1839, Documents diplomatiques* (Brussels, 1929), p. 12; also *Bescheiden in Zake de Tusschen Nederland en Belgie, etc.* ('sGravenhaage, 1929), pp. 13-15.

[68] Hertslet, *Map of Europe by Treaty*, vol. i, p. 78.

ciples governing international rivers, set forth in the same act.[69] At the time of the attempted settlement of the problem of the independent status of Belgium in 1831 a new act, implementing the 1815 arrangement, was drawn up at Mayence by five of the German states, France and the Netherlands.[70] This agreement subsisted until 1868, when it was replaced by the Convention of Mannheim, drawn up by the same parties.[71]

The Franco-Prussian War, involving two of the signatories, apparently was considered not to have affected this agreement, since it was not mentioned in the treaty of Frankfort [72] at the end of the war. Alsace-Lorraine was substituted for France, however, as a riparian. The convention of Mannheim was still in effect in 1914 when war broke out, and although partially suspended during the period of hostilities was never terminated. The Versailles treaty provided that the convention " shall continue to govern navigation as from the coming into force " of its provisions,[73] thus avoiding any statement as to the status during the war of the old convention, but subjected the latter to certain changes specified in the peace treaty, including the substitution of an international Central Commission for the old riparian commission set up before the war.[74] The status of the rules for navigation on international rivers, as set forth in the General Act of Vienna, was not mentioned until the convention setting up

[69] Arts. cviii-cxvi.

[70] March 31, 1831, Hertslet, *op. cit.*, vol. ii, p. 848.

[71] October 17, 1868, *Brit. & For. State Papers*, vol. 59, p. 470.

[72] May 10, 1871, Hertslet, *op. cit.*, vol. iii, p. 1954.

[73] Art. 354. This article states that "as from the coming into force" of the treaty, the old provisions "shall continue to govern"; an apparent contradiction in terms.

[74] Art. 355. For Holland's consent to the Versailles arrangements see the *Bulletin de l'Institut intermédiaire international*, 1921, vol. iv, p. 341.

a Régime for Navigable Waterways of International Concern was drawn up in 1921.[75] This convention, while not mentioning the General Act, stated that the parties were "desirous of carrying further the development of the international régime of navigation on internal waterways, which began more than a century ago, and which has been solemnly reaffirmed in numerous treaties."[76] The Statute attached to the convention, however, modified somewhat the provisions of the General Act, particularly in taking the control of navigation away from the riparians alone.[77]

We find, then, that the 1868 convention survived one war between its signatories, with no provision for its renewed application. But in the case of a general war the parties deemed it necessary to insert in the subsequent peace treaty a provision for renewal, without stipulating whether the convention had meanwhile been suspended or abrogated. The different treatment accorded the 1868 convention in 1871 and in 1919, may be accounted for on several grounds. In 1871 one of the belligerents was eliminated as a riparian by the war; there was therefore no need of making a new arrangement with that riparian. The question of commerce and navigation on the river was not involved in the issues of the war, nor did the war indicate the need of making any changes in the statute of navigation. In 1919, on the contrary, the revision of the entire system of international control of river navigation was under consideration and the negotiators of the peace treaties were engaged in drawing up a complete plan of international organization. Apart from the situation existing on the Rhine itself, and the dislocations caused by the war, there was thus a more general reason for a statement of the new rules governing the situation.

[75] April 4, 1921, *League of Nations Treaty Series*, vol. vii, p. 36.

[76] Preamble.

[77] Statutes attached, arts. ii and xi.

Elbe

The application to the Elbe of the general provisions concerning international rivers was accomplished by the convention of 1821,—to which the riparian states were parties,[78]—modified in 1844[79] and 1863[80] by subsequent agreements. It was the latter which controlled navigation during the wars of 1864[81] and 1866,[82] but neither of these wars, though the belligerents were all parties, appears to have affected the validity of the convention, as it was not mentioned in the peace treaties and was in effect thereafter. In 1870 the North German Confederation, which had absorbed all the parties to the earlier conventions except Austria, and the latter state, abolished the river tolls by bilateral convention.[83]

There were no further changes in the Elbe treaty régime until after the war of 1914-18. The problem of the wartime status of the Elbe conventions was simpler than with the other rivers, since only Germany and Austria—who were allied—were riparians, but no mention was made in the peace treaty of such status. As in the case of the other rivers, the peace treaty merely concerned itself with the problem of future navigation, stating that "pending new agreements" "the international agreements and regulations at present governing the navigation of the Elbe shall be provisionally maintained in force."[84] There is implicit in this statement an acceptance of the fact that the war had resulted in at most

[78] June 23, 1821, Hertslet, *Map of Europe by Treaty*, vol. i, p. 671.

[79] April 13, 1844, *ibid.*, vol. ii, p. 1036.

[80] April 4, 1863, *Brit. & For. State Papers*, vol. 55, p. 938.

[81] Between Denmark and Austria and Prussia.

[82] Between Austria and Prussia and Italy.

[83] June 22, 1870, Hertslet, *op. cit.*, vol. iii, p. 1876.

[84] Art. 345.

suspending part of the prewar agreements, but no attempt was made to indicate which provisions were included.

Conclusions

The experience of the past century with international control of waterways would indicate that a rather clearly defined body of rules governs the interpretation of the parties concerning the effect of war on conventions establishing or defining such control. The basis of such control until 1921 was the rules set down in the treaty of Vienna of 1815, these rules not requiring any renewal after a conflict in order to retain their binding force. It has not been deemed necessary to reestablish prewar provisions after a war between signatories to river conventions where control of the river has not been a cause of the war [85] or where the river was not in the path of military operations.

But the parties to the river conventions appeared to hold a general conflict such as that of 1914-18 created contingencies which required reconsideration of the provisions regulating international rivers. There is evidence in the negotiations that a continuance of the old régime until a new one was established was considered essential, and therefore that there could be no sweeping away of old conventions. But it was also made clear that a statement of the effect of war on these old conventions was to be avoided.

The postwar conventions indicate that at present the parties have accepted, as a rule of communications conventions, that such conventions should remain in force in time of war so far as the rights and duties of neutrals and belligerents permit, and that revision of these conventions shall be made easy if there is a general demand for such revision. These

[85] See Rule 2 of the draft drawn up by the Institute of International Law at Christiania in 1912, *Annuaire de l'Institut de Droit International* (1912), vol. 25, p. 648.

provisions go far to clear up the uncertainties concerning the wartime and postwar status of such conventions from which they suffered in past periods of conflict.

Railways

The matter of chief concern among the European States in connection with the railroad situation after the Armistice was to reestablish communication across the frontiers closed by the war. The Berne convention of 1890,[86] with its successive additional agreements,[87] had governed international traffic before the war, but had been denounced by a number of the signatories near the end of the period of hostilities or immediately thereafter.[88] These denunciations were not effective until the end of December 1919, but unless some arrangement had been made at once there would have been no international agreement in force thereafter governing the relations between the different railroad systems. In March the Peace Conference took up the problem, and it became immediately evident that the majority of the Allied and Associated Powers who were parties to the Berne convention and its successors, whether these Powers had denounced the conventions or not, were of the opinion that the conventions were still in force and had therefore survived the war.[89] It must be borne in mind that Europe was still operating under the Armistice provisions, the treaty not having yet even been

[86] October 14, 1890, *Brit. & For. State Papers*, vol. 82, p. 771.

[87] July 20, 1893, *ibid.*, vol. 85, p. 750; July 16, 1895, *ibid.*, vol. 87, p. 806; June 16, 1898, *ibid.*, vol. 92, p. 433; September 19, 1906, Martens, *Nouveau recueil général, 3me série*, vol. iii, p. 920.

[88] Belgium, December 3, 1918, *League of Nations Treaty Series*, vol. ii, p. 302; France, Italy, Serbia and Rumania, Basdevant, *Traités de la France*, vol. iv, p. 161, note.

[89] *Cf.* Miller, *Diary*, vol. xi, Commission on International Régime of Ports, Waterways and Railways, *passim*. *Cf.* also Stieler, "Der internationale Eisenbahnverband", *Völkerrechtsfragen*, 1926, pp. 6-7.

signed. Italy proposed that if a new convention could not be approved before the end of the year, when the denunciations of the Berne convention were to become effective, that convention should be "prolonged" until "replaced" by a new one.[90] Belgium and France declared "the maintenance of the Berne convention to be indispensable for the present."[91] The provision as finally embodied in the treaty (Art. 366) was for the "renewal" of the whole series of conventions from 1890 to 1906.

Meanwhile the problem was being handled by direct negotiation between the parties to the convention. France, which had denounced the 1890 convention at the end of 1918, because of objections to certain of its provisions, proposed to put it into force with modifications before her denunciation became effective.[92] This proposal met with objections, so she substituted another, to retain the old agreement intact, except for the denunciatory provision, which was to be changed from a one-year notice to three months, with a renewal for one year only. This plan was carried into effect by the withdrawal of the denunciations, the withdrawals stating that it was the mutual understanding of the parties that from then on required notice should be only three months.[93]

That the question whether the convention had survived the war was of little moment in the minds of the parties concerned appears from the fact that although the denunciations had been made while the state of war still existed, the withdrawals of these denunciations were made after the Treaty of Peace had come into effect, and in several cases were stated to have been made so that the convention might come

[90] Miller, *Diary*, vol. xii, p. 384.

[91] *Ibid.*, vol. xi, p. 316.

[92] *League of Nations Treaty Series*, vol. 18, p. 247.

[93] *Ibid.*, p. 254.

again into effect in accord with the terms of the treaty. This is apparently another case where the parties failed to concern themselves with legal questions whose solution was not essential to the handling of the matter directly in hand.[94]

St. Gothard Railway

Previous to the war a series of conventions dealing with the building and operation of the railway through the St. Gothard tunnel, and connecting Germany with Italy through Switzerland, had been drawn up between these three states;[95] the treaty signed in 1909 governed this situation when the war broke out. Through traffic ceased, of course, when Italy and Germany became opposing belligerents.[96] But in the opinion of Italy and Switzerland, at least the 1909 convention survived the conflict, since these two states drew up a working arrangement while the war was in progress "to modify partially and temporarily" its provisions.[97] The treaty of Versailles apparently conceived that the convention was still in force, as it provided that Germany would accept Switzerland's denunciation, after the latter's agreement with Italy on its terms, any time within ten years from the coming into force of the Versailles treaty.[98]

[94] Italy protested that depreciation of exchange and abnormal transport conditions precluded extension of the Berne convention to the countries of Eastern Europe, even though they were parties to the convention, and though the peace treaty called for its renewal. Application appears to have been gradually resumed with the resumption of traffic.

[95] June 20, 1870, Martens, *Nouveau recueil général des traités*, vol. 19, p. 99; January 27, 1871, *ibid.*, p. 101; October 28, 1871, *ibid.*, p. 103; March 12, 1878, *ibid., 2me série*, vol. iv, p. 676; October 13, 1909 with *procès verbal, Brit. & For. State Papers*, vol. 105, p. 639.

[96] *Cf. Railway Age Gazette*, vol. 57, p. 850, and vol. 62, p. 1454.

[97] July 1, 1918, Martens, *Nouveau recueil général des traités, 3me série*, vol. xii, p. 310.

[98] Art. 374, Versailles.

Sealing of Railroad Wagons through the Customs

Two protocols setting up regulations concerning the Sealing of Railroad Wagons through the Customs were signed in 1886 [99] and in 1907.[1] In the treaty of Versailles the 1886 convention was included among those of an economic and technical character which were "alone to be applied" [2] between Germany and the Allied and Associated Powers.[3] A further recognition of the two conventions appears in Art. 370 of Versailles, which provides that Germany must provide apparatus facilitating the free passage of trains belonging to the parties to these two conventions [4] into and out of Germany. There is no provision, as in the other cases considered, in favor of the neutral states parties to these conventions who were not signatories of the peace treaties; in this case Switzerland, Denmark, Norway, Sweden and the Netherlands are left out, and they would thus appear to be deprived of the advantages of Article 370. Otherwise the similar provision in the articles mentioned in favor of neutrals would appear to be redundant.[5]

[99] May 15, 1886, Martens, *op. cit., 2me série*, vol. 22, p. 42.

[1] May 18, 1907, *ibid., 3me série*, vol. ii, p. 878.

[2] Art. 282.

[3] The 1907 convention was not mentioned, but as it was a modification of that of 1886 and had been ratified by all the parties to the latter its application might be understood even though not expressed.

[4] Art. 370.

[5] Among the conventions specified in Article 282 of the treaty of Versailles which were to be applied between Germany and the Allies was that concerning the Technical Unity of Railways, signed in 1886. As a matter of fact there appears to have been little occasion even for suspension of this convention during the period of the war, inasmuch as the standardization of equipment having been accomplished previous to the war, there was little occasion to change it during that period. The convention being designed to facilitate the interchangeability of equipment, but not to effect interchange, its provisions were not affected by the cessation of traffic between the belligerent countries. (For text of this convention see *Deutsches Reichsgesetzblatt*, 1887, p. 111.)

Air Navigation

As these conventions are all of postwar origin, they have not yet had their baptism of fire, and its effect on them must remain a matter of conjecture. It is clearly the design of the parties to the general convention of 1919,[6] to the Spanish American convention of 1926[7] and the Pan-American Convention on Commercial Aviation[8] that these agreements should survive a war, inasmuch as all contain a provision that they shall remain in force in wartime so far as the rights and duties of belligerents and neutrals permit.[9] Conventions regulating international traffic are apt to require at least partial postwar revision in the light of experience which a general war brings, but provisions stating general principles, such as that contained in all these conventions to the effect that the air above a state's territory is subject to its sovereignty, would be less likely to suffer revision than those regulating the form and manner of issuing of pilot's licenses.

Transit

Transit conventions, like the air navigation conventions, are a postwar development, and so have not been exposed to the vicissitudes of a general peace conference. The discussions at Barcelona in 1921,[10] when the general convention on Freedom of Transit was drawn up,[11] indicate that the parties intended that, whatever suspension might be necessary in the application of the convention's provisions in wartime, its life

[6] October 13, 1919, *League of Nations Treaty Series*, vol. xi, p. 174.

[7] November 1, 1926, Hudson, *International Legislation*, vol. iii, p. 2019.

[8] February 20, 1928, *U. S. Treaty Series*, no. 840.

[9] Art. 38 of first two conventions, art. 29 of last.

[10] Barcelona Conference on Communications and Transit, *Verbatim Report* (Geneva, 1921), pp. 106-7.

[11] April 20, 1921, *League of Nations Treaty Series*, vol. vii, p. 12.

was not to be limited by the outbreak of even a general war. As in many of the more general postwar conventions, detailed provisions for denunciation and revision are made,[12] so the vexing question of termination is avoided. Should there be a large number of denunciations either during or immediately after a general war, as might well happen, an appeal by one-third of the parties would result in a revisory conference,[13] which might take place, as did the one which drew up the convention, soon after the peace conference had settled more pressing problems. We would then have a clear history of the fate of these conventions through a war period; that is, suspension between the parties, belligerent and neutral, during the period of war, to the extent that their rights and duties required, but the life of the convention unaffected, and a postwar revision and replacement by a new convention taking into account the changed conditions which a general war always brings about.

Telephone, Telegraph and Cables

The international telegraph conventions begin to appear near the middle of the nineteenth century, several being drawn up to provide for individual telegraph lines before the signing of the first general convention, in 1865, setting up rules governing the international transmission of messages.[14] The first general agreement was drawn up in 1865, and was revised in 1868,[15] 1872[16] and 1875.[17] From that time on, though the regulations attached to the 1875 convention were

[12] Arts 8, 9; Statute arts. 7, 8.

[13] Art. 9 of Convention.

[14] May 17, 1865, *Brit. & For. State Papers*, vol. 56, p. 294.

[15] July 21, 1868, *ibid.*, vol. 59, p. 322.

[16] January 14, 1872, *ibid.*, vol. 66, p. 975.

[17] July 10-22, 1875, *ibid.*, p. 19.

frequently modified,[18] the convention itself remained as it stood.

The German States and France were parties to the 1865 convention when the Franco-Prussian War broke out, but in the treaty of peace nothing was said about the telegraph convention. It was applied in practice, however, before the signature of the peace treaty, in building a line from Paris to Versailles "according to the ordinary rules of international service",[19] and without any special provision the convention was thereafter maintained in force by both France and Germany. In 1877, by a special treaty, the convention was declared to be "again in force" between France and Germany.[20]

During the period between 1914-18, telegraphic relations between the neutrals and belligerents were maintained, and the Central Bureau established by the convention remained in operation and collected payments from the members.[21] There was thus merely a suspension of the application of some of the convention's provisions, though this partial suspension was not limited to the relations between belligerents, the lines between neutrals crossing belligerent territory of course being affected by wartime regulation as well. With the cessation of hostilities traffic was gradually resumed and conducted under the rules of the prewar conventions. The peace treaties avoided, as elsewhere, any determination of the wartime status of the conventions, providing merely that

[18] July 28, 1879, *ibid.*, vol. 70, p. 62; July 17, 1885, *ibid.*, vol. 76, p. 597; June 21, 1890, *ibid.*, vol. 82, p. 869; July 22, 1896, *ibid.*, vol. 88, p. 1120; July 10, 1903, *ibid.*, vol. 97, p. 736; July 11, 1908, *ibid.*, vol. 102, p. 214.

[19] Rolland, *Correspondance postale et télégraphique dans les relations internationales* (Paris, 1901), p. 373.

[20] DeClercq, *Recueil des traités de la France*, vol. xii, p. 56. *Cf.* Otto Kunz, *Die internationalen Telegrafen- Unionen* (Stuttgart, 1924), p. 133.

[21] *Ibid.*, p. 135.

the 1875 convention and the 1908 regulations attached thereto were to be applied, on certain conditions, between the Allied and Associated Powers and Germany.[22] Inasmuch as the conventions were given partial application during hostilities, and were gradually resuming full application pending the period of operation of the peace treaty, the provisions of the latter partake rather of an amendment to an existing convention than the revival of one already terminated.

The more limited telephone and telegraph conventions mentioned above shed some light on the matter. A number of these were denounced or replaced shortly after the war, without mentioning the effect of war on them.[23] But the fact that several of such conventions involved transit across belligerent territory rendered them inapplicable during the war. Had the war terminated these conventions there would have been no need of the denunciation resorted to; it would appear therefore that even complete suspension did not involve termination, express denunciation being required.

It would appear to be the sentiment of the parties to telephone and telegraph conventions that the suspension of commercial intercourse between belligerents involved the suspension of the application of some of the provisions of treaties regulating telephonic and telegraphic communication. It appears equally well established that in the absence of specific arrangement in a peace treaty such provisions may be automatically restored to full force, and that barring possible changes involving impossibility of performance they may be regarded as continuing in force unless denounced.

[22] Art. 283 of Versailles, 235 of St. Germain, 218 of Trianon, 162 of Neuilly, 99 of Lausanne.

[23] See *League of Nations Treaty Series*, vol. xi, p. 437; vol. xv, p. 341; vol. liv, p. 434.

Cables

During the course of the conference which drew up the convention of 1884 for the Protection of Submarine Cables, the English delegates early took the position that during a war the convention was to be suspended in regard to belligerents, but was to remain in effect for the other Powers.[24] Their proposal was stated in the convention in the form that " it is understood that the stipulations of this convention shall in no wise affect the liberty of action of belligerents." [25]

It would appear plain from the above that the signatories to this and its supplementary conventions intended that these agreements were to be merely suspended during wartime as between opposing belligerents, and that they were to survive and reassume their prewar status at the resumption of peacetime relations. They were however submitted to the general régime of being "applied" along with twenty-five other conventions or groups of conventions, by Article 282 of Versailles. The presence of a clause declaratory of the treaty's status in wartime failed to result in any distinction from treaties having no such clause, when provision was being made for postwar status. This appears to be additional evidence that the terms used in the Versailles treaty lack significance as a determining factor regarding the attitude of its negotiators toward the effect of war on these treaties.

Postal Communication

Of the original Universal Postal Union convention of 1874 and its subsequent modifications, the conventions of 1891, 1897 and 1906 with the additional agreements concerning parcel post, money orders, and other matters, were in

[24] October 20, 1882; *cf.* Rolland, *op. cit.*, p. 411.

[25] March 14, 1884, Malloy, *Treaties, etc. of the United States*, vol. ii, p. 1949.

force for one or more of the members of the Union at the outbreak of the war in 1914.[26] As has already been noted, these conventions received partial application, even between belligerents, during the war period, and were gradually resuming their prewar application from the time of the Armistice.

The peace treaties provided that the three agreements mentioned above should be "applied" between the defeated Powers and Allies,[27] but gave no indication whether this "application" was to constitute a new agreement. But the old conventions were modified by a stipulation that the defeated Powers should accept conventions drawn up by the newly created states as well as the renewed application of the old conventions.[28] In spite of any implication to the contrary contained in these provisions, the peace treaties appear to have merely testified to the suspension of these conventions between opposing belligerents. The conventions were fully applied thereafter, both between the Allies and between neutrals and both groups of belligerents, without any treaty stipulation, and inasmuch as there had also been partial suspension between these latter groups, and partial resumption before the peace treaty even between opposing belligerents, it would seem to have required more specific provision to have brought about a complete new treaty relationship.[29] The matter ceased to have lasting importance, however, in view of the new conventions drawn up in 1920,[30] replacing the old as between the signatories.

[26] Art. xxix of the 1906 convention terminated the preceding convention so far as incompatible with the new treaty, but this stipulation was of course not binding on those States not accepting the new convention. *Cf. infra*, p. 240.

[27] Art. 283 of Versailles; and corresponding articles of the other treaties.

[28] *Ibid.*

[29] Bühler, *Der Weltpostverein* (Berlin, 1930), p. 169.

[30] November 30, 1920, *Brit. & For. State Papers*, vol. 114, p. 430.

PUBLIC HEALTH CONVENTIONS

The movement for the international control of epidemic diseases, begun in the middle of the last century, resulted in the drawing up of a number of conventions and the establishment of several international bodies to control such epidemics and disseminate information regarding their incidence and spread. Such agreements were made in 1892,[31] 1893,[32] 1894,[33] and 1897.[34] In 1903[35] a general convention was drawn up to coordinate and supplement these four, and to provide for the establishment of a permanent international bureau. This bureau was established by a supplementary convention in 1907,[36] and began its meetings in 1909.[37]

During the period between 1914 and 1918 most of the provisions of these conventions were suspended in their application, but statistical information was gathered from whatever sources were available and the official bulletin of the central bureau was published regularly. The central bureau recommenced its sittings even before the Versailles treaty was signed, and attempted a full resumption of its prewar activities, including the revision of a convention signed in 1912 but not ratified when war broke out.[38] The peace treaty provided for the application of all the conventions up through

[31] January 30, 1892, *Brit. & For. State Papers*, vol. 84, p. 12.

[32] April 15, 1893, *ibid.*, vol. 85, p. 7.

[33] April 3, 1894, *ibid.*, vol. 87, p. 78.

[34] March 19, 1897, *ibid.*, vol. 89, p. 159; June 30, 1897, modifying the convention of Apr. 3, 1894 (*supra*), *ibid.*, vol. 87, p. 81.

[35] December 3, 1903, *ibid.*, vol. 97, p. 1085.

[36] Dec. 9, 1907, Malloy, *op. cit.*, vol. ii, p. 2214.

[37] *Bulletin de l'Office internationale d'hygiene publique*, 1909, introductory article.

[38] January 17, 1912, Malloy, *op. cit.*, vol. iii, p. 2972. *Cf.* also *Bulletin*, 1919, extraordinary session of June 3, 1919.

1903, between the Allied and Associated Powers and Germany.[39]

The provisions of the sanitary conventions were largely suspended during the war, but the parties to them did not conceive that they were terminated. Early in 1918 the accession of Greece to the 1907 convention, published in the bulletin of the Bureau,[40] indicates that there was no termination of this convention, an indication borne out by the resumption of activity of the Bureau before the signature of the treaty of peace.

CONVENTION ESTABLISHING THE INTERNATIONAL INSTITUTE OF AGRICULTURE

In 1905 a convention was drawn up establishing an International Institute of Agriculture for the collection and dissemination of information regarding the raising of agricultural products, the convention being signed and ratified by thirty-seven states.[41] From the beginning it was the battleground of conflicting national interests, and its efficiency was never as great as its founders had hoped. It did, however, continue to function during the period from 1914-18, though with its activities greatly limited.[42] As rapidly as possible after the Armistice the functions of the Institute under the treaty were resumed.

This treaty was included in the group of those which were to be "applied" between Germany and the Allied and Asso-

[39] None of the Central Powers was a party to the 1907 convention establishing the Central Bureau, so unless Germany was to be forced to become a party there was no need to mention this agreement in the Versailles Treaty.

[40] February 7, 1918, *Bulletin*, 1918, p. 253.

[41] June 7, 1905, Malloy, *op. cit.*, vol. ii, p. 2140.

[42] Hobson, *International Institute of Agriculture* (Berkeley, 1931), p. 73.

ciated Powers,[43] and so joins this group the question of whose survival was not settled. As has been indicated, there was never a complete cessation of the "application" of the convention, and it would thus appear to have survived.

TREATIES CONCERNING INDIVIDUAL RIGHTS

Industrial Property

During the peace conference there was considerable difference of view regarding the postwar status of the prewar industrial property conventions. None of the Powers had denounced any of the conventions, and the Central Bureau was still functioning. A memorandum prepared for the American delegates by a committee of legal experts held that "it is the best opinion of publicists that agreements such as the existing international conventions . . . revive automatically upon the declaration of peace. It would probably be best to incorporate such a provision in the treaty. . . ." [44] A draft provision was later submitted to the effect, however, that "all international conventions and treaties concerning industrial or literary property between the contracting parties, or between two or more of them, in force August 1, 1914, and all personal rights of nationals derived therefrom, shall be recognized as having continued in full force and effect and are confirmed." [45] This would indicate that the conventions had not been suspended, while the former view indicates that they had.

The final wording, however, came closer to the first conception than to the latter. Article 286 of the treaty of Versailles states that the prewar conventions "will again

[43] Art. 282.

[44] November 22, 1918, Miller, *Diary*, vol. ix, p. 65.

[45] *Ibid.*, Appendix A, "Suggested Sections of General Treaty regarding Patents, Trademarks and Copyrights".

come into effect as from the coming into force of the present Treaty, in so far as they are not affected or modified by the exceptions and restrictions resulting therefrom."

This was not true, however, of the treaty of St. Germain, Article 237 of which states that the two prewar conventions to which Austria was a party " shall be applied as from the coming into force of the present Treaty, insofar as they are not affected or modified by the exceptions and restrictions resulting therefrom." The same wording appears in Article 220 of the Treaty of Trianon with Hungary.

A consideration of the status of these conventions during the war would indicate that the draft provision of the American delegation was more nearly in accord with the facts than was the clause which found its way into the treaty. The most that can be said is that a number of parties to the convention unilaterally modified some of its provisions during the war, but there appears to have been no intent on the part of any one of them to consider the convention to have been terminated, nor even entirely suspended. The Bureau continued to function and the contributions continued to be paid. Many of the states concerned did not modify the convention at all, and none of the belligerents rejected any but a few of its provisions. That it was repeatedly violated by the belligerents may be maintained, and the peace treaty took cognizance of these violations and provided either for their condonation or that indemnification should be made (see arts. 306-11 of Versailles).

The difficulty with the peace treaty provisions regarding these conventions is that first, the peace treaties were bilateral, and second, that they did not include all the parties to the prewar conventions. If, as the peace treaty implies, the conventions were not in force during the war, the question arises whether the provision putting them again into force means also among the Allied and Associated Powers as well as between them and Germany. That was probably the intent, though it is not expressed. The second difficulty, which left the belligerents which were parties to the convention in a different position from the non-belligerents, was rectified in the treaty of Berne of 1920,[46] which extended the rights and privileges of Versailles to the states which were not parties to the peace treaties.

Literary and Artistic Property

The war of 1914-18 was the only one up to that time in which belligerents on both sides were parties to the conventions concerning Literary and Artistic Works, so it furnished the sole test of the ability of these agreements to survive a war.[47] Unfortunately the treaties of peace shed little light on the attitudes of the parties toward this question. There appears to be no particular principle guiding the decisions taken, and the expressions used are far from exact. Just as during the war, the decisions taken seem to be the result of a pressing need to start the peace machinery operating, rather than the setting up of a principle in international law.

The articles of the treaty of Versailles, which serve as a model for the other treaties, are 286, which provides that the conventions of 1886, 1908 and 1914 " will again come into effect . . . in so far as they are not affected or modified by the exceptions and restrictions " cited in that instrument,[48] and 306 to 311 describing the " exceptions and modifications " which include the maintenance of acts in virtue of war measures, the possibility of such acts in the future, the

[46] June 30, 1920, *League of Nations Treaty Series*, vol. i, p. 60.

[47] *Cf. Droit d'auteur*, 1914, p. 118 *et seq.*

[48] It is worth noting that the French text appears to differ somewhat: "... seront remis en vigueur et reprendront leur effet ... dans la mesure où ils ne seront pas affectés ou modifiés ..." *Cf.* Chabaud, *La Propriété littéraire et artistique* (Paris, 1921), *passim*, for discussion of these articles.

prolongation of delays for priority and exploitation, the prohibition of legal actions against violators, and provision against future German competition. Austria,[49] Hungary,[50] Bulgaria [51] and Czechoslovakia,[52] which were not members of the Union, were obliged by their treaties to adhere.[53]

This series of arrangements possesses the peculiar property of being a modification of a convention without the consent of all the parties to it. The members of the Union who did not sign any of these peace treaties were no more bound by these arrangements than were the non-signatories of the previous modifications of the original agreement by the later ones. In the case of the Industrial Property conventions this difficulty was remedied by the convention of 1920,[54] extending to the non-signatories of the Peace Treaties the same privileges as those granted to the signatories, but there has been no such arrangement in the case of intellectual prop-

[49] Art. 239 of St. Germain.

[50] Art. 221 of Trianon.

[51] Art. 166 of Neuilly.

[52] September 10, 1919, Malloy, *Treaties, etc. of the United States*, vol. iii, p. 3699, art. 20.

[53] A memorandum prepared at the Peace Conference by Joseph Bailey Brown, one of the legal advisers on industrial property questions for the American delegation, states: "it is believed that treaties having to do with such vested private property rights as patents, trade marks and copyrights are in the class which is not annulled by a declaration of war, but which may be treated as suspended, or as remaining in full force and effect at the choice of the belligerents... the parties are certainly at liberty to consider the treaties as revived after the conclusion of peace, and very probably as a matter of law in the absence of any stipulations to the contrary, all the treaties referred to would be automatically revived and continue after a formal peace is made... it would seem entirely proper to keep all of these agreements (between the United States and Germany) in effect for the future... In fact, if held to be absolutely annulled on account of the war, there is little doubt that similar agreements would be made to take their place." (Miller, *Diary*, vol. vi, p. 328.)

[54] *Cf.* section on Industrial Property conventions, *supra*, p. 184.

erty. It was not until 1928 that a new general arrangement was reached.[55]

The wartime and early postwar history of these conventions illustrates clearly the uncertainty of states concerning the rules governing treaties in wartime. It appears to be generally conceived that private rights deserve protection during hostilities, but not to the point where there is interference with the conduct of the war. On the other hand, any measures taken detrimental to such rights result in reprisals by the enemy, a procedure whose results may be more disastrous than leaving these private rights intact. The result is that treaties concerned are neither maintained in force, entirely suspended, nor terminated, between the belligerents. With the return of peace there is equal difficulty. If the convention has been suspended or terminated, then the measures contrary to it are not invalid, yet if claim is to be made on behalf of nationals for infringements during the war period then the convention must be conceived as having been in force. To avoid this dilemma a sort of general amnesty was declared for all acts committed during the war period, and the conventions were considered suspended so far as was necessary to cover such acts with oblivion. Unfortunately the problem was not settled in drawing up the postwar conventions in 1925 and 1928, and a new war would presumably soon raise the problems of the old.

Private International Law

Of conventions concerning private international law there were three signed in 1902, Conflicts of Law in the Matter of Marriage,[56] in Matters of Divorce and Separation,[57] and

[55] June 2, 1928, Hudson, *International Legislation*, vol. iv, p. 2463.

[56] June 12, 1902, *Brit. & For. State Papers*, vol. 95, p. 411.

[57] *Ibid.*, p. 416.

regulating the Guardianship of Minors,[58] and three in 1905, regarding the Effects of Marriage on the Rights and Duties of Married Persons in their Personal Relations and their Property,[59] the Deprivation of Civil Rights and Analogous Measures of Protection[60] and the convention on Civil Procedure.[61]

There was some diversity of opinion during the war as to the status of these conventions, though in general they were given application, in many cases even as between belligerents. The peace conference, however, failed to take up the question of any but the convention on civil procedure, which it was indicated " the High Contracting Parties shall apply, so far as concerns them ",[62] with the exception of France, Portugal and Roumania. The fate of the other treaties is not indicated, though there appears to have been no reason for exempting them from consideration while dealing with the convention on Civil Procedure.

As a matter of practice, the states which were parties to these conventions have continued to apply them since the war, and in 1923 and 1924 protocols of adhesion to all of them were opened, and a number of states have since adhered.[63] It would thus appear that these conventions had never lost their binding character, and that the effect of the war was merely to suspend the application of certain provisions between some, but not all, of the belligerents. So far as the provision of the Versailles convention regarding the convention relating to Civil Procedure affected the relations of the states con-

[58] *Ibid.*, p. 421.

[59] July 17, 1905, *ibid.*, vol. 116, p. 666.

[60] *Ibid.*, p. 770.

[61] *Ibid.*, vol. 99, p. 990.

[62] Art. 287 of Versailles, 238 of St. Germain, 221 of Trianon.

[63] November 28, 1923, *League of Nations Treaty Series*, vol. 51, pp. 210-239.

cerned, it apparently served only as a record of the denunciation of that convention by France, Portugal and Roumania.

CONCLUSIONS

Until 1919 there appears to have been little consideration given to the status of conventions during the intermediate period between the cessation of hostilities and the legal resumption of peacetime relations, probably because the question had never previously assumed the importance it did at that time. It was obviously impossible for the whole body of international relationships to remain in a period of suspended animation through a period as long as that governed by the various Armistices from 1918 to 1923 and the provisions of these Armistices, detailed as they were, did not cover most of the matters which before the war had been the subject of international agreement.

The practice of states during this period indicates that they did not adopt any definite theory concerning the status of treaties during such an interval. Where the military authorities did not assume control, the civilian authorities in most cases set about rebuilding the old relationships so far as possible on the prewar treaty basis, pending a definitive arrangement. This was possible in varying degree, depending on a variety of factors, such as the need for immediate reestablishment, the physical possibility, the changed relations between the parties, etc. Though this was a period during which states might have availed themselves of an opportunity for suspension of their treaty obligations, it is noteworthy that there was a tendency toward as complete resumption of observance as possible.

In considering the eventual disposition concerning the provisions of prewar conventions, it is essential to keep in mind the place and function of war in its relation to such conventions. It frequently has happened that treaty settlements have become so unsatisfactory to states that when negotiations have failed to change such arrangements they are willing to resort to war to produce such a change. The events of the war may so displace the relative balance of forces between the belligerents that arrangements which were relatively satisfactory when war broke out cease to be so when it is over. Frequently too, the fact that the end of hostilities involves calling a conference, makes possible the consideration of questions which in themselves would have been deemed insufficient reason for such a step. The cessation of hostilities is indication that the belligerents are ready to proceed with negotiations for resumption of those international relationships established by treaty.

It is clear that a theory of uniform termination would leave the very complicated and sensitive machinery of international relations in a state of chaos, to the general detriment of all concerned. To consider all prewar conventions as reviving with the termination of hostilities would serve as a starting point for negotiators, and the tendency toward such a conception appears to stand out from the peace treaties of the past century. But essentially the results of war are unpredictable, and as states utilize peace conferences for clearing the ground for new settlements, their purpose would be defeated if the freedom of the negotiators in handling treaty questions were limited by established rules. In practice, states appear to operate along the lines indicated below. They appear not to be prepared to adopt any general theory concerning the effect of war on treaties, and to treat the status of prewar conventions as a matter of policy rather than of international law.

The nature of the peace conference affects the handling of the problem of the pre-war conventions. If a peace conference includes the Great Powers and a powerful part of the smaller ones it assumes the character of an international regulatory body, as did those of Westphalia in 1648, Vienna in 1815, and Paris in 1919. In such a case it assumes wide liberty in dealing with prewar treaties, even modifying those to which non-belligerents are parties. If, on the contrary, the conference is confined to representatives of two or a small number of Powers, its efforts are directed chiefly toward the reestablishment of relations between the belligerent states, and the negotiators obviously do not concern themselves with broad general policies concerning the body of states as a whole.

The nature of the treaties themselves also makes a difference in their treatment. If the obligations which a treaty imposes are of a technical nature and identical for all the parties, or embody general principles for the guidance of states, the usefulness of the treaty is frequently not impaired by the events of the war, and the treaty will be applied when the war is over. On the other hand, if a treaty includes only provisions imposing different obligations for the different parties, and its drafting has involved political bargaining, it is apt to be revalued in the light of the changes brought about by the war, and either modified or terminated. Where a treaty contains both sorts of stipulations, the former are apt to be allowed to stand while the latter are subject to modification as indicated. Treaties embodying accepted rules governing the conduct of war are believed to continue in force without any express provision in the treaty of peace. There appears to be no other class of treaty to which this rule has been applied; some peace treaties have failed to specify the status of international union treaties after a war, when in practice such treaties have been accepted as having survived, but the peace treaties of 1919-23 made minute provisions in this regard.

Where the solution of questions concerning a prewar treaty of a technical nature appears fraught with difficulty, the peace treaty frequently provides that a revisory conference shall be called within a limited period of time. This is unlikely to prove true in regard to the revision of political settlements, for the victors here are anxious to exert their preponderant influence while it remains unquestioned.

Since 1919 there have been a few instances of provisions concerning the effect of war on treaties, but these are confined chiefly to the field of communications and transit, and almost entirely to conventions dealing with technical matters. It is certainly too early to assume that it is yet the intent of parties to provide either for the survival or the failure to survive in wartime of any more than very limited categories of international agreements.

CHAPTER III

Termination by Denunciation After Notice

It has always been an accepted rule that bilateral conventions could not be terminated by denunciation by one of the parties without the consent of the other. The principle was so well understood that denunciation of a treaty by one of the parties has even been followed by a declaration of war by the other party in order to compel observance. Even with the growth of the use of multipartite agreements and the accompanying increase in the number of parties to such agreements during the nineteenth century there was no increased disposition to permit unilateral denunciation.

The belief of nations concerning the right of unilateral denunciation was apparently first expressed in treaty form in the Declaration of London of 1871, following Russia's attempt to denounce the Black Sea treaty she had signed in 1856. The Declaration states that the parties "recognize that it is an essential principle of the Law of Nations that no Power can liberate itself from the engagements of a Treaty nor modify the stipulations thereof, unless with the consent of the Contracting Parties by means of an amicable arrangement." [1] This principle appears to be generally accepted in so far as it applies to treaties dealing with political rather than with technical matters, and containing stipulations for different rights and obligations for the different parties.

The principle is subject, however, to such modifications as the parties to a treaty choose to provide. In a number of cases, in treaties of the sort mentioned above, unilateral

[1] January 17, 1871, *Brit. & For. State Papers*, vol. 61, p. 1195.

denunciation has been permitted, but operates to release the other parties. Of such a sort was the prolongation of the Triple Alliance of Austria-Hungary, Italy and Germany in 1891,[2] and again in 1902,[3] and 1912,[4] which stated that the treaty should be renewed at the end of six years "if not denounced by one or another of the High Contracting Parties". The Washington treaty for the Limitation of Naval Armament stipulates that it shall continue in force "until two years from the date on which notice of termination shall be given by one of the Contracting Powers, whereupon the Treaty shall terminate as regards all the Contracting Powers".[5] But this provision is modified by that in the succeeding paragraph, providing that within a year of the time such notice is given all the Contracting Parties shall meet in conference. The treaty between the Central American States for the Limitation of Armament, signed in 1923, terminates with the second denunciation, but not with the first, an arrangement accomplished by providing that it will remain in force for the States which have not denounced it "provided they be not less than four in number".[6]

Such treaties as these concern matters which have always been considered as falling in the "political" class. Similar provisions are found in certain treaties of a commercial nature which also impose obligations varying with the different parties. Into this group fall the conventions of the Sugar Union. The 1902 convention of the Union permitted unilateral denunciation, which, while not releasing the other parties automatically, gave them the right of denunciation

[2] May 6, 1891, *ibid.*, vol. 121, p. 1020, art. xiv.

[3] June 28, 1902, *ibid.*, p. 1022, art. xiv.

[4] December 5, 1912, *ibid.*, p. 1023, art. xiv.

[5] February 6, 1922, *U. S. Treaty Series*, no. 671, art. xxiii.

[6] February 7, 1923, Hudson, *International Legislation*, vol. ii, p. 942, art. viii.

until the 31st of October of the same year. There was a provision that if any of the other parties availed themselves of this right the Belgian Government should call a conference to determine what measures should be taken.[7] The 1907 renewal of this convention provided that failure to ratify before the first of February of the succeeding year should be considered equivalent to denunciation, and should have the effects of such denunciation specified above, unless the majority of the parties should decide otherwise.[8] In the 1912 renewal it was provided that any party might withdraw from the Union on a year's notice, from September 1, 1918, and in such case the right of denunciation of the other parties was to come into effect as specified above.[9]

In accordance with this provision, France gave notice on August 22, 1917.[10] The following year Great Britain denounced the provisions by which she was still bound.[11] Belgium, Holland and Switzerland followed the year after.[12] In spite of the provision of the convention calling for a conference of the remaining signatories, due presumably to the fact that the remaining signatories were opposing belligerents, no conference was called. Instead, the Belgian Government communicated the denunciations to the remaining signatories when the war was over and peace was re-established and secured their consent to the dissolution of the Union.[13]

[7] March 5, 1902, Martens, *Nouveau recueil général, 2me série*, vol. 31, p. 272, art. x.

[8] August 28, 1907, *Brit. & For. State Papers*, vol. 100, p. 482, art. i.

[9] March 17, 1912, *ibid.*, vol. 105, p. 392, art. v.

[10] *Ibid.*, vol. 111, p. 652.

[11] *Ibid.*, vol. 113, p. 936.

[12] *Ibid.*, vol. 112, pp. 983, 993, vol. 113, p. 1189.

[13] *Moniteur belge*, September 6-7, 1920, p. 73. Temperley considers the convention terminated on August 31, 1918; see *History of the Peace Conference*, vol. v, p. 81.

A treaty concerning commercial matters with similar detailed provisions for unilateral denunciation is that dealing with the Abolition of Import and Export Restrictions, signed in 1927.[14] Unilateral denunciation is permitted on a variety of grounds; any of the parties are free to denounce it after five years; a long series of temporary exemptions having been included in the convention, any of the parties is free to denounce the convention after three years if such temporary exemptions or any of them are still in force; the convention having provided for the consideration of reservations at a meeting the succeeding year, it is stipulated that any party might denounce the convention after five years if the effect of the exceptions in any of these reservations has, in its view, impaired the effects of the convention.[15] If in turn denunciations should likewise impair these effects, the Secretary-General of the League is authorized to summon a conference to consider the situation thereby created.[16]

Unilateral denunciation is also permitted to the parties to the conventions on the Exportation of Hides and Skins and of Bones, signed in 1928.[17] Here denunciation is permitted on two grounds; one-third of the states may demand that a revisory conference be called, and if the conference fails to carry out such a revision, or if the revision is unsatisfactory to any state, that state is free to denounce the convention;[18] and any state is free to denounce the convention on twelve months' notice after five years from the convention's entry into force. As indicated in the convention on Import and Export Restrictions, if any party feels that denunciation has created a new situation it may cause

[14] November 8, 1927; *League of Nations Treaty Series*, vol. 97, p. 393.

[15] Art. 18.

[16] Art. 19.

[17] July 11, 1928, *ibid.*, vol. 95, pp. 358, 374.

[18] Art. vi of Hides and Skins convention; art. x of Bones convention.

the Secretary-General of the League to call a new conference, and, if dissatisfied with the result, may denounce the convention unilaterally.[19]

A number of multipartite treaties provide for an unrestricted right of denunciation by any party resulting, if availed of, in the release of all. Of this sort are the conventions establishing telephone or telegraph communication across several states,[20] the Central American convention of 1907 providing for Future Conferences,[21] and the 1886 conventions providing for the Exchange of Official Documents and Official Journals.[22] A large number of the telegraph conventions mentioned were denounced after the war, but have generally since been replaced by others.

A small number of treaties provide that when the number of denunciations reduces the number of states to a certain figure the convention is terminated. A reduction to ten signatories terminates the convention concerning Economic Statistics, signed in 1928;[23] reduction to twenty-four produces the same effect in the case of the 1931 convention concerning Narcotic Drugs.[24] In both cases the convention provides that a fraction of the signatories may bring about a conference to revise the convention, a provision which might operate to forestall termination by successive denunciations.[25]

[19] Art. vii of former, art. xi of latter.

[20] *Cf.* convention of March 30, 1889, *Brit. & For. State Papers*, vol. 81, p. 11. Most of such conventions drawn up in the eighties of the past century included similar clauses.

[21] December 20, 1907, Malloy, *op. cit.*, vol. ii, p. 2416, art. v.

[22] March 15, 1886, *ibid.*, pp. 1959, 1962; arts. x and iii respectively. See also Passports and Visas convention of January 27, 1922, art. xvii, Hudson, *International Legislation*, vol. ii, p. 787; also the exchange of notes concerning the Assignment of High Radio Frequencies, February-March, 1929, *U. S. Treaty Series*, No. 777A.

[23] December 14, 1928, League of Nations, *Doc. C.505.M.167.1929.II.*

[24] July 13, 1931, *idem*, *Doc. C.455.M.193.1931.XI.*

[25] Art. 16 of former, art. 33 of latter.

A long series of conventions signed by the Central American States provide that successive denunciations shall not terminate the convention until the number of parties is reduced to two.[26] As noted above, the convention on the Limitation of Armament, signed at the same time, makes the same provision in the case of four signatories.[27] The Protocol on the Accession of the United States to the Protocol of Signature of the Statute of the Permanent Court, opened for signature in 1929, provides that withdrawal by the United States on the one hand, or by two-thirds of the parties on the other hand of their acceptance of the conditions attached by the United States to its adherence to the Protocol of Signature of the Statute of the Permanent Court should serve to terminate the 1929 protocol.[28]

There would seem to be no reason why such a provision for the release of all the signatories in case of a large number of denunciations should not have been included in other conventions providing for unilateral denunciation. In a number of cases conventions contain provision that they shall go into effect when ratified by a number of states as small as two.[29] In such a case it might be presumed that when denunciations brought the states down to the number necessary to bring the convention into effect it should be terminated. In many instances, of course, the need for such provision is obviated by other stipulations calling for periodic revision, or revision on demand of a part of the signatories.

In the case of the 1931 Narcotic Drugs convention men-

[26] *Cf.* conventions of February 7, 1923, *Conference on Central American Affairs* (Washington, 1923), p. 296 *et seq.*

[27] *Ibid.*, p. 339.

[28] September 14, 1929, Hudson, *op. cit.*, vol. i, p. 591, art. viii.

[29] *Cf.* art. vii of convention of November 28, 1919, concerning Employment of Women Before and After Childbirth, Martens, *op. cit.*, *3me série*, vol. 19, p. 76., and corresponding provisions in other Labor conventions.

tioned above, the provision for termination when denunciation has brought the number of parties down to twenty-four may work to general disadvantage. The same convention contains a provision that it shall come into effect with twenty-five ratifications including four of the eight principal states concerned,[30] yet no such distinction is made in regard to denunciations. Should successive denunciations leave twenty-four states including the eight placed in the special category mentioned, it would probably still be of considerable value to that group, yet in spite of themselves they would find the convention terminated. But in this convention, as in many others providing for unilateral denunciation, a provision for a revisory conference on demand of one-third of the signatories is included,[31] a provision of which the remaining states would probably avail themselves should denunciations become common.

Somewhere around one-third of the multipartite treaties signed since 1885 have contained a provision permitting unilateral denunciation while leaving the treaty binding on the remaining signatories. This number includes the great bulk of the technical conventions imposing identical obligations on all the parties. It includes the labor conventions, the communications and transit conventions, the conventions on matters of private international law, the Hague conventions, and a great many others. With the exceptions noted above and a very few others it does not include those conventions dealing with political matters and imposing differing obligations on the different parties. With the exceptions noted above also, these conventions fail to provide that any given number of denunciations shall operate to terminate the convention. In the majority of treaties of the technical type, however, there is some complementary provision for periodic

[30] Art. 30.

[31] Art. 33.

revision, or for a revisory conference on demand of a given number of signatories, thus affording means to forestall wholesale denunciation due to dissatisfaction with the treaty's provisions.

A large part of the group of treaties mentioned above as dealing with technical subjects in which the signature of each of the parties is not necessarily a consideration, provide either that the parties may denounce the treaty separately for any colony, dominion, mandated area, or other territory under its sovereignty, jurisdiction or other control, or that colonies and dominions at least may denounce on their own behalf.

To give a measure of stability to the type of convention permitting unilateral denunciation, a provision is usually inserted that such denunciation may not take place until after a minimum period of years, usually not less than three [82] and sometimes running at high as fifteen.[83] A large number of conventions which, in spite of the fact that they impose identical obligations on all the parties, touch on matters which lend themselves to uniform regulation with some difficulty, provide that they may only be denounced at periodic intervals. Such are the conventions concerning matters of private law,[84] the conventions concerning railway goods traffic,[85] the public health and sanitary conventions,[86] those

[82] *Cf.* art. lx of the Railway Goods Traffic convention of October 14, 1890; *Brit. & For. State Papers*, vol. 82, p. 771.

[83] *Cf.* Latin Monetary Union convention of December 23, 1865; *ibid.*, vol. 56, p. 207, art. xiv.

[84] *Cf.* Civil Procedure convention of July 17, 1905, *ibid.*, vol. 99, p. 990, art. xxix.

[85] *Cf.* Railway Goods Traffic convention of October 23, 1924, *League of Nations Treaty Series*, vol. 77, p. 367, art. 62.

[86] *Cf.* International Sanitary convention, April 15, 1893, *Brit. & For. State Papers*, vol. 85, p. 17, art. iv.

of the Latin Monetary Union,[37] the Congo tariff convention [38] and others.[39]

The possible disadvantage of a right of denunciation commencing after a given period of years was made clear in the discussions at the drawing up of the Covenant of the League of Nations. The French delegates on the Commission drafting the Covenant successfully contended that a provision that there might be no withdrawal for a given number of years might well involve a general withdrawal at that time, and that it was wiser to permit unilateral denunciation at any time.[40] The special circumstances applying in that case do not necessarily apply always, and in practice a combination is used of an initial period during which no denunciation is allowed, followed by a period during which unilateral denunciation may take place at any time.

The usefulness of the provision for unilateral denunciation is apparent. It facilitates the securing of the consent of doubtful states to conventions aiming at universality, by removing the fear that changed conditions will make continued adherence inconvenient or even dangerous. When treaties are subject to periodic revision it permits those states which are not content with the terms of the revised convention to continue to give effect to the old, with the assurance that they may withdraw their adhesion to the old

[37] *Cf.* Latin Monetary Union convention, note 33, *supra,* art. xiv.

[38] December 22, 1890, *ibid.*, vol. 82, p. 81, art. v.

[39] This type of provision for periodic opportunity for denunciation is frequently used in conventions of a political type as well. The renewals of the Triple Alliance in 1891, 1902 and 1912 all provided an opportunity for unilateral denunciation every six years. (*Brit. & For. State Papers,* vol. 121, pp. 1020-1023.) The treaty of Guaranty of the Integrity and Independence of Norway of 1907 might be denounced every ten years. (*Brit. & For. State Papers,* vol. 100, p. 536, art. iii.)

[40] *Cf.* Miller, *Drafting of the Covenant* (New York, 1928), vol. i, p. 342 *et seq.*

at any time that adhesion to the new appeared desirable. It minimizes the value of shrewd bargaining in conferences, inasmuch as any state which is discontented with the result may shortly free itself from its obligations.

The same arguments in favor of unilateral denunciations of technical conventions apply against those primarily dealing with contentious political matters. The essence of the latter being the creation of a stable situation, unilateral release in many cases would operate to defeat the intent of the parties. A broad extension of the use of such provisions in such conventions is not to be anticipated under present conditions. Even in the treaties of this type in which the provision for unilateral denunciation is included, the parties have generally refrained from utilizing their right. The Sugar Convention is a notable exception, and in this case generally termination followed. Two states, Brazil and Costa Rica, have availed themselves of the right of release from their obligations under the Covenant of the League.[41] but in this case the number of parties being large, and neither of the states being among those whose participation was most vital, their denunciation was not followed by that of others. Where the intent of the parties can be carried out without the participation of the denouncing state, denunciation appears not to have been followed by termination.

[41] Costa Rica announced her withdrawal on Jan. 1, 1925, to take effect on Jan. 1, 1927. Brazil gave similar notice on June 12, 1926, and Spain on Sept. 8 of the same year. In March 1928, before the required two years' period after notice had expired, Spain announced that she would remain a member. (*Cf.* G. Howard-Ellis, *Origin, Structure and Working of the League of Nations* (London, 1928), p. 105; also League of Nations, *Official Journal*, April, 1928, pp. 405, 432; May, p. 603; June, p. 778. On March 27, 1933, Japan gave the required two years' notice (*cf. Bulletin of International News*, of March 30, 1933, London). Mexico announced her withdrawal on December 3, 1932 (*cf. Official Journal*, March, 1933, p. 395).

CONCLUSIONS

A consideration of the action of states in permitting or refusing to permit unilateral denunciation by treaty provision indicates that the character of the treaty is the determining factor. As indicated elsewhere, it is rarely possible to place all the provisions of a treaty in a single category, but in the case of treaties dealing with a small number of subjects a distinction can frequently be made on a basis of whether there is identity of rights and obligations between the parties, or a difference between them in this respect; or on a basis of the subject matter,—that is, whether it concerns the relations between states themselves or their nationals.

In general those treaties setting up differing rights and obligations for the different parties are not apt to provide for unilateral denunciation. The same is true if the drafting of the convention has involved a considerable amount of diplomatic bargaining in order to secure the participation of one or of several states. In the cases of both these types of treaties, if such a provision is made it is frequently accompanied by a statement that denunciation by one of the parties releases all the others, or by a provision that in such a case all the parties should meet to confer on their subsequent action. The principle enunciated in the Declaration of London of 1871 concerning unilateral denunciation of treaties appears to have been intended to apply to this type of treaty. The signature of each of the parties appears to be accepted as a consideration for that of all the others.

On the other hand, if the subject matter of the convention is technical, and the rights and obligations of the parties are identical, the withdrawal from participation of one or a few of the states is less apt to affect seriously the value of the convention to the others. A considerable number of such treaties permit separate denunciation for colonies, dominions, or other territories under the sovereignty or jurisdiction of a party. In such conventions it appears equally clear that the participation of any party is not necessarily a consideration for the participation of the others. In view of the rarity of a provision concerning how many denunciations shall serve to terminate the convention, it appears equally true that the participation of no given number of states is a consideration for the continued participation of the remainder.

CHAPTER IV

Termination by Superseding Treaty

THE PRINCIPLE OF UNANIMOUS CONSENT

Introduction

Termination of multipartite treaties comes about more frequently through subsequent agreement among the parties than by any other method. In such a case the question frequently arises whether it is essential for all the parties to the original agreement to participate in the later settlement. In practice there have been numerous deviations from the principle of unanimous consent, and it is essential to discover whether there is an indication of well defined principles governing such deviation.

Up until the nineteenth century the question was of minor importance. The most important settlements, such as those of Westphalia (1648),[1] Ryswick (1697),[2] Utrecht (1713)[3] and Aix-la-Chapelle (1748)[4] were made either in the form

[1] The Westphalia settlement consisted of ten treaties, the first one signed in 1646 and the last in 1650, the most important of which were signed on October 24, 1648, between France, Sweden, the Emperor and the Princes of the Empire. These treaties may be found in Dumont, *Corps diplomatique universel*, vol. vi, pt. i, p. 360 *et seq.*

[2] The settlement of Ryswick consisted of six separate bipartite treaties, to one or more of which Great Britain, France, Spain, Portugal, the United Provinces and the Emperor were parties. See Dumont, *op. cit.*, vol. vii, pt. ii.

[3] The settlement of Utrecht and Rastadt consisted of nineteen bipartite treaties to which seven of the European states were parties. See Dumont, *op. cit.*, vol. viii, pt. i.

[4] The Aix-la-Chapelle settlement consisted of a preliminary treaty, three definitive treaties to which France, Great Britain and the United Provinces

of a group of bilateral agreements or were signed by a smaller number of states. They were largely terminated piecemeal by subsequent treaties; consent of the original parties was sometimes obtained without difficulty, and when refused, war was frequently resorted to. The subsequent treaty generally contained a provision to the effect that the remaining parts of the original treaty were confirmed as they stood.[5] During the seventeenth century these confirmations appear to have been based on the necessity of assuring the preservation of these treaties against encroachment, principally on the part of France. In the eighteenth century the unchanged portions of earlier treaties were confirmed " so far as the parties to the present treaty are concerned ",[6] a phrase due to a somewhat more general participation in multipartite treaties, with an evident recognition of the principle that parties to the earlier treaty not participating in its revision could not be bound without their consent. Through all the seventeenth and eighteenth century the sentiment appeared to be growing, however, that a territorial base and a charter of international principles was being built up in which all the states had a greater or lesser interest, an interest which could not be eliminated merely by agreement between those states which had set up any particular part of the treaty network on which the whole structure was based.

At the time of the settlement of Vienna in 1815 this principle took more definite shape. This settlement, like the earlier ones of 1648 and 1713, was made up of a number of

were parties, and to which a number of other states acceded, and a treaty for the execution of these three to which five states were parties. See *Traités publics de la royale maison de Savoie* (Turin, 1836-61), vol. iii, p. 33 *et seq.*, and Wenck, *Codex juris gentium,* vol. ii, pp. 333 *et seq.*

[5] *Cf.* Aix-la-Chapelle, October 18, 1748, art. 3; *Traités publics de la royale maison de Savoie,* vol. iii, p. 51.

[6] *Cf.* Defensive Alliance between Sardinia, Hungary and England of September 13, 1743, art. ii; *ibid.,* vol. iii, p. 7.

separate agreements to which in few cases all the states represented at the conference were parties. But unlike the earlier settlements, these separate agreements were all attached to one General Act as Annexes, and all the principal states represented at the Congress were made parties to this Act.[7] As will be seen subsequently, the question whether such an arrangement resulted in making the consent of all the signatories of this Act necessary to the revision of the separate Annexes, to which they had only been parties as signatories of the former, caused a good deal of trouble, but no one appears to have denied the validity of the principle of unanimous acceptance of revisory stipulations.

What might appear to be a renewed acceptance of the principle occurred in the signing of the Declaration of London of 1871, in which seven states including the Great Powers agreed that no Power might liberate itself from the engagements of a treaty, nor modify its stimulations, without the consent of the contracting Powers.[8] But in view of the attendant circumstances, the design of the parties appears to have been to deny the right of unilateral denunciation rather than to declare the rule of unanimous consent, and their own practice in proceeding to the revision of treaties without securing the consent of the minor signatories would leave some doubt of their design to give sweeping support to that rule.[9]

From that time on the principle of unanimous consent was little discussed until the peace conference in 1919. The conference was frequently troubled by the fact that certain states such as Russia and the Netherlands, which were not participating in the conference, were parties to important prewar

[7] *Brit. & For. State Papers*, vol. ii, p. 7.

[8] Hertslet, *Map of Europe by Treaty*, vol. iii, p. 1904.

[9] *Cf.* Protocols of Conference of London, *Brit. and For. State Papers*, vol. 61, pp. 1198-1227.

treaties which appeared to call for revision. For the most part the problem was at least temporarily solved by ignoring Russia [10] and making arrangements for securing the subsequent consent of Holland.[11] But the intent of the states represented at the conference apparently was to accept the principle, modifying its application to the extent that reluctant consent or absence of concerted objection was not allowed to prevent the solution of the problems at hand.[12]

The question was brought up again in 1930, at the time of the attempted revision of the Statute of the Permanent Court of International Justice. The Protocol of Revision stipulated that it should enter into force on September 1 of that year if the Council of the League was satisfied that those states concerned which had not already ratified the amended statute had no objection.[13] Among such states Cuba indicated her unwillingness to accept this arrangement, and her action was sufficient to defeat the project.[14] During the discussion which followed, criticism was made of the provision that acceptance was implied in the absence of an expression of dissent, rather than that express unanimous acceptance was necessary, on the ground that such a pro-

[10] *Cf.* British suggestion at the Paris Peace Conference, when the question which states should participate in the revision of the 1839 treaties concerning Belgium was under discussion, to the effect that Russia was for the moment "non-existent"; British memo., Miller, *My Diary of the Peace Conference*, vol. v, p. 33.

[11] Treaty of Versailles, art. 354.

[12] *Cf.* President Wilson's handling of the question of the Monroe Doctrine in drafting the Covenant of the League of Nations; Miller, *Drafting of the Covenant*, Commission on the League of Nations, Tenth Meeting, *Minutes* (English), pp. 324; Fifteenth Meeting, pp. 384.

[13] September 14, 1929, art. 4; Hudson, *International Legislation*, vol. i, p. 582.

[14] Hudson, "Revision of the Statute of the Court", *Foreign Affairs*, vol. ix, p. 344.

vision was an innovation in the history of international agreements.[15]

Since 1918, however, a type of treaty has become common which, while providing for its own revision, stipulates that the unrevised convention shall remain binding in the relations with those parties to it which fail to ratify the new.[16] This arrangement obviates the paralyzing effect of the principle that unanimous consent to any revision is required, without abolishing the principle. Though the field of usefulness of such treaties is limited, they constitute a recognition of the fact that, as the number of parties to multipartite conventions grows, the possibility of securing unanimous acceptance of modifications diminishes.

In order to determine the validity of the principle of unanimous acceptance and whether the deviations from it are subject to other well-defined principles, it will be necessary to consider the specific applications of the former and the circumstances under which the latter took place. Up until the past few decades there were only rare instances where the parties indicated in the convention itself[17] their design to observe the principle, and there are frequent indications that the intent differed with different parties. Nevertheless these differences of intent may frequently be coordinated in modifying rules, some of which are now recognized and others still taking shape.

[15] League of Nations, *Document C. L. 194(a).1930.V.*

[16] E. g. the convention concerning Industrial Property, of June 2, 1911; Malloy, *Treaties, etc. of the United States*, vol. iii, p. 2953, art. 18.

[17] Art. xvii of the Berne convention of September 9, 1886, stipulates that "aucun changement à la présente Convention ne sera valable pour l'Union que moyennant l'assentiment unanime des pays qui la composent." *Brit. & For. State Papers*, vol. 77, p. 22. This provision was repeated in the subsequent conventions of November 3, 1908, and of June 28, 1928.

The General Act of the Congress of Vienna

The political circumstances of the time of the Vienna settlement were of primary importance in determining the parties to the various arrangements of which it is composed. At the opening of the congress there was a sharp discussion as to which states were to participate in the drawing up of the new arrangements. The four principal allies, Great Britain, Austria, Prussia and Russia, were inclined to take the matter into their own hands, and probably would have done so had it not been for the skilful work of Talleyrand, who succeeded in using the German States and the minor allies,—Spain, Portugal and Sweden,—for strengthening the claim of the other states at the conference, including France, to participate.[18] As a result the seven allies and France were signatories of the General Act, the same parties, with the exception of Spain, which had been signatories of the preliminary treaty of peace of the preceding year.[19]

This General Act was composed of three types of provisions. There were a number of separate treaties and declarations dealing with a variety of questions, only four of which were signed by all the parties to the General Act,[20] but which were all attached to it "as integral parts of the Arrangements of the Congress". A large part of the stipulations of these Annexes, together with numerous other provisions characterized as being of a "superior and permanent interest"[21] were joined in a general convention to which the

[18] *Cf.* Protocols of Conference, *Brit. & For. State Papers*, vol. ii, pp. 553-773, *passim*.

[19] Treaty of Peace of May 30, 1814, *ibid.*, vol. i, p. 151; art. xxxii.

[20] XIA, Declaration concerning the Helvetic Confederation; XII, Protocol of Conference concerning Cessions by Sardinia to Geneva; XV, Declaration of Eight Powers, relative to the Slave Trade; XVI, Regulations concerning the Free Navigation of Rivers.

[21] Preamble.

parts described above were annexed. There was thus an overlapping of provisions, some of those of "superior and permanent interest" being included both in the body of the Act and in one or another of the Annexes. Article 118 of the General Act provides that the Annexes should have "the came force and validity as if they were inserted, word for word, in the General Treaty." In addition to the various groups of signatories involved in the Act as a whole and in the different Annexes, the whole arrangement was submitted to all the states signatory to any part of it, and eventually received the acceptance of all.[22]

A fourth type of provision was added in November, 1815, five months after the signature of the General Act, when Great Britain, Austria, Prussia and Russia drew up a treaty establishing a British protectorate over the Ionian Islands, and stated that it "shall be considered as forming part of the General Treaty concluded at Vienna".[23] In order to conform to the principle of unanimous consent, the treaty provided for the accession of all the states parties to the original peace treaty in 1814 and of those which were parties to the General Act. In an effort to gain the consent of two other states whose interest in such a settlement must be presumed, Turkey and the Two Sicilies were also invited to accede.[24]

We have in this treaty an indication of the transition from the principle that the Vienna settlement concerned all those states who had been belligerents in the precedent war, to the principle that those states whose interest in the maintenance of certain parts of that settlement was slight need not be consulted when modifying it, provided the Great Powers,

[22] *Cf.* Flassan, *Histoire du Congrès de Vienne* (Paris, 1829), vol. ii, p. 326.

[23] Hertslet, *Map of Europe by Treaty*, vol. i, p. 337.

[24] Art. viii.

which were chiefly responsible for the settlement, were satisfied. The definitive treaty of peace, signed a few days after the Ionian Islands treaty, was signed only by the five Great Powers;[25] Spain acceded two years later, but neither Portugal nor Sweden appear to have been consulted in spite of the fact that the convention brought about several modifications in the General Act.[26] This was the last appearance of Spain, too, among the signatories of arrangements involving the provisions of the General Act of Vienna.

No denial of the principle of unanimous acceptance of changes appears to have been made at any time, but in practice it was frequently violated. A consideration of subsequent changes in the Vienna settlement shows the difficulty encountered by states in attempting to square theory with practice.

The first Annex to the General Act[27] was in the form of a treaty between Russia and Austria concerning Poland. The second was a very similar treaty on the same subject between Russia and Prussia.[28] In 1831 Russia suppressed the Polish constitution for which provision had been made in these conventions, and England protested Russia's action on the ground that inasmuch as the other parties to the General Act had not been consulted there had been a violation of that Act. Russia did not deny that a change in the Annex involving a contractual provision would have involved the participation of the Powers, but claimed that the grant of the constitution had been a spontaneous act of the Emperor, and that its withdrawal could not therefore affect the validity of the convention. She had obtained the assent of Austria and Prussia before acting, and appeared to feel that she was

[25] November 20, 1815, *Brit. & For. State Papers*, vol. iii, p. 280.

[26] *Cf.* art. ix.

[27] May 3, 1815, *ibid.*, vol. ii, p. 56.

[28] *Ibid.*, p. 63.

thus secure in case of a charge of breach of her obligations.[29]

In 1846 when the Third Annex,[30] concerning the Free City of Cracow, was terminated by the annexation of that city to Austria, that state took the same position as that of Russia discussed above. England and France both protested the annexation on the grounds that they had a right to be consulted as parties to the Act of Vienna. Austria replied that the Act gave no additional validity to the Annex, which was a tripartite treaty between herself, Russia and Prussia, and hinted that the principle of unanimous consent had not always been observed by the protesting states. She announced that, in her view, the consent of Russia and Prussia having been obtained she had no further obligation to consult the other parties to the Act. The fact that most of the provisions of the Cracow Annex had been embodied in the "principles of superior and permanent interest" as well as in the Annex appears not to have affected Austria's stand, as she stated that the Act was more a piece of evidence than a treaty, and at most might be held to give merely the right to the parties to intervene in case of disagreement among the signatories of the Annex.[31]

One of the principal tasks of the Congress of Vienna had been the constitution of the German Confederation. The result of these labors of the Congress was the Ninth Annex to the General Act,[32] consisting of the Constitution, in the form of a treaty to which the members of the Confederation were parties, and the inclusion of a large part of the Constitution among the "principles of superior and permanent

[29] *Cf.* Russia's reply to Great Britain's protest; Hertslet, *op. cit.*, vol. ii, p. 885.

[30] May 3, 1815, *Brit. & For. State Papers*, vol. ii, p. 74.

[31] *Cf.* correspondence between France and Great Britain and Austria, *ibid.*, vol. 35, pp. 1072-1105.

[32] June 8, 1815, *ibid.*, vol. ii, p. 114.

interest ". The Confederation was dissolved by the Austro-Prussian treaty of 1866,[33] but this treaty made no mention of the rights of the other signatories of the General Act. The states which had fought against Prussia during the war acceded,[34] and Prussia absorbed a number of the other signatories of the Annex.[35] The President of the Diet of the Confederation and the King of Hannover protested against the dissolution of the Confederation as a violation of the General Act,[36] but none of the other parties to that Act appear to have taken official notice of such protests, or to have claimed any rights of their own.

At the time of the annexation of Cracow by Austria, she replied to England's protest by citing the violation of the principle of unanimous consent in 1839 by the latter state in the case of Belgium.[37] Annex X of the General Act[38] had set up an arrangement for the union of Belgium and Holland and defined the position of Luxemburg in relation to the latter. This arrangement was modified by the Recès général of Frankfort in 1819,[39] without the consent of the Netherlands, which had been a party to the Annex, or of France, Portugal, Spain or Sweden, which had been parties to the General Act. A more serious modification, and the one cited by Austria, had taken place in 1839,[40] without the consent of the last three states named. The last arrangement was frankly an affair of the Great Powers, with no

[33] August 23, 1866; *ibid.*, vol. 56, p. 1050.

[34] Bavaria, Württemberg, Baden, Hesse-Darmstadt.

[35] Hannover, Hesse-Cassel, Nassau, Frankfort.

[36] Hertslet, *op. cit.*, vol. iii, p. 1742.

[37] *Cf.* note 31, *supra.*

[38] May 31, 1815, *Brit. & For. State Papers*, vol. ii, p. 136.

[39] July 20, 1819, *ibid.*, vol. vii, p. 3.

[40] April 19, 1839, *ibid.*, vol. 27, pp. 990, 1000.

reference to the Act of Vienna, and Austria was correct in her contention that if she had been guilty of a violation in 1846 all the Great Powers had been equally guilty in 1839.

In 1860 a dispute arose concerning the revision of Annex XIA,[41] which contained the provision for the neutralization of Switzerland, and the Protocol of Conference, drawn up later in 1815,[42] which had extended that neutralization to Upper Savoy, then a part of Sardinia. This extension was embodied in a definitive treaty of peace in the fall of 1815, signed by the five Great Powers. Switzerland protested the cession of this territory to France in 1860 on the ground that such a cession violated the terms of the treaty.[43] The matter was settled by France's agreement in the treaty of cession that she would accept the territory on the conditions under which Sardinia held it, and that she must come to an understanding with the Powers represented at the Congress of Vienna and with Switzerland, giving them the guaranties stipulated in the old treaties. This was a clear recognition of the principle of unanimous consent, a recognition which was lacking in the other cases discussed.[44]

From the instances cited above the other modifications of the Vienna settlement, several conclusions may be drawn concerning the view of the parties to that settlement on the question of the necessity of unanimous consent. First, that within a very short time after the date of signature the General Act and the Annexes ceased to be considered by all the parties as an indivisible whole. Second, where the parties to each of the Annexes considered that they must be consulted in case of revision of that Annex, they appeared

[41] March 20, 1815, *ibid.*, vol. ii, p. 142.

[42] Hertslet, *op. cit.*, vol. i, p. 326.

[43] *Ibid.*, vol. ii, pp. 1415, 1435.

[44] March 24, 1860; *Brit. & For. State Papers*, vol. 50, p. 412, art. ii.

frequently to be of opinion that the assent of the other signatories of the General Act was not necessary to termination or revision of the Annex in question.[45] Where revision affected stipulations included both in an Annex and in the body of the Act such inclusion appears never to have been made the occasion of special consideration. In revising or terminating parts of the General Act, it was frequently the practice not to consult those parties whose interest was slight or might be safely disregarded.

Those provisions of the Annexes which were also included in the body of the Act, and characterized as of " superior and permanent interest " appear to have been clothed with a guaranty whose significance was that their revision might be considered as a matter of general concern. Austria and Russia failed to accept this view in dealing with Poland and Cracow, though England and France recognized it. The latter states appeared to feel that " general concern " meant that of the Great Powers, and as time went on that view appears to have prevailed. Within a few years of the signing of the General Act no one appears to have given further thought to the principle of unanimous consent in revising the Vienna settlement, except in a few cases such as the Savoy settlement, and even here the conference which was to have furnished France the assent of all the parties was never held.[46] Yet in spite of the actual disregard of the principle there is nowhere in the discussions a denial of its validity, and frequent affirmations of its existence. Nor is there anywhere a statement that the consent of the Great Powers, as such, to revision of the provisions of general concern is sufficient or even necessary, although this was the

[45] Three of the parties to the General Act, Spain, Portugal and Sweden, appear never to have been consulted in regard to any revision, nor to have protested because they had not been.

[46] Hertslet, *op. cit.*, vol. ii, p. 1448.

principle on which much of the treaty revision throughout the nineteenth century was based.

Treaties Involving the Public Law of Europe

As has already been indicated, the concept that certain treaty arrangements were of interest to other states than the signatories, since they formed a sort of charter of European law on which the political stability of the continent was based, had been growing all through the seventeenth and eighteenth centuries. During the early part of this period the interest of no state appeared to be more than regional; that is, there was no one state which claimed a right to be consulted in making new arrangements concerning any part of Europe. The period of the Napoleonic wars appears to have been the time when the concept first commenced to take definite shape that a small group of powerful states had an interest in the settlement of any important European problem. The corollary to this principle, that a state outside this group which was party to a general arrangement need not always be consulted in a revision of that arrangement, received practical application immediately after the settlement of Vienna, with the elimination of Spain, Portugal and Sweden, all signatories of the General Act, from subsequent conferences for amending that Act. There was never apparent any belief that these states had no right to demand to be consulted, but in the absence of such demand there appeared to have been no disposition to consider that their consent was necessary to modifications of stipulations to which they had been parties if that of the Great Powers had been secured.

The disposition to recognize the particular interest of the smaller states in treaties concerning them was manifested pointedly in the treaty of peace at the end of the Crimean

War, signed in 1856.[47] Provision was made here for the admission of Turkey to "the public law and system of Europe".[48] There was no explanation given of the phrase, but its significance in the view of future developments appears to have been that Turkey's right was recognized to participate in future arrangements concerning southeastern Europe.

The avoidance of exact definition of these terms allowed for their free application to any exigency which arose. But by 1914 their significance so far as treaty arrangements were concerned was reasonably clear. The exact content of the public law of Europe was never established, but so far as it was expressed in treaties it included much of the treaty of Vienna and such regional arrangements as were made in 1839 for Belgium and Holland, and in 1856 for the Near East, the regulations concerning the Danube in the same treaty, and in general those treaty stipulations covered by a multipartite guaranty.[49]

The Concert of Europe was a term apparently signifying the common action of the European states to protect the charter known as the public law of Europe.[50] Its significance from the point of view of treaties appeared to be that those states particularly interested in any part of that charter were generally consulted in any revision. The status of a Great Power usually involved consultation on all such questions, while the lesser Powers participated in the discussion of revision of those treaties dealing with questions immediately concerning them.

In view of the absence of tribunals for the enforcement

[47] March 30, 1856, *Brit. & For. State Papers*, vol. 46, p. 8.

[48] Art. vii.

[49] *Cf.* Satow, "Pacta sunt servanda", in *Cambridge Historical Journal*, 1925, p. 303.

[50] *Cf.* Bluntschli, *Droit international codifié* (Paris, 1895), arts. 110, 113.

of treaty provisions the system had much to recommend it, but it is difficult to square its practical working with the principle of unanimous consent to revision. One weakness of the system lay in the fact that neither the interests nor the importance of states remained static, and their claim to participation in treaty arrangements on the basis either of their interest in the question or their power to force consideration of their demand might thus be constantly open to question. Frequently a claim was made for participation in treaty revisions too, on the basis that all the parties must be consulted, when in effect even the claimant state did not appear to intend to include all the original parties in the revision. Examples of this incongruity of view are found in the revisions of parts of the Vienna Annexes, such as those relating to Cracow and Savoy, discussed above.

In this connection an examination of the Declaration of London of 1871 is fruitful. It is there stated that the Great Powers plus Turkey " recognize that it is an essential principle of the Law of Nations that no Power can liberate itself from the engagements of a Treaty, nor modify the stipulations thereof, unless with the consent of the Contracting Powers by means of an amicable arrangement ".[51] As has been noted elsewhere, the parties to this declaration had themselves participated in the modification of treaties, and continued to do so, without the consent of all the parties. If they had intended to observe the principle of unanimous consent as implied here it would always have been possible for a single state, of whatever importance, to block any progress toward the revision of treaty stipulations if such state happened to be a party thereto. The result must inevitably have been that powerful states would restrict carefully the number of states participating in treaty arrange-

[51] *Brit. & For. State Papers,* vol. 61, p. 1198.

ments, to limit the possible use of the veto power when revision was contemplated.

The design of the parties would appear definitely to have been somewhat different. The conference which drew up the declaration had been called to block Russia's attempt to modify the provisions of an important treaty by her unilateral act, and their purpose would appear to have been rather to declare that unilateral denunciation could not be accepted as a principle, and to provide for general consultation of the Great Powers at least when a treaty which might be considered as forming part of the public law of Europe was to be changed.

That the Declaration was not intended as an endorsement of the principle that unanimous consent was necessary to revision by subsequent treaty is indicated by later events in the Near East, the region whose affairs were discussed at the 1871 conference. The principles of unanimous consent and of the Concert of Europe coincided in 1878, when revision of the 1871 arrangement of Near Eastern affairs took place with the consent of all the parties, but in 1908 Austria upset the provisions of the 1878 arrangement relating to Bosnia-Herzegovina by her unilateral act, securing the consent of the principal Powers thereafter. In 1912 the Balkan States upset it further without obtaining the consent of the parties until afterward. After the war of 1914-18 Russia was not a party to, and even expressed her dissent from, most of the arrangements revising the old, yet the changes were made, and Russia has since tacitly given her acquiescence. None would be inclined to doubt the validity of these arrangements on the ground that unanimous consent to the revision of the 1878 treaty had not been obtained when they were made, so long as the balance of power was preserved and the Concert of Europe was not broken up.

The principle involved in the Concert of Europe which

permits a Great Power to participate in the settlement of questions with which its connection may appear to be only indirect, received tacit recognition in 1867 when Italy was invited to participate in the settlement of the Luxemburg question.[52] Italy had not been a party to the treaties which were to be revised, and the status of Luxemburg did not appear to have been a matter of great concern to her. Yet her representative was invited to participate. No mention is made of her status as a Great Power, yet from that time on Italy took part in all the conferences to which the Great Powers were invited.

There is no particular difficulty from the point of view of treaty arrangements in such a case, but when through loss of the Great Power status, as was the case with Austria after the war of 1914-18, or through the end of participation in the Concert, as was the case with Russia after 1917, the conflict between the principle of unanimous consent and of the Concert of Europe becomes evident. The fact that the former principle had been repeatedly recognized, while the latter had been only tacitly accepted as a rule of conduct, made the application of the latter difficult in the treaty revisions immediately after the war. Austria's transition to the status of a small Power was made by the same instrument by which she renounced her rights under most of those arrangements to which she was a party by virtue of her former status. The peace conference, however, failed to provide for Russia's consent to revision, and thus abandoned the principle of unanimous consent in this case, presumably operating on the principle that if a Great Power chooses not to participate in the Concert the latter may go on without her.

[52] The president of the Conference, Lord Stanley, stated that Italy's presence at the Conference "would contribute to the success of its deliberations". The Italian delegate replied that "we had not, like other Powers, a prior right to take part in the Conference. We owe it to a mark of deference on their part." *Ibid.*, vol. 60, pp. 497-8.

That this principle was not entirely satisfactory to all the states concerned, however, was made evident in 1926, when Belgium and the Netherlands attempted in cooperation with France and England to provide for the revision of the 1839 treaties. This treaty,[53] which was never ratified, contained a provision for Russian accession, presumably in view of the fact that she was a party to the old arrangement. As the treaty never went into effect, the invitation to Russia was never extended, so what her action would have been in such a case can only be a guess.

Russia has, however, made her own position reasonably clear. In 1917 she denounced all secret treaties, on the ground that they had been made for the benefit of landed proprietors and capitalists. Immediately following the war she signed treaties with China, Persia and Turkey terminating all the treaties of the old régime with those countries. But beyond this she has made no disposition concerning the prewar treaties to which she was a party. In 1924 she stated that most of these treaties had been either expressly or tacitly abrogated without her consent in the relations between the other parties, and that revival by her would therefore result in two conflicting sets of obligations on the part of the other parties. She expressed the sentiment that all the treaties should be reconsidered, and in fact made to Great Britain a direct proposal for such reconsideration.[54]

[53] Bescheiden in *Zake de Tusschen Nederland en Belgie* ('sGravenhaage, 1929), pp. 13-15.

[54] "La rupture extraordinairement prolongée des relations politiques avec tous les Etats du monde, qui suivit la révolution de 1917, et les changements survenus entre temps dans tout l'ensemble des engagements internationaux, ne permettraient certainement pas une reconstruction pure et simple de l'ensemble des traités des anciens gouvernements russes. Peu d'entre eux pourraient, en effet, être mis en execution sans qu'il s'en suivit une collision avec le réglement ultérieur des mêmes questions qui survint après 1917 sans la participation de l'une des parties engagées dans ces traités..." Communication to the *Bulletin de l'Institut inter-*

There has been no such reconsideration as suggested, and the fact remains that Russia's consent to the revisions which have taken place has never been obtained. The bridge across the gap between the two principles discussed which has been used in other cases is apparently in use here, namely, that when a revision takes place, the failure of any party to the earlier arrangement to protest when not consulted may operate to defeat its subsequent right to do so, provided that the negotiations or the treaty resulting therefrom are brought to the knowledge of that party. The fact, however, that Russia's signature appears on most of the treaties which might be considered as forming the public law of Europe between 1815 and 1914 and that her status as a Great Power is unchanged may later operate to bring the other parties to these arrangements to seek Russia's accession to their modifications.

Where a treaty dealing with a matter of general interest serves to increase the special interest of certain of the parties while diminishing that of others, the result may be that the latter may be in fact eliminated from participation in revision of the treaty, without of course losing the right to protest such elimination. An example in point is furnished by the Franco-German treaty of 1911,[55] which modified certain provisions of the Act of Algeciras of 1906.[56] As is usual in such cases, however, provision was made to invite the accession of all the parties to the Algeciras Act.[57] There appears to have been some disposition on the part of these parties to protest this procedure, but the validity of the new arrangement was not seriously contested.

médiaire international, 1924, vol. xi, pp. 154-5. *Cf. London Times* of February 2, 3, 8, 10 and May 17, 29, 1924.

[55] November 4, 1911, *Brit. & For. State Papers*, vol. 104, p. 948.

[56] April 7, 1906, Malloy, *Treaties, etc. of the United States*, vol. ii, p. 2157.

[57] Art. xiv.

The following principles concerning treaties appear to be involved in the concept of the public law and Concert of Europe:

1. Certain states may have interests widespread enough to give them a right to participate in a revision of any treaty involving the public law of Europe.

2. Failure of one or more signatories of a treaty to participate in a revision need not render that revision invalid.

3. Failure to assert the right to participate when the revision is public knowledge appears to be equivalent to an implied acceptance of the new settlement by a non-participating party to the revised treaty.

4. The public law of Europe is of such a character that the enforcement of an unrevised treaty embodying part of that law, as between the non-signatories of a revision of such an instrument, is generally incompatible with the new agreement, with the result that the new agreement may operate in practice to prevent the carrying out of the old even for the non-signatories of the new arrangement.

5. A change in the status of a state from small to Great Power or vice versa, or any of several other changes in circumstances may change the position of a state in the Concert of Europe to the extent that the importance of its consent in the case of a given revision may become vital or negligible.[58]

The Peace Treaties, 1919-23

The Versailles settlement did but little to improve on the weaknesses of the Vienna arrangement of a century earlier in regard to its own modification. The structure of the later

[58] In 1919, Clemenceau, in a note to Paderewski transmitting the treaty to be signed by Poland under art. 93 of the treaty of Versailles, indicated his conception of the development of the public law of Europe under the aegis of the League of Nations; *cf.* Miller, *My Diary of the Peace Conference*, vol. xiii, p. 215 and see *supra*, p. 54.

settlement is less confusing, it is true, being composed of five peace treaties, quite separate and distinct from each other, instead of the cumbersome arrangement of a series of general provisions followed by a large group of annexes signed in almost every case by different sets of parties. A number of the less controversial provisions of these later treaties may be revised by groups of states or other bodies without the unanimous consent of the signatories of the treaty. But in other respects the later arrangement is more likely to lead to confusion. The number of parties to the Versailles treaty is twenty-eight, as compared with eight in the former treaty, making the probability of unanimous consent to change correspondingly slighter. The five peace treaties in the later group were signed at intervals extending over four years, although dealing in many cases with the same subject matter, and making a good deal of confusion over a considerable period concerning the status of many of the subjects treated. The division of the parties into two groups, the Allied and Associated Powers and the Principal Allied and Associated Powers, would have avoided much of the difficulty caused by the failure so to divide the parties to the Vienna treaty, were it not for the fact that very little use was made of the division to determine which provisions might be revised by either group.

Undoubtedly one reason for this failure to differentiate between two types of provision in this way was due to the design of the parties to set up permanent arrangements. That much of the treaty would call for revision before any long interval was in the minds of certain of the negotiators at the time,[59] yet aside from the provision of Article XIX

[59] *Cf.* statement of J. C. Smuts after signature of the Versailles treaty, Temperley, *History of the Peace Conference*, vol. vi, p. 582; also the statement of Lord Robert Cecil in the House of Commons, July 21, 1919, on the Treaty of Peace bill, Hansard, *Parliamentary Debates*, 5th ser., vol. 118, col. 991.

that the Assembly of the League might recommend the reconsideration of treaties which had become inapplicable, there is no provision made for revising the great bulk of the provisions for these treaties. Such provision as was made, however, for the revision of a small part of the treaties' stipulations, indicates an appreciation of the fact that some means must be found for maintaining the provisions of treaties in accord with the current needs of the international community, by permitting revision by some other process than negotiations resulting in unanimous consent of a large number of parties to the change. A brief resumé of the provisions for modification shows how the problem was met.

Versailles

The parties to the peace settlement of Versailles [60] avoided one of the dangers encountered by the Vienna settlement of 1815 by providing for the replacement of certain parts through separate action of variously constituted bodies.

The first twenty-six articles, comprising the Covenant of the League of Nations, can be amended on ratification of the change by all the States whose members compose the Council and a majority of those whose members compose the Assembly.[61] This procedure constitutes revision not by the parties to the original convention, but by a group of constantly changing composition.

All the general articles relating to most favored nation treatment by Germany of the Allied states,[62] those concerning ports, waterways and railways,[63] and the prohibition of regular river service by German boats between two ports

[60] *Treaties, etc. of the United States*, vol. iii, p. 3329.

[61] Art. 26 of the treaties of Versailles, St. Germain, Trianon and Neuilly.

[62] Art. 280.

[63] Art. 378.

of an Allied state,[64] are limited to five years' duration, after which they are subject to revision by the Council of the League, unless that body decides to extend the period.

The labor provisions of the treaty may be changed by a vote of two-thirds of the delegates at the General Conference of the International Labor Organization, upon ratification by the states composing the Council and three-fourths of the members of the League.[65]

Customs regulations imposed on Germany by Articles 264-70, inclusive, Allied fishing and navigation rights in German territorial waters, and the prohibition of inspection of Allied fishing boats in the North Sea [66] might be amended by the Council of the League after five years, or extended beyond that period, after one year's previous notice of the proposed change or extension.

Article 276, preventing exemption of German nationals from restrictions imposed on Allied nationals, was to remain in force beyond a five-year period for an additional period of five years, if the Council should so decide by majority vote.

The régime for international rivers set up by the treaty (Arts. 332-337) was to be superseded by one drawn up by the Allied and Associated Powers and approved by the League.[67]

The rest, and by far the largest part, of the treaty is not subject to any specific revisory process. Article XIX of the treaty provides that the Assembly of the League might advise the reconsideration by the Members of the League of treaties which have become inapplicable, a provision which might apply to this treaty as well as another, but

[64] Art. 332.

[65] Art. 422.

[66] Art. 271 and 272, revision provided in art. 280.

[67] Art. 338.

which in practice has not been so applied. But the Versailles treaty has not escaped modification in parts for the revision of which no provision was made in the treaty itself. Annex I to Part VIII of the treaty, dealing with decisions of the Reparations Commission, was modified in 1924 by a protocol signed by France, Great Britain, Italy, Japan, Belgium and the Serb-Croat-Slovene State.[68] The protocol provided that its decision should be notified to the Powers signatory of the Treaty and to the Reparations Commission, but contains no other recognition of the rights of the non-participating states.

Article 428 provided that the troops of the Allied and Associated Powers were to occupy the Rhineland in whole or in part until 1935, unless Germany should have complied with all the undertakings resulting from the treaty. In 1929, before such compliance, Germany, Belgium, Great Britain, France and Italy arranged by treaty for the evacuation of the Rhineland, with no recognition of the rights of the other parties to the Versailles treaty.[69]

By Article 232 of the treaty of Versailles, Germany undertakes to make compensation for all damage done to the civilian population of the Allied and Associated Powers and their property during the war. The conditional release from this obligation was drawn up in 1932 in the form of a treaty to which only the beneficiaries from reparations and Germany were parties, and there was no provision for accession by any states except Germany's creditors.[70]

It would appear that modification of the Versailles treaty is to be made in much the same manner as the Vienna settle-

[68] January 22, 1925, Martens, *Nouveau recueil général des traités, 3me série*, vol. xiv, p. 771.

[69] August 30, 1929, *League of Nations Treaty Series*, vol. 104, p. 489.

[70] Cmd. paper, 4126 Misc. 7 (1932); Protocol re entry into force, Cmd. 4129, Misc. 8 (1932).

ment. Clearly there is no feeling that all the parties must participate in the revision of every part of it, nor even that their accession must always be provided for. The other parties to the Versailles treaty are not, it appears, disposed to assert any right to participate in the revisions already made. It has been maintained that the disarmament clauses may only be modified by agreement among the parties to the Versailles treaty, and it is probable that a number of the signatories who have accepted other revisions tacitly without participation would be more insistent about participating in a revision of these clauses. But the principles built up under the Concert of Europe in regard to participation in revisory conferences would still appear to be of frequent application.

Other Peace Treaties Besides Versailles

The minorities provisions, appearing in the St. Germain,[71] Trianon,[72] Neuilly[73] and Lausanne treaties,[74] can only be modified with the consent of a majority of the Council of the League, provided however that the British Empire, France, Italy and Japan agree not to withhold their consent if the amendment is assented to by a majority of the Council. It is not made clear whether this majority is to be made up without counting the four states mentioned, or whether, a majority being lacking without their votes, they are obligated to cast them in favor of such modification. In practice this provision has never been tested, however.

The provisions of Article 327 of the treaty of St.

[71] Malloy, *Treaties, etc. of the United States*, vol. iii, p. 3149, arts. 62-9.

[72] *Ibid.*, p. 3539, arts. 54-60.

[73] *Brit. and For. State Papers*, vol. 112, p. 781, arts. 49-57.

[74] *Ibid.*, vol. 117, p. 543, arts. 37-45. The effect of these provisions is to give to a state represented on the Council, but not a party to any of these treaties, the right to participate in preventing the parties to these treaties from modifying the minority provisions. Thus in 1934 Guatemala might participate in blocking such action.

Germain, covering the operation of telephone and telegraph lines between Austria and Czechoslovakia, may be revised by Austria and Czechoslovakia alone, and after ten years in case of disagreement, by an arbitrator designated by the League Council.

Freedom of transit is broadly defined by Article 284 of St. Germain as it is to be granted by Austria to the persons and property of Allied nationals, but it is provided that a new Convention drawn up by the Allied and Associated Powers is to be substituted for the provisions of Article 284.

Article 189 of the treaty of Trianon permits the Reparations Commission to alter the dates specified for carrying out its provisions.

Article 306 permits the Czechoslovak Railway Administration and the Hungarian railway administrations involved to alter the provisions of this article concerning the routes for through trains to the Adriatic.

Article 211 of the treaty of Neuilly permits termination of Bulgaria's obligations under the section dealing with aerial nagivation by adhesion to the convention relative to Aerial Navigation with the consent of the Allied and Associated Powers.

We have then a wide variety of bodies which were granted power by the parties to these treaties to revise them. They are as follows:

Council of the League of Nations; unanimously plus half the Assembly;[75]

Council of the League of Nations; majority;[76]

Council of the League of Nations; no majority specified;[77]

[75] First twenty-six articles of Versailles, St. Germain, Trianon and Neuilly.

[76] Treatment of Allied nationals, art. 276, Versailles; see also art. 280.

[77] Customs, shipping, Versailles, arts. 271-2; see also art. 280.

Council of the League of Nations; plus International Labor Conference and three-quarters of the Assembly; [78]

Council of the League of Nations; majority not including Great Britain, France, Italy and Japan; [79]

Allied and Associated Powers; plus the League of Nations; [80]

Allied and Associated Powers; alone; [81]

Governments represented on the Reparations Commission; [82]

Hungary and Czechoslovakia; [83]

Railway administrations of Hungary and Czechoslovakia; [84]

Arbitrator designated by the Council.[85]

There was thus in these agreements a realization of the wisdom of facilitating modification of certain parts of these treaties without resorting to the cumbersome and sometimes dangerous method of a conference of the parties. In thus securing in advance the assent of these parties to other forms of modification, much of the difficulty involved in adapting conventions to new conditions is avoided.

[78] Part. xiii, Versailles.

[79] Minorities provisions, St. Germain, art. 69. The other peace treaties provide for the modification of their minorities clauses by action of the majority of the Council, the Allied and Associated Powers represented thereon agreeing not to withhold assent to a modification agreed to by such majority. (*Cf.* art. 60 of St. Germain.)

[80] Versailles, régime for international rivers, arts. 332-337.

[81] Versailles, art. 354, final paragraph.

[82] Versailles, art. 234.

[83] Trianon, art. 310; similar provision between Austria and Czechoslovakia, St. Germain, art. 327.

[84] Trianon, art. 306.

[85] St. Germain, art. 327, par. (6).

Conventions Concerning International Waterways

A deviation from the principle that the parties to a convention should also be parties to its revision occurs in the case of international rivers. The rule in question is contained in the General Act of Vienna, and stipulates that regulations concerning navigation on rivers separating or traversing two or more states should be drawn up in common by those states.[86] The design of the parties to this stipulation would appear from the text to be that the rule should be applied to all such rivers, but in practice it was only applied to given rivers specifically, and this was done sparingly. Furthermore, the rule did not specify that no one except such riparians was to participate in drawing up the regulations, and in view of later treaty arrangements in which participation of non-riparians in the regulation of such navigation was specifically provided,[87] the parties to the Vienna Act appear not to have intended to lay down such a rule.

The principle was applied to the Elbe by the General Act of Vienna itself,[88] but it was not until 1821 that the statute of navigation was drawn up.[89] This statute stipulated that revision of its terms should be made only by a committee on which all riparian states were represented.[90] So far as the regulation of navigation was concerned, the principle was observed, though the toll provisions for the river were

[86] *Brit. & For. State Papers,* vol. ii, p. 162.

[87] E. g., European Commission of the Danube, Treaty of Paris, March 30, 1856; Hertslet, *Map of Europe by Treaty,* vol. ii, p. 1250, art. xvi. It was not originally intended, however, that this Commission should control navigation.

[88] May 18, 1815, forming Annex iv of the General Act, art. xvii, *ibid.,* vol. i, p. 134.

[89] Act of June 23, 1821, *ibid.,* vol. i, p. 671.

[90] Art. 30.

the work of a different group of states, all the riparians not being represented.[91] When the tolls were finally abolished, however, in 1870, it was done by Austria and the North German Confederation, the sole remaining riparians.[92]

The General Act of Vienna itself provided a statute of navigation which was signed by all the riparians [93] for the Rhine. The statute included a provision for the organization of a Central Commission composed of representatives of the riparian states and which was to draw up navigation regulations in accordance with the principles of the Vienna Act. In 1831 these regulations were drawn up by the riparians, with a proviso that there could be no change except by common consent,[94] and in 1868 the regulations were revised in accordance with this principle.[95]

With the transfer of Alsace-Lorraine to Germany in 1871 France ceased to be a riparian, and in accordance with the Vienna principle she should have lost the right to participate in drawing up navigation regulations on the basis of her rights as a riparian. In this case, if the provision of the 1831 regulations for revision by "common consent" is taken to mean "common consent of the riparians" rather than "common consent of the parties to the arrangement concerned" France would lose her right derived from the 1831 arrangement to participate in a revision. In practice the former interpretation was accepted; after the transfer of Alsace-Lorraine to Germany, the regional Government of Alsace-Lorraine passed an act to put the regulations into

[91] The treaty of June 22, 1861 (*Brit. & For. State Papers*, vol. 51, p. 27) concerning the Redemption of the Brunshausen Toll, was signed also by Great Britain, Belgium, Brazil, Spain, France, the Netherlands, Portugal, Russia, Sweden and Norway, all non-riparians.

[92] June 22, 1870, Hertslet, *op. cit.*, vol. iii, p. 1875.

[93] Annex xvi B of the General Act of Vienna, *ibid.*, vol. i, p. 78.

[94] March 31, 1831, *Brit. & For. State Papers*, vol. 18, p. 1076.

[95] October 16, 1878, *ibid.*, vol. 59, p. 470.

effect,[96] and in 1898, when the police provisions of the 1868 regulations were revised, Alsace-Lorraine was a party and France was absent.[97]

The principle of the Vienna Act was applied to the Danube by the treaty of 1856,[98] and the succeeding year a statute of navigation was prepared by the riparian states.[99] Due to a protest by the non-riparian signatories of the 1856 treaty, caused by the fact that the provisions of the Vienna Act were not observed, this Act of Navigation was never put into effect.[1] The treaty of 1856 confided to a commission composed of representatives of the parties to the 1856 treaty the task of freeing the mouths of the Danube from obstacles to navigation. In 1864 this commission, having accomplished part of its task, set up provisional regulations for navigation on the lower river,[2] and followed this by a definitive Public Act the following year.[3] This Public Act stipulated that its provisions should continue in force until replaced by definitive regulations set up by common action of the riparians, as stipulated in the treaty of 1856.

Württemberg and Bavaria, the upstream riparians, were not represented on the European Commission; hence regulation of navigation on any part of the river by the Commission constituted a violation of the principles of the Vienna Act. It is true of course that the parties to the Public Act

[96] *Rheinurkunden* ('s-Gravenhage, 1918), vol. ii, p. 200, document 401.

[97] June 4, 1898, Martens, *Nouveau recueil général, 2me série*, vol. 29, p. 113.

[98] March 30, 1856, Hertslet, *op. cit.*, vol. ii, p. 1256.

[99] November 7, 1857, *Brit. & For. State Papers*, vol. 57, p. 786.

[1] Protocols of Conference, August 9 and 16, 1858, *ibid.*, vol. 48, pp. 105, 123.

[2] November 21, 1864, *ibid.*, vol. 54, p. 558.

[3] November 2, 1865, *ibid.*, vol. 55, p. 93.

made it clear that they intended such regulation to be temporary only. Had Württemberg and Bavaria claimed the right to participate in the work of the Commission, the basis of their claim would be a convention to which they were not parties, that is, the Paris convention of 1856. The application of the provisions of the Vienna Act to the Danube was the work of the same group of states which tacitly set these provisions aside in failing to assure the participation of the upstream riparians. There was no provision in the Vienna Act as to what group of Powers was to declare that the provisions of that Act should thenceforth be applied to any given river, but on the principles underlying the public law and Concert of Europe the Powers assembled at Paris would have had the power to do so. There is a question whether, once having applied the Act to the Danube, these states had the right to set it aside even tacitly. In 1871 the question was reduced to purely academic interest by the absorption of the upstream riparians in the German Empire, which was a party to the arrangements made by the European Commission, by virtue of being a successor state to Prussia. In 1878, when Serbia became a riparian, the situation arose again, and was not regularized until the abortive treaty of Bucharest in 1918.[4]

At the Peace Conference in 1919 there was much discussion as to what was to be done with the prewar river conventions, and whether the old Vienna principles were to apply. The Commission on Ports, Waterways and Railways suggested that no rivers should be considered as international merely because they had been declared so in the past, but that those which were to have that status should be specifically mentioned in the peace treaties. In furtherance of that principle, but without its specific recognition,

[4] May 7, 1918, Martens, *Nouveau recueil général, 3me série*, vol. x, p. 867.

the Elbe, Oder and Niemen were declared international,[5] and provision was made for a future conference which was empowered to give that status to others.[6] The peace conference did not attempt a revision of the provisions of the Vienna Act, the establishment of general principles being left to the future conference mentioned.[7]

In 1921 this conference was held, and while mentioning that the development of the regime of international waterways began at Vienna, it neither repudiated nor specifically adopted the principles of the Vienna Act.[8] So far from repeating the stipulation that navigation on international rivers should be regulated by the riparian states, however, it made specific provision for regulation where riparians were not parties. Inasmuch as over forty states participated in the work of this conference it is to be presumed that by general consent the rule established by Vienna no longer exists.

MODIFICATIONS OF TREATIES EFFECTIVE FOR CONSENTING PARTIES ONLY

The growth during the last half of the nineteenth century in the number of conventions imposing uniform obligations

[5] Treaty of Versailles, art. 331.

[6] *Ibid.*, art. 338.

[7] *Cf.* discussion in Committee on Ports, Waterways and Railways of the Paris Peace Conference, in Miller's *Diary*, vol. xi, *passim*. Chargueraud, Secretary-general of the Committee, stated that "until the meeting of the Commission to be summoned within a year after the ratification of the Treaty of Peace, there would be no rivers declared international ipso facto by reason of their present status. The only international rivers would be such . . . as were named and described in the annex." *Ibid.*, p. 245.

[8] *League of Nations Treaty Series*, vol. vii, p. 12, preamble. Compare with statement made by Chargueraud in 1919: "It was true that a departure was being made from the principles established in 1815, but in 1815 it was not possible to foresee the importance of irrigation and hydraulic power." *Ibid.*

on all the parties in the form of regulations, and in the number of states which were parties to such conventions, made the problem of securing unanimous consent to revision very difficult, and the necessity of its solution more pressing. In an increasingly large proportion of these treaties the solution was found by providing that the revised convention should replace the old for the signatories of the latter only, leaving the provisions of the old binding between the old signatories and between them and the signatories of the new.

This sort of arrangement is possible only in those cases where there is no direct and serious conflict between the two sets of regulations, and in practice has been confined almost entirely to conventions concerning the conduct of war [9] or regulating individual rights in commerce and industry.[10] In the former type the principles established have been changed very little, the practice under those principles merely being changed in accordance with the experience of the intervening period. A noteworthy example of the latter type is found in the industrial and literary and artistic property conventions, which have been frequently revised, at times three successive conventions having been thus in effect at the same time. In practice, however, the situation does not ordinarily remain so complicated; frequently the states not immediately ratifying the new tacitly adopt part or all of its provisions in dealing with those states which are parties to the new, and as accession is always left open there is a gradual absorption of all the non-ratifying states so that the

[9] See the Hague convention of Oct. 18, 1907 concerning the Pacific Settlement of International Disputes (*United States Treaty Series*, No. 536), art. 91, which replaces the convention of similar title of July 29, 1899 (*ibid.*, No. 392).

[10] *Cf.* the convention for the International Protection of Industrial Property, of June 2, 1911, Malloy, *Treaties, etc. of the United States*, vol. iii, p. 2953, art. 18, which replaced for those ratifying it the convention of March 20, 1883.

final termination of the old conventions creates no great change.[11] The advantages of this method of gradual termination are evident; there is an avoidance of all violent transition from one set of conditions to another, no compulsion, and a gradual adaptation of states to the new conditions at varying rates of speed.

The shortcomings of the method are equally apparent. It sometimes happens that only one state is still bound by the old set of rules, but legally all the others must observe those rules in dealing with that state. The fact that states not bound by the later convention sometimes adopt the new regulations nevertheless leads to confusion in case of dispute. But the chief drawback is the limited field in which the method can be applied. In conventions where the obligations of the parties differ, there can be no withdrawal of one party without upsetting the balance of rights and obligations for the others. Even in the case of a convention where the obligations of all the parties are identical and the convention is of an administrative type, there can be no drastic change in the administrative organs or in the regulations without inducing a conflict between the two treaties rendering impossible the task of maintaining both sets of provisions in force at the same time.

Many of the conventions under discussion contain a provision for their own revision by a future conference on demand of a certain proportion of the parties,[12] a provision which would obviate any breakdown in the execution of either the old or new treaty due to the incompatibility of their respective provisions. The combination of the provisions for universal accession, for gradual replacement of

[11] Until 1923 the Industrial Property conventions of 1883, 1891, and 1911 were in force for one or more of the parties; *La Propriété industrielle*, 1923, p. 1.

[12] *Cf.* Universal Postal Union convention of June 28, 1929; *League of Nations Treaty Series*, vol. 102, p. 245, art. 14.

a previous convention by optional acceptance of its revision, for individual denunciation after notice, and for revision on demand of a fraction of the parties gives the conventions containing these provisions great elasticity and a correspondingly longer life.

MODIFICATIONS EFFECTIVE FOR ALL THE PARTIES

An important derogation from the principle of unanimous consent was made in the 1878 convention of the Universal Postal Union. In the interval between the congresses provided for in the convention, any administration might propose the revision of any article of the convention. When the consent of two-thirds of the administrations had been obtained to the revision of any except those articles declaring the principles on which the Union was based the revised article was declared to be binding on all the administrations.[13]

This method of revision was limited to those changes which might be necessary between the general conferences provided for in the treaty, and was further restricted to minor regulations, as distinct from those declaring the principles on which the union was based. The alternative to acceptance of the revised provision was withdrawal from the Union, a matter of considerable disadvantage to the withdrawing state. A state which felt itself injured by the operation of this revisory process had of course the right to air its grievance at the succeeding general conference.

Since the war several other conventions of a statutory nature have adopted this plan of revision by less than unanimity. The statutes of the International Hydrographic Bureau may be amended in conference with the consent of two-thirds of the member states. Between conferences, the Directing Committee may either make its own decisions and

[13] *Cf.* art. 20 of the Universal Postal Union convention of June 1, 1878, Martens, *Nouveau recueil général, 2me série*, vol. iii, p. 699.

report them to the members, or, in more important matters, may send a circular letter to the members, who vote by majority on the first ballot or by plurality on the second.[14]

The annexes to the 1919 convention on Aerial Navigation may be modified by three-fourths of the votes of the parties, but, as the votes of the states are weighted, such modification may require the consent of something less than half of the states which are parties. The majority must include three of the five principal parties to the convention.[15] This is one of the few instances where the relative difference in importance between states has been recognized in providing for the revision of a convention. The importance of the use of this method of revision is diminished in this case, however, by the fact that the provisions of these annexes are confined to technical matters of registration, identification papers, etc.

In most cases in which provision is made in treaties for modification by less than unanimity with such modification binding on all the parties, it is found in regulations and statutes attached to conventions, which do not ordinarily deal with matters where the right of participation is of great moment to all parties. But in drawing up the plan for the League of Nations a serious inroad was made on the unanimity rule. The problem of unanimous consent to modifica-

[14] Art. 64, Statutes of International Hydrographic Bureau, signed June 21, 1921, Hudson, *International Legislation*, vol. i, p. 663.

The Rules for the Organization of General Conferences on Communications and Transit (Hudson, *op. cit.*, vol. i, p. 617, art. 16) may be amended by two-thirds of the members of the League, excluding altogether non-member states which are participating in the Communications and Transit Organization of the League. Technically this might permit of revision by less than a majority of the participating states, but as there are but few participating states which are not members of the League there is no such actual possibility. In any case these rules are not set up in the form of a treaty, merely governing the acts of conferences called to set up treaty arrangements.

[15] Protocol of June 30, 1923, *League of Nations Treaty Series*, vol. 78, p. 441.

tions of the Covenant was discussed at the time of its drafting, and the discussion brought out the hesitancy of the parties in adopting the principle that such consent was unnecessary to revision. A universal League was envisaged, however, and it was realized that unanimous consent would be very difficult to obtain, and that it was practically certain that if the Covenant was to be maintained in force it would at some time have to be revised.

Larnaude, one of the French delegates on the Commission which drew up the Covenant, was in favor of limiting the sovereignty of states in so far as was required to eliminate their right to insist on unanimous consent to revision. The American delegates held to the principle that a revision was a new engagement, and was subject to the consent of the American Senate to its ratification. Venizelos of Greece proposed a division into "fundamental" and "non-fundamental" provisions, such as that which is found in the constitution of Greece. He suggested that the amendatory process might be made easier for the latter than for the former. Makino, one of the Japanese delegates, felt that such a proposal would never be acceptable to the Commission. The proposal was then made that revision might be made by less than unanimity, but that a state which had not consented to the revision might then withdraw from the League. Objection was made to this proposal on the ground that the withdrawal of a Great Power might throw the League into confusion.[16]

The compromise now embodied in the Covenant concerning its amendment was then reached; namely, that ratification by the members of the Council must be unanimous, while that of the Assembly need only be by majority. The Covenant failed to provide, however, for any method for

[16] *Cf.* discussions in Miller, *Drafting of the Covenant*, vol. i, pp. 71, 203-6, 293, 342-3, 379, 398-9, 456; vol. ii, pp. 358, 457.

voting on amendments, confining itself to the solution of the problem of ratification. But an amendment was voted by the Second Assembly providing that future amendments of the Covenant should be accepted by the Assembly by a three-fourths majority, including all the representatives of states represented on the Council and present at this session, and this procedure has since been followed, though this amendment itself has not been ratified by the required number of states.[17]

Similar recognition of the difference in importance between the participation of states was given in the provision for amending the Labor Section of the peace treaties. These provisions may be changed, after action by the General Conference of the International Labor Organization, upon ratification by the states composing the Council and three-fourths of the members of the League.

It will be noted in these two cases that not only is it unnecessary to obtain the consent of all the parties to the treaty which is to be revised, but where a member of the Council of the League of Nations is not a signatory of the peace treaties it is necessary to obtain the consent of a state which was not even a party to the original treaty.

The procedure for amending the Covenant and Labor Sections of the peace treaties approximates to a limited extent that described in the modification of the public law of Europe. In that less well defined procedure the consent to revision of those Powers having general interests is usually obtained, as well as that of states having a particular interest in the problem involved. But unanimity of consent of the parties to the revised convention is not obtained or sought, in many cases. The alternative to acceptance of the revision, however, differs from that in the case of amendments

[17] League of Nations, *Official Journal*, Special Supplement, No. 6, October, 1921, p. 9.

to the Covenant; a dissatisfied state in the latter case may withdraw from the League,[18] while in the former the alternative is a protest which, if ineffective, might be followed by war. In the case of the Covenant, should membership in the League become increasingly desirable the result observed in the case of the postal conventions would probably follow; that is, the disadvantages of denunciation would be great enough to induce the states who had failed to consent to revision to refrain from denunciation. Experience would tend to show that in the process of amending the public law of Europe the principle of unanimous consent gives way to one which recognizes a difference in the importance of the consent of states on the basis of the importance of the state itself and on the extent of its interest in maintaining the solution of the problem. In the provisions for amending the Covenant and the Labor sections of the peace treaties the same difference was recognized by distinguishing between the consent of the states represented in the Council and those in the Assembly only.[19]

MODIFICATIONS — POSITION OF ADHERING AND ACCEDING STATES

For a variety of reasons the original parties to a treaty have frequently been disposed to permit the accession of other states. During the sixteenth and seventeenth centuries. when the European states were consolidating their respective positions, and first one and then another appeared to threaten existing arrangements, the treaties of alliance of the threatened states frequently contained a provision that other states whose support was not obtained when the convention was drawn up might accede later. As successive settlements of

[18] Art. 26 of the Covenant.

[19] It will be recalled that at the time the Council was intended to contain a majority of Great Powers.

frontier and dynastic disputes commenced to build up a sort of charter of European law, those states who were interested in maintaining its provisions against the encroachments of any of their number, frequently drew up treaties of guaranty or alliance or both, inviting all those interested in maintaining the peace of Europe to accede. In the case of such a general invitation it was usually provided that the unanimous consent of the original parties was necessary before accession was permitted. The invitation was sometimes confined to one or a few states, and then no special action was necessary to permit the accession of those states.[20]

Generally, where the significance of accession was explained in the treaty, it was held to constitute participation in all the rights and obligations of the treaty, which would necessarily include the right to participate in revision on an equal basis with the original signatories. Practically the question was not of great importance, as the treaties were seldom terminated in this way, and because in spite of the frequency with which the clause appears accessions were rare. The provision for general accession did serve, however, to indicate which provisions or treaties were considered as of general interest.

The nineteenth century saw a broadening of the field of international activity regulated by multipartite treaties, and with it the development of certain definite principles governing accession. During this period the treaties providing for general accession may be divided roughly into two categories, the first, those providing for a common rule for the

[20] *Cf.* art. xii of the Quadruple Alliance of Denmark, Brandenburg, the United Provinces, and Brunswick-Luneburg, of October 25, 1666, Dumont, *Corps diplomatique universel*, vol. vi, pt. iii, p. 122, for general invitation. *Cf.* art. xvi of the Triple Alliance of Great Britain, Denmark and the United Provinces, of January 20, 1701, *ibid.*, vol. viii, pt. i, p. i, for an invitation of specific States.

conduct of states, such as the Declaration of Paris of 1856,[21] and the second those providing for international administration or international standards of measurement, such as the establishment of the Institute of Agriculture[22] or the convention of 1875 for the unification of the metric system.[23] In the former type the treaty makes no provision for its own termination. In the latter type there is provision for unilateral denunciation after notice, applying equally to acceding and to ratifying states,[24] thus making it possible for states to become or cease to be parties as they will.

In addition to those treaties providing for general accession there is a more limited group in which the right of accession is based on the principle of the earlier period already discussed; that is, to secure the support of states whose participation is desired but which, for any reason, failed to participate when the treaty was drawn up. Such a provision is proportionately much rarer than in the earlier period. There are also a very few treaties providing for the accession of those states which by virtue of participation in an earlier treaty on the same subject might claim the right to participate in its revision, but for any reason did not do so.[25] The function of the provision here is to clear up any outstanding claims and to secure unanimous acceptance of the revision.

After 1918 the majority of multipartite conventions were

[21] April 16, 1856, *Brit. & For. State Papers*, vol. 46, p. 26.

[22] June 7, 1905, *U. S. Treaty Series*, No. 489.

[23] May 20, 1875, *ibid.*, no. 378.

[24] Art. 13.

[25] *Cf.* art. viii of the Ionian Islands treaty of November 5, 1815, Hertslet, *op. cit.*, vol. i, p. 337. "All the Powers which signed the Treaty of Paris of the 30th of May, 1814, and the Act of the Congress of Vienna of the 9th of June, 1815, and also His Majesty the King of the Two Sicilies and the Ottoman Porte, shall be invited to accede to the present Convention."

of the two types described above in the opening paragraph. A large share of these were left open for signature for a considerable period, after which date they were open to accession only.[26] In such cases the significance of distinction between ratification and accession seems to have disappeared. These treaties sometimes provide that the ratification of as few as two states brings the treaty into effect,[27] so that the significance of later ratifications would seem to be no different from that of accessions, since the rights and obligations of ratifying and acceding states are the same. Some of these conventions provide that they may be revised on demand of a third of the parties,[28] and here as elsewhere the position of the acceding state does not differ from that of the ratifying state so that both are included in computing the fraction necessary to demand revision.

Though there would seem to be no difference between ratifying and acceding states under treaties of a legislative type setting up the same obligations for all the parties, under those where the obligations of the parties differ accession may have the effect of a guaranty rather than of participation in all the rights and obligations under the convention. But in such cases the interests of the acceding state are apt to be important enough so that there would be no disposition not to allow the acceding state to participate in any revision, even apart from its legal right to do so as a party to the convention.

[26] Convention of July 11, 1928, concerning the Export of Bones, *League of Nations Treaty Series*, vol. 95, p. 373, art. 9.

[27] *Cf.* art. 28 of the draft convention of June 28, 1930 concerning Forced Labor, *International Labor Conference*, 1930, vol. i, pt. iii, p. 858.

[28] *Cf.* art. 33 of the convention of July 18, 1931, for the Limitation of the Manufacture and the Regulation of the Distribution of Narcotic Drugs, League of Nations, *Document C.455.M.193.1931.XI.*

CONCLUSIONS

The need of changing the stipulations of conventions is constantly making itself apparent. The increasingly wide participation of a large number of states is meanwhile making unanimity more difficult to attain. Such widespread participation is apt to result in the inclusion of parties whose power of veto is theoretically as great as the others, but whose interest in maintaining the treaty's provisions in force may be very slight or practically non-existent.

Moreover, there appears to be no general rule concerning the necessity of unanimous consent to revision. The administrative or technical type of treaty in which the obligations of all the parties are identical solves the problem by providing for revisory conventions which are binding only on those accepting the revision, thus making it possible for two or more conventions concerning the same matter to remain in existence simultaneously. The confusion which might result from such a condition is diminished by the tendency of those states not having accepted the revised convention to modify the execution of the old sufficiently to avoid friction with the new.

Such an arrangement is not possible, however, where the rights and obligations of the parties under the treaty differ. In such cases certain of the parties have sometimes drawn up a revisory treaty without the consent of the remainder, occasionally inserting a provision for their subsequent adhesion. In such a case the parties to the new treaty generally ascertain in advance whether the opposition from the non-participating states is apt to be of a serious nature, and ordinarily do not proceed in such a case unless prepared in advance to resist any pressure from such states, so it rarely happens that there is any objection by the latter. Particularly in treaties of general settlement, those signatories to the treaty which are least interested in the revision of any given part are not consulted, and do not insist in participating in such revision.

The insertion of a provision for a revisory conference after a stated interval, on any of various pretexts, on the demand of one or more of the signatory states, offers a prospect of change to dissatisfied states, and such a provision appears with increasing frequency even in conventions where the obligations of the parties differ, and unanimous consent to change is a matter of importance to all the parties. It has been maintained that too easy revision would do away with any international stability, but as international relations are dynamic and not static, a means must be provided to keep the treaty regulation of these relations in close accord with the changes occurring in them.

CHAPTER V

Termination of Parts of Treaties

The question whether treaties are to be considered as an indissoluble whole, and therefore whether the termination of any single clause might render the treaty as a whole either voidable or void, or whether part of the treaty might be terminated without affecting the rest, has been given consideration by writers from the time of Grotius. The difficulty has arisen chiefly because of the difference between theory and practice. For those writers who have adopted a close analogy between treaties and private law contracts,[1] the former view has been accepted, but the adoption of this theory in practice would have resulted in rendering most of Europe's treaties of general settlement at least voidable almost as soon as they had entered into effect.[2] Those who accepted the theory that part of the treaty might be terminated without affecting the rest[3] were also confronted with a serious obstacle; namely, that treaties generally being the result of negotiation, the balance between rights and obligations for each of the parties might be seriously upset by the termination of even a single clause, and if it were to be permissible thus to destroy the balance set up by negotiation the value of negotiation would be greatly diminished.

To overcome this difficulty, certain writers attempted to

[1] *Cf.* Phillipson, *Termination of War and Treaties of Peace* (London, 1916), pp. 205-6.

[2] *Cf.* discussion of the General Act of Vienna, *infra*, p. 254.

[3] *Cf.* Rühland, "Einfluss des Kriegsbeginns auf Staatsverträge", *Niemeyer's Zeitschrift für internationales Recht*, 1924, p. 74 *et seq.*

separate the clauses of treaties into two groups—those which were vital to the maintenance in force of the treaty, and the violation or termination of which would operate to render the treaty either voidable or void, and those which did not have that effect.[4] For the latter type, the remedy in case of violation or denunciation was the payment of damages, but where impossibility of performance had supervened, no remedy was provided. But the question which clauses should fall in each category was always difficult of solution; it might be resolved by arbitration or by the Permanent Court of International Justice, but in treaties themselves there is rarely any indication of the design of the parties concerning such a division.

The presumption would be then that in the absence of such a provision, a violation of a single clause would render the treaty voidable. The difficulty of reconciling the need for changes with the interdependence of all the clauses of a treaty has frequently troubled text writers, but in general the conclusions arrived at are of limited value as applied to multipartite treaties.[5]

The greater number of all but the most recent writers have based their views on bipartite treaties, and in most

[4] *Cf. Wolff, Jus gentium* (Magdeburg, 1749), § 432; de Martens, *Précis*, § 59 (Paris, 1864); see also the view of Grotius, *De jure belli ac pacis*, lib. iii, ch. xx, § 35.

[5] Grotius (*De jure belli ac pacis*, lib. ii, ch. xiv, § 15) recognized the difficulty of reconciling the need of change in conventions with the inevitable upsetting of the balance between rights and obligations when one or more clauses of the convention were violated or terminated. He held that "each of the articles of a convention has the force of a condition, the non-fulfilment of which renders the treaty void", but added that "the clause is sometimes inserted that the violation of a single article is not to annul the whole treaty, in order that one of the contracting parties may not be able to free itself of its obligations upon the smallest provocation".

Vattel (*Droit des gens*, bk. ii, pt. xiii, § 202) attempted such a reconciliation, but apparently with bipartite conventions in mind.

cases on those in the limited field included in the treaty relations of a half century or more ago, such as alliances, commerce, subsidy and cession. The attempt to discover what rules may govern separability of provisions in the wider modern field, and where as many as fifty states are participating in drawing up conventional arrangements, would have been of a much more complicated nature had not their greatly increased number and the simultaneously increasing frequency with which the problem was dealt with in the treaty itself, simplified the drawing of general conclusions.

The separability of the clauses of multipartite treaties in wartime has been discussed in detail elsewhere.[6] It will be recalled that belligerent states in many cases largely overlooked the contractual nature of their engagements, and either enforced or suspended the enforcement of treaty provisions either on the basis of the compatibility of enforcement with successful prosecution of the war, on the basis that, as war was an affair between states only, individual rights under treaties could not be affected, or more simply on the basis of reciprocity of enforcement on the part of enemy states. Executed and executory provisions were for the most part considered to be separable, since the former had exhausted their force when carried into effect. The primary assumption on which all separability was based was that the parties to a treaty when drawing it up did not intend that in wartime any part of a treaty should affect to a greatly adverse degree the successful conduct of the war. To have put this intent in the form of a clause in the treaty would have resulted in rendering abuse likely, and such expression was therefore not resorted to. But it appears nevertheless to be implicit in most conventions.

[6] In chapter I, Termination in Wartime, under Guaranties, International Unions, etc., *supra*, pp. 55, 74, etc.

The parties to such conventions did not propose, however, to allow this wartime lack of balance to continue indefinitely, and one of the functions of peace treaties has been the redressing of that balance. It is in the provisions of the peace treaty that there is to be found the interpretation by the parties to a prewar treaty of their new relationship in the fields covered by such prewar arrangements. A simple renewal or confirmation of all the provisions of a treaty indicates that in the field or fields covered by that treaty the parties conceive that the original bargain is satisfactory in the light of postwar conditions. Such renewal except where provisions of a legislative sort are concerned, ordinarily indicates that the political balance of the Powers concerned has not been changed; in the case of legislative clauses it indicates merely that the convenient moment for revision which a peace conference brings, found the parties content to confine termination to the method permitted by the clauses usually contained in such treaties.

Treaties of general settlement present a special problem. Dealing as they do with a great variety of matters quite unrelated one to another, and in which the interest of each of the signatories varies greatly, it is difficult to consider them as an indivisible whole. In practice they are not treated as such, and recently the parties themselves have given increasing recognition to the need of arranging for separate treatment of different sections. A consideration of the history of such conventions indicates the wisdom of such action.

Up until the settlement at the end of the Napoleonic wars, most of the general settlements in Europe consisted of a series of bipartite arrangements,[7] with occasionally one or

[7] E. g., Westphalia, Utrecht, Ryswick, and Aix-la-Chapelle. See Introduction to chapter iv on Termination by Superseding Treaty, *supra*, p. 254.

more States adhering to some one or other of them. When revision of any part of such treaties was necessary it was simple to conduct negotiations with the few parties concerned, and even though their consent might be difficult to obtain by peaceful means, it was easier than would have been the case with a larger number of parties. The treaties were generally terminated piecemeal, and without determining exactly which clauses remained unaffected. These remaining parts, however, were reconfirmed in each new settlement by providing that the ancient treaty was " hereby confirmed except as modified by this present Act ".[8] As these earlier conventions rarely attempted to settle problems concerning the community of states as a whole—that community not yet forming a cohesive group, and the concept of international legislation in the form of treaties still being nebulous—such partial amendment did not involve the question of the interest of such a community in the settlement.

Beginning with the General Act of the Congress of Vienna, however, a change took place. The five Great Powers directed the settlement, and thereafter all considered themselves interested in any changes made in it, no matter what other states might be involved. In making the settlement these Powers attempted to reconcile two conflicting ideas; first, that they must settle a heterogeneous collection of special problems widely scattered both as to the interests and as to the territory involved,—second, that these settlements must be tied up together, in order to indicate the collective interest in their maintenance. This double task was accomplished by setting up the hybrid instrument known as the General Act. It consists of a series of seventeen Annexes, representing the separate settlement of each of the principal problems, and a collection of special provisions,—

[8] *Cf.* treaty of Peace between France, Great Britain and Spain of February 10, 1763, art. ii; Martens, *Recueil des traités*, vol. i, p. 33.

culled for the most part from these Annexes, and characterized as being of a " superior and permanent interest ".[9]

The destruction of this settlement began almost at once, and continued through the century. A number of the Annexes were terminated separately, and when terminated apparently pulled down with them the corresponding provisions which had been given a place among those of a " superior and permanent interest ". An attempt set on foot by Napoleon III in 1863 [10] to gather up the remaining fragments in a new convention was blocked almost at its inception by Great Britain, and the process of disintegration continued until most of the treaty had been terminated. During this process no one seems to have claimed that such piecemeal destruction had resulted in destroying the original contractual balance; such objection as was made was based on the fact that one or another of the original parties had not previously been consulted, though even in such cases no one appears to have considered the consent of all the original parties was necessary.[11]

The settlements of the Near Eastern questions made in 1856,[12] 1871[13] and 1878 [14] followed somewhat the same process. When Russia attempted unilateral denunciation of part of the 1856 settlement, the protest of the other parties was based not on the resulting upset of the contractual balance, but on the illegality of the attempt to denounce a convention unilaterally.

The condemnation of unilateral denunciation was based

[9] Preamble.

[10] Hertslet, *op. cit.*, vol. ii, p. 1575 *et seq.*

[11] See section on the General Act of the Congress of Vienna in chapter iv, Termination by Superseding Treaty, *supra*, p. 211.

[12] March 30, 1856, *Brit. & For. State Papers*, vol. 46, p. 8.

[13] March 13, 1871, *ibid.*, vol. 61, p. 7.

[14] July 13, 1878, *ibid.*, vol. 69, p. 749.

on a principle similar to that of the inseparability of the clauses of a treaty, both involving the question of the consideration for the signature of each of the parties. The participation of each of the parties was generally considered to depend on that of the others, and the acceptance of each of the clauses of a treaty to depend on that of each and all of the other clauses. Therefore, whenever one of the parties attempted unilateral denunciation, or when one or more of the clauses of a treaty was terminated, the consideration for each of the parties was affected, and their unanimous consent to the new consideration was required.

A considerable modification of the above principles has, however, recently taken place. In the legislative type of treaty, which is constantly becoming more common, in which the rights and obligations of the parties are identical, these two elements involved in the consideration of the parties are generally of diminished importance. The consent of the parties to any given clauses was less frequently given in consideration for the acceptance of other clauses by other parties, and the participation of any one state was more rarely dependent on that of any other single state.[15] In other treaties not of this type the consent of certain of the parties was obviously less important to the parties involved than was that of others,[16] and the acceptance by some of the parties of certain clauses in many cases must have had little bearing on the acceptance of other clauses.[17] The determination, however, of those clauses or signatures which were

[15] There are exceptions however; the Narcotic Drugs convention of 1931 (League of Nations, *Document C.455.M.193.1931.XI*) is notable.

[16] E. g., the consent of Portugal was less important to the parties to the General Act of Vienna than was that of France.

[17] E. g., the acceptance by Great Britain of the Mandates section of the Covenant bore little relation to her acquiescence in the clause calling for the punishment of the Kaiser, contained in the same treaty.

not essential to any one of the parties, when not indicated in the treaty itself, obviously might involve great difficulty.

The peace settlement after the war of 1914-18 recognized the fact that piecemeal termination would probably result, and that provision should be made for some method for accomplishing it. An analysis of the treaty of Neuilly,[18] as typical of the group of treaties included in this settlement, will indicate how it was done.

It was provided that the first twenty-six articles, comprising the Covenant of the League of Nations, might be modified separately by action of the States composing the League.[19] The minorities clauses of Part III might be modified by action of the League Council.[20] Part IX contained a number of economic clauses which were to remain temporarily in force, and were then subject to termination by the Council.[21] Part X, dealing with aerial navigation, was to terminate either when Bulgaria entered the League, or on a specified date, or when Bulgaria adhered to the 1919 convention on aerial navigation.[22] The section of Part XI dealing with the régime for international railways and with freedom of transport might be revised separately by the Council of the League of Nations.[23] Part XII dealing with labor might be revised by action of the Labor Conference, accepted by the states represented in the International Labor Organization.[24]

There was no precise indication, however, of any method of revising or terminating a large part of the treaty. But

[18] Signed November 27, 1919; *Brit. & For. State Papers*, vol. 112, p. 781.

[19] Covenant, art. 26.

[20] Art. 57.

[21] Art. 160.

[22] Art. 211.

[23] Art. 247.

[24] Art. 284.

the Second Part, dealing with boundaries, that part of the Third concerning cessions of territory, and the Fifth, concerning Prisoners of War and Graves, exhausted their force when once carried into effect. A large part of the Economic and Financial Clauses,[25] including those parts dealing with Reparations, might be expected to terminate through specific performance within a time limit indicated in the treaty. Yet another category of provisions, including those dealing with the status of inhabitants in ceded territories, and the penalties attached to non-performance under certain clauses, remained executory for an unlimited period.

There appear thus to be three broad classes of provisions in such treaties; first, those of which the treaty itself provides the means for their termination; second, those which, by their nature, will terminate by specific performance within a limited period; third, those setting up executory obligations of indefinite duration. The first two classes present no difficulty from the point of view of this discussion. The upsetting of an established balance of rights and obligations can occur only when a provision of the last category is terminated, and even here the difficulty arises chiefly from the fact that there is seldom unity of intent among the parties to a treaty concerning the time when the provisions of indefinite duration in a treaty are to be terminated.

The discussion at the peace conference in 1919 concerning the status of the guaranty of Belgian neutrality contained in the 1839 treaties indicated the uncertain attitude at that time of the states concerned, in regard to the separability of clauses. This settlement of 1839 itself was a modification of one of the Annexes of the General Act of Vienna of 1815.[26] It consisted of a treaty between Belgium and Holland containing a series of territorial provisions, a

[25] Parts viii and ix.

[26] Annex x.

régime for navigation on the Scheldt, a provision for the demilitarization of Antwerp and for neutralization of Belgium, and two other treaties, between the five Great Powers and Belgium and Holland respectively, which contained a guaranty of all the clauses of the first treaty.[27] In view of the experiences of the war, Belgium sought to secure the consent of the Powers not alone to the termination of her neutralized status but also to that of the entire treaty. She had no difficulty in obtaining the consent of the Great Powers to the termination of the neutralization provision, but none of them displayed any interest in her attempt to modify the territorial provisions as well. As a compromise these five Powers and Belgium consented to the separation of the treaty's clauses, uniting to consider the neutralization provision as terminated while the other clauses remained in force.[28] There appears to have been no admission, however, that separation of this sort was in accordance with legal practice.

The practice of considering separately the clauses of a treaty of general settlement, when changes become necessary, has been continued since 1919. A number of the sections of each of the peace treaties have been terminated or revised without affecting the validity of the remainder of the treaty, or even recognizing that its validity might have been affected thereby. The provisions for the evacuation of the Rhineland in the Versailles treaty[29] and the reparations clauses in all the peace treaties except Lausanne[30] have been either

[27] *Brit. & For. State Papers*, vol. 27, pp. 990, 1000.

[28] *Cf.* abortive treaty of 1926 between France, Great Britain, Belgium and the Netherlands, to which Austria, Hungary, Germany and Russia were invited to adhere; *De Herziening der Verdrangen van 1839*, Diplomatike Dokumenten (Brussels, 1929), p. 26. Compare with preamble to Locarno treaty of 1925; *Brit. & For. State Papers*, vol. 121, p. 923.

[29] Art. 429.

[30] Part viii of Versailles, St. Germain, Trianon; part vii of Neuilly.

modified or terminated. In spite of this fact, any projected modification of the disarmament provisions appears to be considered as endangering the existence of the remainder of the treaty.[31] As a matter of fact it might involve political consequences which would have that result, but there would appear to be precedent for the termination of that section without legally affecting the remainder of the treaty in any way.[32]

Provision for separability of clauses is not confined to peace treaties. The protocol annexed to the Railway Goods Traffic convention of 1924 allows exceptions to be made by any party to the enforcement of certain provisions only, for a period not exceeding four years, " in view of the fact that the respective value of the currency used in the various States is liable to sudden fluctuations ".[33] The 1890 convention for Suppression of the African Slave Trade, while permitting modifications by common consent, stipulates that such modification shall be "without prejudice to" certain articles.[34] These articles, concerning the arms traffic, liquor duties, and the search of slave trading vessels, may be terminated independently of the rest of the treaty. One part of the provisions of the Universal Postal Union conventions may be

[31] The provisions noted above authorize the modification of certain specified parts of a convention without affecting the validity of the rest. In one instance permission is granted to modify any provision; the procès-verbal of signature of the convention of 1906 concerning the Pharmacopeial Formulas for Potent Drugs (Malloy, *Treaties, etc. of the United States*, vol. ii, p. 2209) reserved the rights of any of the parties to introduce such modifications into the convention "as the progress of medical and pharmacal science may render necessary from time to time".

[32] See discussion of termination of various sections of General Act of Vienna, chapter iv, Termination by Superseding Treaty, *supra*, p. 211.

[33] October 23, 1924, *League of Nations Treaty Series*, vol. 77, p. 30, art. ii.

[34] July 2, 1890, *U. S. Treaty Series*, no. 383, art. 97.

modified between general conferences by unanimous consent, while another part may be modified with the consent of but two-thirds of the parties.[35]

The problem of securing the adaptability to new conditions by revision of part of the clauses of a treaty was solved in the conventions establishing or maintaining international unions. The method used here was the drafting of a new convention retaining those provisions of the old which appeared suitable to the parties, and replacing the remainder by new provisions, the parties to the old conventions being free either to adopt the new convention or remain bound by the old.[36] Although technically in such a case there was no modification so far as the states bound by the unrevised convention were concerned, the mere fact that subsequent to the revision the states bound by the new convention were maintaining two sets of provisions in effect, sometimes quite divergent in certain provisions, would appear to have reduced the value of the old convention to those states still bound by it. Usually this difficulty is reduced in importance by the gradual adoption of the new provisions in practice by those states not yet having ratified the new convention, and by their subsequent eventual adhesion thereto.[37]

[35] Convention of June 1, 1878, art. 20; Martens, *Nouveau recueil général, 2me série*, vol. iii, p. 699.

[36] To what extent Article xix of the Covenant might accomplish such adaptation to new conditions has not yet been made clear. A recommendation to the parties to the effect that only certain clauses of a treaty had become inapplicable might facilitate the process of readaptation, whereas a declaration of the general inapplicability of an entire treaty might serve to strengthen the determination of certain of the parties to maintain it in force. The trepidation of the French Government concerning the possibility that a revision of the disarmament clauses of the Versailles treaty might bring the entire treaty into discussion is a case in point. *Cf.* Industrial Property convention of June 2, 1911, art. 18; *Treaties, etc. of the United States*, vol. iii, p. 2953.

[37] When the Postal Convention of July 4, 1891 was signed, Honduras,

In the case of the union conventions whose revision is accomplished in this way, the question of the balance between rights and obligations of each party is less important than in treaties of general settlement. In the case of conventions dealing with only one or a few important subjects, and among only a small number of states, and where the rights and obligations of each one of the parties are conditioned very closely on those of each of the others, such piecemeal termination occurs only with the consent of all the parties. In such a case, if partial revision appears called for and consent is refused, in the absence of a provision in the treaty itself there is no legal means of compulsion.[38]

The effect of separating the clauses of a treaty appears to differ with the character of the clause as well as with the character of the treaty. For example, clauses concerning boundaries and cessions of territory appear to have exhausted their effect once their stipulations have been carried out. Other clauses, such as those calling for progressive evacuation of territory, are capable of fulfilment within a limited period of time. There is a third type, setting up an obligation which if not perpetual is at least of indefinite duration. These three types of clause are frequently found in the same treaty, though one type or another may predominate. Treaties setting up differing obligations for each party frequently contain all three. Treaties establishing uniform rules which might apply to the international community as a whole more frequently include the first only in

which was a party to the convention of June 1, 1878 (superseded by the 1891 convention), failed to sign or accede to the latter. She put its provisions into effect, however, without taking such action. Paraguay, although not a party to either of these conventions, put the latter into effect without acceding.

[38] *Cf.* art. 16 of treaty of July 7, 1911, concerning the Protection of Fur Seals (*U. S. Treaty Series*, no. 564); and art. 21 of the treaty for the Limitation of Naval Armament, of February 6, 1922 (*ibid.*, no. 671.).

those provisions establishing a bureau, the rest of the provisions being confined to the third type,—those of indefinite duration. The problem of determining when the balance of rights and obligations is upset is much simpler in the latter case, where obligations under the treaty are more nearly of the same duration.[39]

The problem is more complicated in the case of the treaty to which only a small number of states are parties and where the obligations of each are closely conditioned on those of the others. It is frequently difficult to determine whether the consent of a party to the insertion of a provision which is executed immediately, such as a cession of territory, is the price for another party's acquiescence in the insertion, for example, of a provision for the protection of minorities. If the minorities provision appears obsolete or otherwise unsatisfactory, it is conceded that the price demanded for its termination by a party interested in its maintenance frequently may not be a provision for a return of the ceded territory, which would undo the effect of the original provision. An instance in point occurred in the attempt to settle the question of Belgium's neutrality in 1919. Belgium insisted that her consent to neutralization was part of the price of her acceptance of the territorial arrangements made at the time. But none of the other parties accepted this thesis.[40] Such acceptance would have involved not merely the termination of the old treaty, which would not have

[39] In internal legislation the United States has provided for separability of the provisions of legislative acts, in the case that any provision of an act or the application of such provision to any person or circumstance is held invalid by the courts. In such a case the remainder of the act, or the application of the provision held invalid to other persons or circumstances, is not to be affected. E. g. *Act to Provide Revenue, etc.*, June 17, 1930, sect. 652, *U. S. Statutes at Large*, vol. 46, pt. 1, p. 763 (H. R. 2667).

[40] Miller, *My Diary of the Peace Conference*, vol. iv, p. 426.

affected the territorial settlement provided therein, but a new international act by Holland—in whom the title to the territory rested—and an indeterminate group of other states as well, whose interests would be affected by such a transfer.

The contractual balance between a provision such as those for the cession of territory and one of indefinite duration would appear to be therefore a somewhat nebulous thing. The former provision is definite in extent and in time; the latter depends largely for its value on the length of time during which it is given effect, and, as the parties do not indicate how long this is to be, the exchange is between two things one of which has a certain and the other an uncertain value. Where this exchange is further complicated by the fact that a large number of parties are involved, greatly increasing the number of considerations and rendering more indefinite the specific bargain between any two of them, it becomes clear why there is so much difficulty in essaying such exchanges in order to satisfy the parties by a new contractual balance.

In modifying treaties of general settlement the balancing of rights and obligations appears to be confined to those comprised within the settlement of one section of the treaty, and within the unexecuted clauses of that section. In the contractual type of treaty between a small number of parties and dealing with subjects of capital interest to the parties, a more delicate balance of rights and obligations having been struck in the beginning, any upsetting of that balance is apt to call for a careful revaluing of the entire treaty. But termination of the treaty in whole or part does not restore the situation changed by clauses involving transfers of territory; a new act of those parties who may have subsequently acquired a title or interest is necessary.

A clear indication of the extent of the interdependence of a treaty's clauses would of course be of great value in this connection, but it is an indication which is seldom given and, due to the delicacy of the negotiations of any but the least controversial technical type of treaty, the practice will hardly be widely extended.

CHAPTER VI

Conference Procedure for Terminating Treaties

In the great majority of cases where old conventions are terminated or modified by new, the work is accomplished by a conference of representatives of the parties to the former treaty. It is important therefore to observe what rules govern this revisory procedure.

Previous to the nineteenth century a large part of the multipartite treaties were either stated by their own terms or implied to be of indefinite duration, hence provision for their revision was the exception. Wars during this period were of frequent occurrence, and the subsequent peace conference setting up new arrangements obviated the need which might otherwise have been felt for provision for definite duration or for revision after a stated period. Occasionally, however, in treaties negotiated for a short period of years only, a provision for renewal with revision was attached. These were not confined to one type of treaty, being found in treaties of commerce, of subsidy and of alliance.[1]

Through the period discussed and until the latter part of the nineteenth century the great majority of treaties consisted of provisions imposing differing obligations on each party and of a highly political nature, and such treaties seldom carry provision for their own revision. In practice, however, revision of these nineteenth century treaties took

[1] *Cf.* art. xiv of treaty establishing the League of the Rhine, August 15, 1658; Dumont, *Corps diplomatique universel*, vol. vi, pt. ii, p. 239; also art. x of Quadruple Alliance of October 25, 1666, *ibid.*, pt. iii, p. 122; also Alliance of January 20, 1701, arts. i, vi, xv, *ibid.*, vol. viii, pt. i, p. 1.

place largely through the medium of conferences, resulting in the drafting of new agreements partially or entirely replacing the old. These conferences were convened on the invitation of one of the parties to the treaty to be revised, the invitation explaining the purpose and extent of the proposed revision. Particularly during the period when only absolute monarchies were represented at such conferences, there was never any doubt concerning the necessity of unanimity. Proposals were not put to a vote; they were abandoned when discussion had disclosed that unanimous approval was not to be expected. The fact that delegates were frequently sovereigns themselves or their personal representatives, made the decisions of the conference the important factor in determining the acceptance of the terms of the revision, inasmuch as approval of terms in conference was the practical equivalent of ratification.[2]

All through the nineteenth century, however, the treaty dealing with technical matters only was becoming increasingly important. At the same time delegates were less frequently personal representatives of their sovereigns, and ratification became increasingly important since the results of the deliberations of the conference had more often to meet the approval of the people's representatives. At the same time the number of states participating in conferences increased, making it more difficult to obtain unanimous approval of the steps taken in the negotiations.[3] To over-

[2] For a discussion of the Westphalia and Vienna conferences see Dunn, *Practice and Procedure of International Conferences* (Baltimore, 1929), first sixty-five pages.

[3] A comparison of the three great congresses of Westphalia, of Vienna and of Paris (1919) makes this clear. The first consisted of meetings of delegates in two separate cities, for the most part meeting in very small groups and never all together; the second consisted of a larger group of states meeting in one place, but the General Act of the Congress was signed by only eight states; the treaty of Versailles was signed by twenty-eight states.

come the difficulties inherent in the new conditions, the old methods were somewhat modified. Advance agreements among the principal states represented concerning the matters to be discussed reduced the importance of the discussions in the conference itself, and also facilitated the securing of unanimous approval when decisions were finally made.[4] The difficulty of securing ratification by those states under representative government was largely overcome by close cooperation between the negotiators of such states and their parliamentary leaders, or the use of the latter as negotiators. Although the rule of unanimous approval of each step taken by the conference was observed, objections were frequently overcome by presenting a united front to the objector and practically forcing agreement. In those cases, however, where opposition was too strong thus to be overcome, no revision was attempted.

The principle of unanimous consent was accepted up until 1914 even in the case of conferences dealing with regulations designed to be applicable to the international community as a whole. However, abstention from voting by some of the parties was considered to offer no bar to the adoption of the proposal under discussion, and occasionally when the number of parties was large and dissent was confined to a very small number of states the project was adopted as though unanimous approval had been obtained.[5]

Where conferences were dealing with the revision of treaties concerned with political questions the matter of the agenda to be put before the conference was of great importance, and opposition was strong to any attempt to modify it extensively. The purpose of these conferences was to relieve such pressure resulting from the old treaty as threatened to disturb the peace, but it was always considered

[4] E. g., the Algeciras Conference in 1906. See Dunn, *op. cit.*, p. 107.

[5] Dunn, *op. cit.*, p. 124 *et seq.*, especially p. 130.

essential to keep the revision within bounds. When the Congress of Berlin met to discuss the treaty of San Stefano the agenda included all the terms of the treaty,[6] but this was an isolated case. On the other hand, an attempt by Napoleon III to call a conference in 1863 for the general revision of the General Act of Vienna met with such opposition that he was forced to abandon the idea.[7]

It was not until the latter part of the nineteenth century that provisions were commonly inserted in treaties providing that the latter should be revised under specified conditions. Such provisions were largely confined to treaties regulating technical questions for a large part of the international community, though there were notable exceptions. But the proportion of treaties of the technical and non-political type containing some sort of revisory provision has grown steadily, and an increasingly large number give an exact description of the revisory method.[8]

An early instance of a provision implying revision of an agreement is that contained in the principles governing international rivers, established by the General Act of the Congress of Vienna in 1815.[9] One of these principles stipulates that regulation of navigation shall be governed by arrangements drawn up by the riparian states by common accord.[10] Here, as in a number of other cases where pro-

[6] Hertslet, *op. cit.*, vol. iv, p. 2735, protocol of June 13, 1878.

[7] *Ibid.*, vol. ii, p. 1575 *et seq.*

[8] In the years from 1815 to 1825, only one of less than twenty multipartite treaties signed during that period contained any provision for revision. During the period from 1865 to 1875, of forty-five treaties examined about half contained such a provision. During the period from 1919 to 1932, of 150 such treaties nearly 100 provided for their own revision, and only eleven contained no provision for termination.

[9] Hertslet, *op. cit.*, vol. i, p. 75.

[10] Art. 1. It has always been within the power of the parties to a

vision is made for revision by common accord, there is no statement that such revision is to be accomplished by the conference method, but in practice it is most commonly carried out in such a manner.[11] In many cases the convention specifies that common accord is to be reached through conference, though frequently the manner of calling the conference and the procedure to be followed are not indicated.

A constantly growing number of treaties rectify this defect by specifying one of several methods of revision. One of these is to provide in each revised agreement for the time and the place of the next revisory conference.[12] Another common provision is that such conferences should take place at stated intervals.[13] A third provides for the assembling of a conference on demand of a fraction, usually a third, of the parties.[14] Sometimes this method is varied to provide for a call if demanded by a given number of signatories, varying from one to ten.[15] Frequently where provision is made for revisory conferences at stated intervals there is an

treaty to revise it by common accord without specific provision to that effect. Such a provision in a convention, however, serves to indicate that the parties did not intend the convention to be of perpetual duration.

[11] When a river is declared international, a commission is usually set up with limited power of control over navigation. But the general rules under which the commission functions are included in treaties drawn up by a conference of states.

[12] November 3, 1906, Wireless Telegraph Convention, *Treaties, etc. of the United States*, vol. iii, p. 2892, art. 11.

[13] June 1, 1878, Postal Convention, Martens, *Nouveau recueil général, 2me série*, vol. iii, p. 699, art. 19.

[14] April 20, 1921, Régime of Navigable Waterways, *League of Nations Treaty Series*, vol. vii, p. 36, art. 9.

[15] E. g., the convention of September 12, 1923, for the Suppression of Obscene Publications calls for revision on appeal by five signatories; *League of Nations Treaty Series*, vol. 27, p. 215, art. 16.

accompanying provision authorizing interim conferences on the demand of a given number of signatories.[16]

Certain conventions require approval of the demand for revision. For example, a number of the conventions drawn up under the auspices of the League of Nations require that the demand for a revisory conference should be submitted to one or another of the organs of the League.[17] The 1925 convention for the Suppression of the Contraband Traffic in Alcoholic Liquors provides merely that the parties "will consider favorably" a demand for revision, without binding themselves to unite in conference.[18]

Arrangements for a future revisory conference are rare in conventions concerning controversial political questions. The treaty of 1922 on the Limitation of Naval Armament is a notable exception, however. It provides for a revisory conference under two conditions; the first, in case of a change of circumstances affecting the requirements of any of the contracting states in respect of naval defense, and the second, after eight years, in order to consider changes necessary in view of possible technical and scientific developments.[19] The 1930 Limitation of Naval Armament Convention also contains a provision for future conference, in this case to be called in 1936 unless a general naval agreement arrived at in the interim should render it unnecessary.[20]

[16] 1878 Postal Convention cited above, note 13.

[17] The Council of the League of Nations may consider calling a revisory conference on demand of one-third of the signatories of the convention for the Simplification of Customs Formalities, November 3, 1923; *League of Nations Treaty Series*, vol. 30, p. 371, art. 30.

[18] August 19, 1925, Martens, *Nouveau recueil général, 3me série*, vol. 20, p. 131, art. 12.

[19] Art. 21.

[20] April 22, 1930, *U. S. Treaty Series*, no. 830, art. 23. The prolongations of the Triple Alliance between Austria-Hungary, Germany and Italy of 1891 and 1902 contained provisions for introducing modifica-

A number of conventions of an economic nature establishing identical obligations for all the parties also contain provisions affecting the parties to highly different degrees. Where such conventions contain provision for revision the terms are as precise as in the type of convention just discussed. An instance of this sort is the 1911 convention for the Protection and Preservation of Fur Seals, to which the United States, Great Britain, Japan and Russia are parties. This convention provided that on the request of any of the signatories a conference should be held forthwith to agree upon an extension of the life of the treaty, with such modifications as should be found desirable.[21] Another is the sugar convention of 1902, which stipulates that if one of the parties should denounce the convention, and any of the others should take advantage of a provision allowing their own denunciation in such a case, the Belgian Government should convoke a conference to decide what steps should be taken, though there was no provision that such steps should involve the drafting of a new convention.[22] The 1928 conventions on the Exportation of Bones and of Hides and Skins provide for revisory conferences on appeal of one-third of the parties,[23] as does the convention on the Abolition of Export and Import Restrictions and Prohibitions.[24] A similar appeal on the part of one-third of the parties to the convention for the Simplification of Customs Formalities

tions under the form of a protocol, by mutual agreement. This provision was not repeated in the 1912 prolongation.

[21] July 7, 1911, *Treaties, etc. of the United States,* vol. iii, p. 2966, art. xvi.

[22] March 5, 1902, Martens, *op. cit., 2me série,* vol. 31, p. 272, art. x.

[23] July 11, 1928, *League of Nations Treaty Series,* vol. 95, pp. 357, 373. Art. 6 of convention on Exportation of Hides and Skins; art. 10 of Bones convention.

[24] November 8, 1927, *ibid.,* vol. 97, p. 393, art. 19.

must receive the approval of the Council of the League of Nations before the conference may be called.[25]

There is less frequently any detailed provision concerning procedure after the conference has been called. A few conventions contain limitations on the extent of the revision; the 1864 convention concerning Drawbacks on Sugar limited revision to these matters which should not constitute opposition to the spirit or principles of the convention.[26] Provision is made in the conventions concerning the Exportation of Bones and of Hides and Skins that if no revision at all or a revision unsatisfactory to one of the parties is made, that party may resume its liberty of action.[27]

The provisions for revisory conferences, except where the date of the subsequent revision was specifically provided, have failed to bring about frequent revision. Even in those cases calling for revision at frequent intervals, the revisory conference has frequently been held over well past the time when it should have met. The Postal Union convention of 1878 called for a revision in five years, but such revision did not take place until 1885.[28] The 1891 convention contained a similar provision, and the convention was held in 1897.[29] The five-year period stipulated in the 1897 convention was stretched to 1906,[30] and the next convention after 1906 was not held until 1920,[31] although the 1906 convention contained the same provision for a conference within five years as did the earlier conventions. None of the conventions dealing with controversial political questions mentioned

[25] November 3, 1923, *ibid.*, vol. 30, p. 371, art. 30.

[26] November 8, 1864, *Brit. & For. State Papers*, vol. 54, p. 29, art. xxi.

[27] *Cf.* note (23), *supra.*

[28] Martens, *op. cit.*, *2me série*, vol. xi, p. 1.

[29] June 15, 1897, *Brit. & For. State Papers*, vol. 89, p. 65.

[30] May 26, 1906, *ibid.*, vol. 99, p. 254.

[31] November 30, 1920, *ibid.*, vol. 114, p. 430.

above has been subjected to revision. In 1927, at the expiration of the term of the Fur Seals convention of 1911, Japan proposed a revisory conference to the other signatories, and secured the assent of Great Britain and Russia; the United States demurred, however, on the ground that the reasons for revision cited by Japan appeared to her insufficient. As Japan did not press the matter further the conference was not held.[32]

But the provisions of Articles 23 and 24 of the Covenant of the League, concerning the League's control of international bureaux and commissions and the League's activities in humanitarian and other fields necessitated the development of procedure for the negotiation and revision of treaties in the fields mentioned. As a first step it was necessary to determine the extent of the League's control over the international bodies already operating or to be set up in these fields. The First Assembly of the League in 1920 decided that its control of international bodies was limited to recommending measures to the states members of such bodies, recommendations which the states were at liberty to reject.[33] Yet in 1921 when the conference on Communications and Transit met, the delegates appeared to consider themselves bound by the League's recommendations, and the attempt to provide for periodic conferences was defeated apparently because the recommendations submitted by the League contained no suggestion for such conferences. The question of unanimous consent to the adoption of provisions was discussed, but an attempt to modify such consent in the manner already adopted by the Labor Conferences (discussed below) was defeated, on grounds both of custom and expediency.[34] By the time the third communications

[32] *Revue générale de droit international public*, 1927, p. 328.

[33] Dunn, *op. cit.*, p. 160.

[34] *Ibid.*, p. 163.

and transit conference was held in 1927, however, tradition held less sway, and procedure suited to the needs of the conference was adopted in the form of a statute and approved by the Assembly. This statute provides that the Advisory and Technical Committee of the Communications and Transit Organization should draw up the agenda of the conference, but the agenda was not to become definitive until adopted by the conference itself by a simple majority, with the exception of new items, which required a two-thirds majority. The final texts must be voted on by a majority of the delegations, and must receive a two-thirds majority of those voting. They must then be submitted to the states for ratification. This statute may itself be revised in general conference by a two-thirds majority of the states voting, and not being cast in the form of a treaty requires no ratification.[35]

The provisions for revision of conventions drawn up by the International Labor Organization also indicate a drift away from the conference procedure of the nineteenth century. These provisions are contained partly in the Labor Section of the Peace Treaties and partly in the labor conventions themselves. They stipulate that after ten years the Governing Body of the International Labor Office shall report on the operation of the conventions and consider the desirability of placing on the agenda of the International Labor Conference the question of their revision or modification. This agenda goes to the members four months before the conference meets, allowing time for the registering of objections and their circulation to the members. The provisions objected to may be kept on the agenda by a two-thirds vote of the conference. The modified convention, in turn, must be adopted by a two-thirds vote of the confer-

[35] September 2, 1927, League of Nations, *Doc. C.558(C)M.200(C) 1927.VIII*; Hudson, *International Legislation*, vol. iii, p. 2107, arts. 8-11.

ence in order to be accepted. It then goes to the states for ratification.[36] At present these draft conventions go into effect with ratification by two members of the Labor Organization; presumably the same procedure will be followed in case of revision.[37] To date, however, this procedure has only once been invoked, due presumably to the fact that the need of revision has not made itself felt to the Governing Body.[38]

Those international unions whose conventions have been most frequently revised have developed what appears to be a generally satisfactory procedure for keeping these conventions up to the current needs of their organization. First, the permanent organization of the union keeps account of the needs of the parties and their desire for changes, and prepares a plan for revision along the lines suggested.[39] Second, the conventions themselves contain provision for periodic conferences, in which representation of the states is generally on an equal basis, the conferences having power of revision. Third, where equality of representation would amount to injustice to the larger states, weighted voting is resorted to or colonies receive separate representation. Fourth, where revision between conferences appears necessary, a conference may be called on the demand of a fraction of the states forming the union, or minor revision may take place merely by diplomatic exchange through the central bureau, unanimous consent not being required always to minor modifications. Fifth, protection is provided for the dissenting parties by requiring ratification of the conventions

[36] Treaty of Versailles, arts. 400-408.

[37] *Cf.* art. 10 of convention concerning the Employment of Women during the Night, Hudson, *op. cit.*, vol. i, p. 412.

[38] International Labor Conference of 1932, *Record of Proceedings*, April 26, p. 300.

[39] Protocol of amendment of art. 34 of the Convention on Aerial Navigation of October 13, 1919, signed June 30, 1923, Hudson, *op. cit.*, vol. i, p. 380.

drawn up by the conference, the non-ratifying states generally maintaining the old convention in force.

To date, however, there appear to be no generally accepted rules for procedure in revisory conferences. The League of Nations Committee of Experts for the Progressive Codification of International Law attempted an exploration of the whole problem of conference procedure, but failed to arrive at any satisfactory results.[40] As the problems considered by such conferences differ in almost every case, the rules of procedure must vary accordingly. Where periodic conferences are provided by treaty, however, procedural rules are generally drawn up, and serve a useful purpose.

Conclusions

The revisory conference has long been recognized as an agency for the revision of treaties, but only recently has there been any wide use of a provision for such revision in the treaty itself. Where used, it is confined almost entirely to treaties primarily technical in character, the parties to a treaty of a political type being generally averse to expressing any intent to modify its provisions.

In the absence of treaty or other provision governing such conferences the procedure involved has shown little change over a half century or more. The conference is called on the initiative of one of the parties to the treaty to be revised, and a statement of the questions to be considered is attached. The parties are represented by plenipotentiaries, decisions are unanimous, and the resultant text is submitted to the respective states for ratification.

But the technical convention providing for its own revision makes wide departures from these rules. Frequently there is provision for calling the revisory conference by some agency not a state and not a party to the convention to be

[40] *Cf.* League of Nations, *Doc. C.196.M.70.1927.V*, p. 105.

revised. Sometimes the agenda is prepared and submitted by such bodies and frequently the entire convention is open to modification. In the case of an international union, the states invited to participate are the members of the union, regardless of whether they were parties to the most recently revised convention or not. The delegates are often not representatives of the Governments of the states of which they are nationals, but appear in another capacity.[41] Frequently there is provision that unanimous decisions are not necessary. The principal point of resemblance between the two types of conference is the necessity of submitting the result to the states concerned for their ratification.

There are several reasons for the differences in procedure. In the former case the interests are primarily those of states, in the latter they are frequently those of individuals, and for that reason the necessity of primary consideration of the effect of decisions on the interests of states is less strong. In the former the rights and obligations discussed vary from state to state, and their precise determination and the consent of all its essentials; in the latter the object of the convention is to establish uniformity of regulation throughout the territory represented by the states which are parties, and such regulation is less apt to work to the disadvantage of any party; therefore unanimity of consent in the conference is less vital, and lack of unanimity less apt to prevent ratification of the resultant convention. In the former the work of the expert is less important than the work of the diplomat; in the latter, the need of the diplomat is often negligible, and therefore the participation in the revisory work of non-state agencies is not a matter of great concern.

It is unfortunate that such considerable difficulties stand in the way of the development of more mechanical and less

[41] For example, the labor and employer representatives in the Labor Conferences.

cumbersome procedure in conferences for revising the political type of treaty. But the individual character of the problem in each case and the great care required for protecting the interests of the parties appear to make the organization of any such procedure extremely difficult if not impossible. Until state sovereignty becomes a much less important factor in international relations than at present, the old system, at least in its main lines, will probably continue in use.

CONCLUSIONS

The practice of states indicates the absence of any large body of recognized rules concerning the conditions under which multipartite treaties are terminated. Yet in spite of this fact we find detailed provisions for termination in only a limited number. Among them, provisions concerning the life span of treaties are most carefully specified in treaties of the international union type and the communications and transit conventions. In these treaties are found provisions for general signature and adhesion; for entry of the treaty into force with but a small number of ratifications; for unilateral denunciation either at any time after a given period or at periodic intervals, or on demand of a fraction of the parties; for revision of certain of the clauses without unanimous consent; and for a conference for general revision of the convention either at regular intervals or after a certain length of time. Some of these conventions also provide for their own suspension in wartime or other emergency. A few provide for automatic termination when denunciations have reduced the number of parties bound below a certain figure. The design of the parties concerning termination is made manifest here under almost any conceivable circumstances, and conventions of this sort are readily adaptable to any contingency likely to arise.

In practice the measures provided in these conventions appear in the main to have accomplished their purpose. The ease with which states may release themselves from their obligations under such conventions appears to have contributed to their general acceptance, yet in practice the provisions for denunciation have seldom been invoked. The conviction informally expressed by any considerable number of the parties that the usefulness of the convention had been impaired has generally proved sufficient to induce the remaining parties to consent to the calling of a revisory conference without making it necessary to invoke the formal provisions of the treaty itself.

The field of application of such treaties is, however, very limited. It is still confined to matters which can be regulated uniformly for all the parties, and the regulation of which can not conceivably threaten their welfare or endanger their safety. In the case of most other treaties, states are more concerned with the establishment of a condition of immediate stability than in providing for future change, and frequently the prevention of future change is the precise aim of the negotiations. In such cases, states are generally unwilling to contract away any rights by treaty except for the purpose of solving a present difficulty. This applies even to the case of peace treaties where defeated states, though forced into an agreement by the victors, concede only as much as is necessary to attain their aim of securing peace. Sometimes provisions are included for meeting future contingencies which do not appear likely to involve serious controversy, but if provision against a remote contingency appears likely to complicate the negotiations, its discussion is generally avoided. Moreover, many of the obscurities concerning the design of the parties in the face of contingencies which later arise are due to the practical limitations of the conference procedure under which these conventions are drawn up. Decisions must be reached within the limits of the time and patience of the negotiators, and sometimes of their mandate from the authorities of their state. It is therefore essential to set up an arrangement which will be at least temporarily stable, and the discussion of those questions of which the settlement cannot be fitted into the frame of these conditions is postponed, in the hope that the progress of events may never make their consideration necessary.

The fact that there are no definite safeguards thrown around the members of the community of states to protect them from the danger of serious injury through unwise or unfortunate treaty provisions also induces states to avoid specifying the particular conditions under which they intend to consider a treaty terminated. It is not to be supposed that a state will voluntarily provide by treaty for its own destruction, and should the operation of a treaty provision threaten to produce such an effect, the state concerned presumably intended when consenting to the treaty that the provision in question should be terminated. In the case of an imposed treaty of peace the design of the victors may have been to compel the defeated state to run such a risk in order to achieve other aims of the victors, and the defeated state may have intended to accept the risk in preference to possible destruction through continuing the war. Yet even here, when such a threat to the vanquished is no longer necessary for the accomplishment of the aims of the victors, the design of the latter to force the vanquished to run the risk of annihilation may give place to a willingness or even a desire to assist in his recovery. At such a time the possibility that the victorious state may have intended not to consent to annihilation must be taken into account.

It is obviously impossible to make provision in treaties against all contingencies, and yet experience indicates that some arrangement should be made for avoiding the confusion attendant on the present method of trusting to the course of events to avoid the necessity of making such provision, or when action is necessary, trusting to negotiations at such a time, and in the event of the failure of such negotiations, to each party's taking action on its own account, and finally possibly, to war. There appear to be three ways in which such arrangement may be made; the first, by accepting the termination of treaties under certain circumstances as due to the operation of international law; the second, by including provisions for termination when drafting the treaty; and the third, by the establishment of recognized methods of adapting it to unexpected situations.

The first method presents great difficulties. It has been held that certain changes of conditions may render treaties obsolete, and that frustration or supervening impossibility of performance may result in termination. But the limits of the field of application of these principles have never been made clear, and there is no immediate prospect of such clarification. A much broader experience with interpretation will be necessary before the import of the rules of international law concerning termination is sufficiently clear to command general acceptance.

In the case of the legislative type of treaty already discussed, confusion concerning termination is practically eliminated by the completeness of the provisions of the treaties themselves. Although the field in which they operate might be extended by multipartite treaty of this legislative type to other subjects where international regulation by such treaties would be possible, such subjects are still either under intrastate control or regulated by bipartite treaties only. The fields of state participation in private commerce, of conflict of laws, and of extradition offer convenient examples.

But even in the field where international activity is regulated by multipartite convention, improvement in the method of such regulation would be possible. Legislative methods adaptable to the international field are capable of development, but in using internal legislation as the basis for suggestions for improving the procedure for drawing up the so-called legislative treaty it is essential to keep in mind the differences between the two. The primary objection to the use of such an analogy lies in the nature of international society; there being no international legislature, it is difficult to speak of international legislation in any exact sense. The Assembly of the League of Nations, though made up of representatives of all but a few of the states, lacks universality through the absence of certain important members of the world community. In the fields where it sponsors international action by treaty it is obliged to delegate the work to a conference called for the purpose, and that conference frequently includes representatives of states which are not members of the League. Thenceforth it is the conference, and not the Assembly, which is responsible for whatever action is taken, and it is the parties to the resulting convention, and not the Assembly, which determine the fate of the treaty.

The next difference lies in the distinction between the units represented. A conference responsible for creating international legislation is composed of representatives of units of international society; each of these units is sovereign, and each must give its consent if it is to be bound. On the other hand, in national legislative bodies in which popular representation is the rule, each member of the legislature ordinarily represents a large number of constituents who have delegated their legislative authority to the body to which he belongs, and who accept the will of the majority of such representatives, as expressed by legislation, as binding on the constituents of all. Moreover, such legislation is put immediately into effect, whereas international legislation requires further action by the respective national authorities before it becomes directly effective.

These differences, however, serve merely to indicate that development of the procedure for creating and revising international legislation will probably take place along its own lines. Should all the members of the international community of states come to be represented in some body such as the Assembly of the League, the development of a standard revisory procedure of a simple nature would be feasible. Such a body could avoid the calling of a large number of conferences, by substituting one or more sessions each year for all the periodic conferences of that year. Such an arrangement need not affect the preparatory work of the international bureaus or the Secretariat of the League of Nations, which now perform much of that preliminary work vitally essential to the drafting of a satisfactory convention; it would merely concentrate the conference work within a short period and in one place.

Such a procedure would not at present be applicable in dealing with the mass of questions not concerning the international community as a whole. In spite of the fact that the number of multipartite treaties of this more limited sort is constantly growing, and thus constantly entailing an increasing number of international conferences involving in each case great preparation and expense, no superior method of dealing with such questions has yet been developed. The variety of questions to be considered, the differing composition of the group of interested parties, and the need of freedom to make rapid and delicate adjustments makes standardization of method in dealing with such questions extremely difficult if not impossible. Much could be done, however, to improve treaty drafting to facilitate the subsequent interpretation of the design of the parties in the face of a new situation calling for such interpretation.

Most of the apparent weaknesses in present methods of drafting any but the legislative type of treaties appear to arise from the unwillingness of states to be precise in explaining their meaning, due to the fact that the experience of states in dealing with the question of termination of multipartite treaties is very limited. A few general principles have gradually developed through practice, but these are apt to change before many occasions arise for applying them. It must be recalled that there are roughly but sixty states in the international community, that most of them have only a short history, and that treaty relations on any broad basis between these states have been in many cases of but recent origin. The fact, too, that states use the treaty as the principal instrument for recording the regulation of every sort of arrangement between themselves, in the field covered by both legislation and contract in the relations between individuals, makes the establishment of rules governing treaties in general as difficult as would be the establishment of rules governing both legislation and contracts in private law.

In the treaty field where political bargaining between the states is of equal or greater importance than technical collaboration, therefore, there has been little change in method over a very long period, and little sign of future progress is evident. Negotiators are always anxious to keep the hands of their governments as free as possible, and although it is evident that the establishment of rules would diminish future occasions for dispute, such standardization would by so much reduce the freedom of the parties represented, and is therefore resisted.

Limited progress has been made, however, since the war. The use of the term "guarantee" was given precision in the treaty of 1921 concerning the Aaland Islands, and in the Locarno pact. Recognition of the fact that states do not intend to cripple themselves in wartime by treaty arrangements appears in the communications and transit and other conventions. But in the fields which are among the most fruitful causes of dispute, little change is noticeable. For example, no clear recognition has been made of the difference between treaties forming part of the public law of Europe, and for which revision is therefore a matter of general concern, and those dealing with the most unimportant matters. Where stipulations of both these sorts are found in the same treaty there is no recognition of the fact that the former are of more consequence than the latter. The result is that when the latter are modified irregularly or are no longer observed, —a matter entailing limited consequences—such action serves as a precedent for similar action concerning the former type of stipulation, which may occasion serious international complications. Nor is there ordinarily any recognition of the varying degrees of concern of the different parties to a treaty in the matter of its termination. The Great Powers, on whose shoulders still rests the principal burden of maintaining the treaty structure on which the present organization of the world is based, are in most treaties placed ostensibly on a par with the other signatories, yet in practice their support of the treaty is ordinarily more essential, and that of certain of the signatories may be quite unimportant.

In a few cases, the necessity of the support of certain states has been recognized, either to bring a treaty into force or to prevent its termination. Yet in general no such distinction between the parties appears, with the result that frequently those states with the greatest interest or those of the greatest importance proceed to the revision or termination of a treaty without reference to any established rule. Yet modification of this practice is very difficult to achieve, due to the fact that the interest of the parties and even their importance do not remain constant necessarily, and if provision were made in an attempt to fix these variable factors, such provision would probably be ignored where not in accordance with the facts at the time when termination or revision took place.

With the great growth of the number of multipartite treaties there is developing also an increasing mass of precedents which in time will assist the development of more precise procedure. Already the beginning of new methods along certain lines has been indicated, and others should follow. The peace treaties of 1919 and 1920 recognized the existence of two categories of signatories by distinguishing between the Principal Allied and Associated Powers and the others, although they failed to indicate any broad general distinction between the two. Except in treaties concerned with technical subjects, however, such distinctions are still rare. In several cases the peace treaties provided for revision by other bodies than the parties themselves, and although this procedure was confined for the most part to the less controversial portions of these treaties, if it should prove successful in practice it might prove capable of extension. The advantage of such a procedure, if feasible, is obvious, as it gives to a body more important and often more cohesive than the states themselves, the task of determining when revision is advisable, and thus avoids the delicate questions of prestige and internal politics involved in obtaining the consent of the parties. The whole conception of entrusting the matter of revision or termination to another authority than the parties to a treaty themselves is, however, still too new for any clear picture of its operation to have developed. Until it is possible for states to run less risk to their own welfare in entrusting their vital affairs to the judgment of their peers than is now possible in international society, it is unlikely that any very decided change in this direction may be expected.

Increased use by states of the interpretative function of the Permanent Court of International Justice, would be helpful. Such action will probably be slow, both because even parties bound by the optional clause are apt to be unwilling to consider the most vital questions as coming within the scope of the Court's functions, through unwillingness to trust their most important interests to an outside body, and because the Court itself might find itself in some difficulty due to the small body of precedent it would have as its disposal for guidance.

At present too, Article XIX of the Covenant of the League, which was intended to aid the process of revision and termination of treaties by peaceful means, has only conjectural possibilities, since it appears to contain such uncertainties and dangers that states are greatly disinclined to consider its use. Even in the few cases where invoked by a state which considered necessary the revision of a treaty as no longer applicable, or as creating a situation the continuance of which might endanger the peace of the world, the Assembly has failed to come to a vote on the matter of a recommendation.

The whole problem whether such a recommendation should be unanimous has thus far not been settled; the League of Nations Commission at the Peace Conference left it in abeyance, and it has never yet been brought to a decision in the Assembly itself. Unanimity including all the parties to a treaty is scarcely to be conceived, since it is unlikely that with such unanimous opinion in favor of change the matter would come before the Assembly at all. Unanimity leaving out the parties to the treaty would indicate an opinion of only limited value in the case of multipartite treaties to which any considerable number of states were parties. For example, changes in territorial provisions are among those which are frequently sought, but which present special difficulties under Article XIX. Unanimity of recommendation in the Assembly is scarcely to be hoped for, as the victim of the change cannot be expected to join in any plan for his own dismemberment. In Europe such territorial provisions are usually included in treaties of general settlement to which a large number of states, including the Great Powers, are parties, and if the parties to such treaties are not to participate in the voting, a recommendation by the remaining states would have little value. A recommendation by a majority, then, with the parties to the treaty participating, appears to be the only remaining possibility. States are still too convinced of the danger of submitting territorial questions to a judgment of their peers for the general acceptance of such procedure to be envisaged in the immediate future.

There can probably be no considerable progress in the field of treaties created and revised primarily by diplomatic negotiators rather than by technical experts until there is a greater sense of security between states than exists today. If the time should come when such security has been attained, it will be safer to use terms in more precise fashion, and to make more detailed provision for the termination of the treaty in the instrument itself, and so when differences of opinion arise between the parties concerning revision, suspension, or termination, these differences may safely be left to such outside bodies as the Assembly or the Permanent Court of International Justice. The outcome of their consideration will be more certain and the disposition of states to avail themselves of their services will be greater. Probably the present slow development is wise. Treaties dealing with the least controversial subjects operate under the most fully developed rules; the others will have rules developed for them, cautiously at first, and then as states become surer of the method, with increasing rapidity.

TABLE OF CASES

BIBLIOGRAPHY

This study is based primarily on treaty texts, protocols of conferences, diplomatic correspondence and court decisions concerning treaties. This material has been supplemented by legal and historical interpretations of the events bearing directly on these treaties. The author has had in view the determination of the current practice of states in dealing with multipartite treaties, rather than an appraisal of theories of the past. The selected bibliography given below is confined to the sources which have proved of the greatest value in making such a determination.

Treaty Collections

Abreu y Bertodano, *Coleccion de los tratados de paz* (Madrid, 1740-1752).

Basdevant, *Traités de la France* (Paris, 1918-1922).

British and Foreign State Papers.

Central American Peace Conference, Washington, 1907. *Tratados y convenciones* (*Publicacion de la Secretaría de relaciones exteriores de la República de Guatemala, 1913*).

de Clercq, *Recueil des traités de la France* (Paris, 1880-1923).

Dumont, *Corps diplomatique et universel de Droit des Gens* (Amsterdam and the Hague, 1726-1731).

——, *Supplément, ibid.,* (The Hague, 1730).

Great Britain, Treaty Series (London, 1892-).

Hertslet, Map of Africa by Treaty, 2nd ed., (London, 1896).

——, Map of Europe by Treaty (London, 1875, 1891).

Hudson, International Legislation (Washington, 1931).

International Labor Conference (Geneva, 1920-).

Koch, *Recueil des traités;* etc. (Basle, 1802).

League of Nations, Treaty Series (1920-).

Léonard, *Recueil des traités, etc.* (Paris, 1693).

Martens, *Recueil des traités, etc.* (Göttingen, 1791-1817).

——, *ibid., Supplément* (Göttingen, 1791-1818).

——, *Nouveau recueil géneral, etc.* (Göttingen, 1843-1875).

——, *ibid., Deuxième série* (Göttingen-Leipzig, 1876-1908).

——, *ibid., Troisième série* (Leipzig, 1909-).

Niemeyer, *Jahrbuch des Völkerrechts, Sonderband,* vol. XI, 1926.

Plason-Neumann, *Recueil des traités et conventions conclus par l'Autriche, etc.* (Leipzig, 1855-1919).

Recueil des traités et conventions conclus par le royaume des Pays-Bas (The Hague, 1858-1859).

Scott, The International Conferences of the American States, 1889-1928 (New York, 1931).

Traités publics de la royale maison de Savoie, etc. (Turin, 1836-1861).

Tratados y convenciones de Washington de 1923 (*Ministero de relaciones exteriores,* Honduras, 1927).

CONFERENCE PROCEEDINGS

For the period beginning with the conference of Vienna, and extending down to 1890, the British and Foreign State Papers supply the abstracts of the minutes of most of the international conferences, both of a technical and a political character. From 1890 on, however, such minutes no longer appear in this series. Sources for minutes of conferences concerning matters of a technical nature, many of which are missing from the British and Foreign State Papers collection, are listed in D. P. Myers, Manual of Collections of Treaties, Harvard University Press, 1922. This book covers the period from the beginning of such technical conferences up to 1920. Unfortunately the minutes of a number of conferences, both of earlier periods and even of the past few years, either have not been preserved or else are not in form available for research.

The period since the war has not yet brought forth a manual indicating sources for conference minutes. The records of the Peace Conferences of 1919 are still far from complete, though Miller, My Diary at the Conference of Paris, contains the minutes of a number of the Committees. Among postwar conference proceedings examined are the following:

1919—Peace Conference; Miller, *op. cit.* (New York, 1924). Ibid, Drafting of the Covenant, (New York, 1928).

1919-1932—International Labor Conferences; Minutes of the International Labor Conference (Geneva, 1920-).

1920-1921—International Conference for the Establishment of a Definitive Statute for the Danube River (Paris, *Imprimerie nationale,* 1921).

1921—*Comptes rendus et textes relatifs à la convention sur la liberté de transit* (Geneva, 1921).

Comptes rendus et textes relatifs à la conventions sur le régime des voies navigables d'intérêt international (Geneva, 1921).

Comptes rendus et textes relatifs au réglement d'organisation des conférences générales et de la Commission consultative et technique des communications et transit (Geneva, 1921).

1922—Conference on the Limitation of Armament, Washington, November 12, 1921, to February 6, 1922 (Washington, Government Printing Office, 1922).

1923—Records and Texts relative to the Convention and Statute on the International Régime of Maritime Ports (Geneva, 1924).

Records and Texts relative to the Convention on the International Régime of Railways (Geneva, 1924).

1923—Conference on Central American Affairs, Washington, December 4, 1922 to February 7, 1923 (Washington, Government Printing Office, 1923).

Records of the International Conference for the Suppression of the Circulation of and Traffic in Obscene Publications, held at Geneva from August 31 to September 12, 1923 (Geneva, 1923).

Proceedings of the Conferences on Customs and other similar Formalities, Geneva, December, 1923 (Geneva, 1924).

1925—*Actes de la cinquième conférence sur le droit international privé (Imprimerie nationale, la Haye, 1926).*

Conference pour la suppression du trafic international des armes (Lausanne, 1925).

1926—Conference of States Signatories of the Protocol of Signature of the Statute of the Permanent Court of International Justice, 1926 (Geneva, 1926).

Conference sanitaire internationale, du 5 jusqu'au 21 juin, 1926 *(Paris, Imprimerie nationale, 1927).*

1927—Records of the Conference for the Limitation of Naval Armament (Geneva, 1927).

1930—Acts of the Conference for the Codification of International Law (The Hague, 1930).

Cinquième congrès international de la navigation aérienne, la Haye, 1930 (la Haye, 1931).

COURT REPORTS

Belgium

Pasicrisie belge, Recueil général de la jurisprudence des cours et tribunaux de la Belgique, (Bruxelles) 1838, 1917, 1921.

France

Journal officiel, 8 septembre, 1915, Conseil des prises.

Clunet, *Journal du droit international, (Paris) 1888, 1915-1919, 1926.*

Journal du palais, Recueil . . . de la jurisprudence francaise, (Paris) 1839 (ii), 1843, 1860.

J. B. Sirey, Recueil général des lois et des arrêts, (Paris) 1854 (i), 1922 (ii).

Germany

Deutsche Juristen-Zeitung (Berlin) 1916.

Entscheidungen des Reichsgerichts in Zivilsachen (Leipzig), 1884, 1885.

Juristische Wochenschrift (Leipzig), 1915, 1924.

Markenschutz und Wettbewerb (Berlin), 1915.

Niemeyer's Zeitschrift für internationales Recht (Berlin) 1922.

Zeitschrift für Völkerrecht (Breslau), 1916.

Great Britain
Law Times Reports, 1914.
Lloyd's Reports of Prize Cases (London), vol. iii.
Reports of Cases argued and determined in the High Court of Chancery, 1829-1931, by James Russell and J. W. Mylne (New York, vol. i.
Times Law Reports, vol. 31.
Trehern, Price Cases during the Great War, etc. (London), vol i.
United States
Court of Claims (1932), vol. 73
Massachusetts Reports, vol. 119
New York Reports, vol. 229
New York Supplement (1911), vol. 164
Supreme Court Reporter,
8 Cranch,
8 Wheaton.
International
Permanent Court of International Justice, Judgments, Series A, no. 14 (Leyden, 1923).
Scott, Hague Court Reports, Second Series (New York, 1932)..
General
Dickinson, Cases and Other Readings on the Law of Nations (New York, 1929).
Hudson, Cases and Other Materials on International Law (St. Paul, 1929).
Fontes juris gentium (Berlin), 1931.
McNair, A. D., and Lauterpacht, H., Annual Digest of Public International Law Cases (London), 1929, 1930.
Scott, Cases on International Law (St. Paul, 1922).
Belgium
Moniteur belge, Sept. 6-7, 1920.
La Révision des traités de 1839 (Brussels, 1929).
France
Journal officiel, May 29, Sept. 8, 1915.
Archives diplomatiques (see *supra,* Conference Proceedings).
Germany
Reichsanzeiger, Aug. 8, 1914.
Reichsgesetzblatt, 1887, 1914-1918.
Great Britain
British and Foreign State Papers (London) 1814-1925, *passim.*
Command Papers
1898, Misc. 2, 9088.
1917, Misc. 2, 8436.
17, 8693.

1918, Misc. 2, 8915.
1923, Turkey 1, 1814.
1932, Misc. 7, 4126.
Misc. 8, 4129.
Hansard, Parliamentary Debates, 3rd series, vol. 165.
5th series, vol. 118.

Netherlands
Bescheiden in Zake de tusschen Nederland en Belgie, etc. (Hague, 1929).

United States
Congressional Record, Jan. 7, 1932.
Diplomatic Correspondence with Belligerent Governments relative to Neutral Rights and Commerce, Dept. of State, European War, American White Book (Govt. Printing Office, 1915).
German Delegates' Observations on Conditions of Peace, Official Summary, Senate Doc. 149, 66th Cong., 1st session, 1919.
Neutrality Proclamations (Dept. of State, 1919).
Notes exchanged between the United States and Other Powers on the subject of a Multilateral Treaty for the Renunciation of War (U. S. Govt. Printing Office, 1928).
State Papers, Foreign Relations, vol. iv.
United States, Foreign Relations, 1898.
United States Treasury, Weekly Health Report, vol. 40.
Statutes at Large
65th Congress, H. R., 4960.
H. R. 13086.
70th Congress, H. R. 7201.
71st Congress, H. R. 2667.

League of Nations Publications

(See also Conference Proceedings, *supra*)
Council Documents, C. 196. M. 70, 1927 V.) (Codification of International Law).
C. L. 194 (a) 1930. V. (Revision of Statute of Permanent Court of International Justice).
Official Journal
1920, Annex 3, Aaland Islands.
October 1921, Special Supplement No. 6, Amendment of Covenant.
March 1933, Mexico's withdrawal.
Records of Plenary Meetings of the Assembly, Dec. 16, 1920.
International Labor Office
Etudes et documents, série i, no. 2, (Geneva, 1931).
Report on the Employment of Women and Children and the Berne Convention of 1906 (London, 1919).

DOCUMENTS AND PERIODICALS CONCERNING INTERNATIONAL UNIONS AND BUREAUS

Droit d'auteur, organe officiel du bureau de l'Union international pour la protection des oeuvres littéraires et artistiques (Berne) 1914-1918.

Bulletin de l'Office international d'hygiène publique (Paris), 1909, 1914-1918.

Annuaire de législation agricole (Rome), 1915-1918.

La Commission européenne du Danube et son oeuvre de 1856 à 1931 (Paris, 1931).

La Navigation du Rhin, organe de publication de la Commission central pour la navigation du Rhin (Strasbourg), 1925-1932.

La Propriété industrielle, Organe officiel du Bureau international de l'Union pour la protection de la propriété industrielle (Berne), 1914-1919, 1923.

L'Union postale, official organ of the Universal Postal Union (Berne), 1914-1918.

Rheinurkunden, etc., Documents concerning Rhine navigation (The Hague, 1918).

Railway Age Gazette (New York and Chicago), vols. 57, 62.

TREATISES AND MONOGRAPHS

Adanya, S., *Régime international de l'Escaut* (Paris, 1929).

Anson, W. R., Principles of the Law of Contract (New York, 1930).

Baker, R. S., Woodrow Wilson and World Settlement (Garden City, 1922).

Baker, J. R., and McKernan, L. W., Selected Topics connected with the Laws of Warfare as of August 1, 1914 (U. S. Govt. Printing Office, 1919).

Baty, T., The Canons of International Law (London, 1930).

Bergbohm, C., *Staatsverträge und Gesetze als Quellen des Völkerrechts* (Dorpat, 1876).

Bertram, H., *Die Aufhebung völkerrechtlicher Verträge* (Leipzig, 1915).

Buckland, W. W., Main Institutions of Roman Private Law (Cambridge, 1931).

Bühler, H., *Der Weltpostverein,* (*Völkerrechtsfragen*) (Berlin, 1930).

Burgsdorf, A., *Die Kriegserklärung und ihre Wirkungen unter besonderer Berücksichtigung des öffentlichrechtlichen und privatrechtlichen Verträge* (Düsseldorf, 1914).

Chabaud, G., *La Propriété industrielle, littéraire et artistique* (Paris, 1921).

Chamberlain, J. P., The Regime of the International Rivers, Danube and Rhine (New York, 1923).

Chitty, J., Law of Nations (Boston, 1812).

Crandall, S. B., Treaties, Their Making and Enforcement, 2nd. ed. (Washington, 1916).
Cumming, C. K. and Pettit, W. W., Russian-American Relations from March 1917 to March 1920 (New York, 1920).
Dennis, W. C., Tacna-Arica (New Haven, 1931).
Dunn, F. S., Practice and Procedure of International Conferences (Baltimore, 1929).
Flassan, G. R., *Histoire du Congrés de Vienne* (Paris, 1829).
Garner, J. W., International Law and the World War (London, 1920).
——, Prize Law During the World War (New York, 1927).
Graves, P. P., Question of the Straits (London, 1931).
Gruber, R. G., *Internationale Staatenkongresse und Konferenzen, ihre Vorbereitung und Organisation* (Berlin, 1917).
Headlam-Morley, Studies in Diplomatic History (London, 1930).
Higgins, A. P., The Hague Peace Conferences and Other International Conferences concerning the Laws and Usages of War (Cambridge, 1909).
Hobson, A., The International Institute of Agriculture (Berkeley, 1931).
Hoijer, O., *Les traités internationaux* (Paris, 1928).
Howard-Ellis, C., The Origin, Structure and Working of the League of Nations (London, 1928).
Hü, H. Z., Treaty Revision under Article Nineteen of the Covenant (New York, 1931).
Jacomet, R., *La Guerre et les traités* (Paris, 1909).
Kao, Yin Tang, International Conferences on Ports and Waterways (New York, 1932).
Kohler, J., *Grundlagen des Völkerrechts* (Stuttgart, 1919).
Kosters, J., and Bellemans, F., *Les Conventions de la Haye de 1902 at 1905 sur le droit international privé* (The Hague, 1921).
Kunz, Otto, *Die internationale Telegrafen-Unionen* (Stuttgart, 1924).
Ladas, S. P., The International Protection of Industrial Property (Cambridge, 1930).
——, The International Protection of Trade Marks by the American Republics (Cambridge, 1929).
Lauterpacht, H., Private Law Sources and Analogies of International Law (London, 1927).
Masters, R. D., International Law in National Courts (New York, 1932).
Maurel, M., *De la Déclaration de guerre* (Toulouse, 1907).
Miller, D. H., Drafting of the Covenant (New York, 1928).
Moore, J. B., International Law and Some Current Illusions (New York, 1924).
Moulton, M., A structural view of the Conference as an Organ of International Cooperation (Highland Park, N. J., 1930).
Phillimore, W. G. F., Three Centuries of Treaties of Peace and their Teaching (London, 1919).

Phillipson, C., Termination of War and Treaties of Peace (London, 1916).

——, and Buxton, N., The Question of the Bosphorus and the Dardanelles (London, 1917).

Pillet, A., *Les Conventions de la Haye du 29 juillet 1899 et du 18 octobre, 1907* (Paris, 1918).

Price, M. P., Diplomatic History of the War (New York, 1915).

Pulling, A., Manual of Emergency Legislation (London, 1914).

Putnam, R., Luxemburg and her Neighbors (New York, 1918).

Renault, L., *Les deux conférences de la paix, 1899 et 1907* (Paris, 1909).

Rolin, H., *Le droit moderne de la guerre* (Brussels, 1920).

Rolland, L., *De La Correspondence postale dans les relations internationales* (Paris, 1901).

Roper, A., *Convention internationale aérienne du 13 octobre, 1919* (Paris, 1930).

Satow, E. M., International Congresses (H. M. Stationery Office, London, 1920).

Scott, J. B., Diplomatic Documents relative to the Outbreak of the European War (New York, 1916).

——, Reports to the Hague Conferences of 1899 and 1907 (New York, 1907).

Sherman, C. P., Roman Law in the Modern World (Boston, 1917).

Shotwell, J. T., Pact of Paris, International Conciliation Pamphlet No. 243 (New York, 1928).

Slavko, R., *Régime international des voies ferrèes et la Société des nations* (Paris, 1925).

Soergel, T., *Kriegsrechtssprechung und Kriegsrechtslehre* (Berlin, 1916).

Stieler, K., *Der internationale Eisenbahnverband* (*Völkerrechtsfragen*) (Berlin, 1926).

Temperley, H. W., History of the Peace Conference (London, 1920-1924).

Triepel, H., *Droit international et droit interne* (Paris, 1920).

Ward, Sir A., The Period of Congresses (New York, 1919).

Woeste, C. F. A., *La Neutralité belge* (Brussels, 1891).

Abbreviations:

A.J.I.L.; American Journal of International Law

Br. Yr. Bk.; British Year Book of International Law

Gr. Soc. Ann.; Grotius Society Annuaire

Rec. des Cours; Hague Academy, Recueil des Cours

R.D.I.L.C.; Revue de droit international et de legislation comparée

R.G.D.I.P.; Revue générale de droit international public

Brierly, J. L., "Some Considerations on the Obsolescence of Treaties", *Gr. Soc. Ann.*, vol. xi (1926).

Dennis, W. C., "Effect of War on Treaties", *A.J.I.L.*, vol. 23 (1929).

Duez, P., "*L'Interprétation des traités internationaux*", *R.G.D.I.P.*, vol. 32 (1925).

Dupuis, C., "*L'Institut de droit international—Session de Christiania, 1912*", *R.G.D.I.P.*, vol. 20 (1913).

van Eysinga, W. J. M., "*l'Entretien de l'Escaut suivant les traités*", *R.D.I.L.C.* (1928).

Fachiri, A. P., "International Court. American Participation; Statute Revision", *Br. Yr. Bk.* (1930).

——, "Interpretation of Treaties", *A.J.I.L.*, vol. 23 (1929).

Fischer-Williams, Sir John, "Permanence of Treaties", *A.J.I.L.*, vol. 22 (1928).

Hershey, A. L., "History of International Relations During Antiquity and the Middle Ages", *A.J.I.L.*, vol. 5 (1911).

Hostie, J., "*Les Actes du Danube et de l'Elbe*", *R.D.I.L.C.*, vol 4 (1923).

——, "*Notes sur le statut relatif au régime des voies navigables d'interêt international*", *R.D.I.L.C.*, vol. 2 (1921).

Hudson, M. O., "Present Status of the Hague Conventions", *A.J.I.L.*, vol. 25 (1931).

——, "Revision of the Statute of the World Court", Foreign Affairs, vol. 9.

Hurst, Sir C., "Effect of War on Treaties", *Br. Yr. Bk.* (1921-1922).

Hyde, C. C., "Interpretation of Treaties by the Permanent Court of International Justice", *A.J.I.L.*, vol 24 (1930).

Kleinfeller, G., "*Der Einfluss des Krieges auf völkerrechtliche Verträge,*" *Niemeyer's Zeitschrift für internationales Recht*, vol. 25 (1915).

LeFur, L., "*Chronique des faits internationaux*", *R.G.D.I.P.* (1898).

McNair, A. D., "Functions and Differing Legal Character of Treaties", *Br. Yr. Bk.* (1930).

——, "*Termination et dissolution des traités*", *Rec. des Cours*, vol. 22 (1928).

Malkin, H. W., "Reservations to Multipartite Conventions", *Br. Yr. Bk.* (1930).

Myers, D. P., "Violation of Treaties by Adverse National Action", *A.J.I.L.*, vol. 2 (1918).

Nolde, B. C., "*La Monnaie en droit international*", *Rec. des Cours*, vol. 27.

Politis, N., "*Accords de Locarno*", *R.D.I.L.C.* (1925).

——, "Effect of War upon Treaties and International Conventions, Project of the Institute of International Law", *A.J.I.L.*, vol. 7 (1913).

Rathenau, W., "*Der gewerbliche Rechtsschutz in Deutschland während des Krieges*", *Recht und Wirtschaft* (1914).

Renault, L., "*Les Unions internationales*", *R.G.D.I.P.*, vol. 3 (1896).

Rolin-Jaequemyns, "*L'Entretien de l'Escaut suivant les traités*" *R.D.I.L.C.*, vol 9 (1928).

Rapisardi-Mirabelli, "*La Classification des traités internationaux*", *R. D. I. L. C.*, vol. 4 (1923).
Röthlisberger, E., "*Die Schicksale des gewerblichen Eigentums im Weltkriege*", *Schweizerische Juristen-Zeitung* (1916).
Ruffini, Fr., "*Oeuvres littéraires et artistiques*", *Rec. des Cours*, vol. 12.
Rühland, C., "*Zur Theorie und Praxis des Einflusses des Kriegsbeginn auf Staatsverträge*", *Niemeyer's Zeitschrift für internationales Recht*, vol. 32 (1924).
Satow, Sir E. M., "*Pacta sunt servanda*", Cambridge Historical Journal (1925).
de Stael von Holstein, L. F. W., "*L'Immunité postale en temps de guerre*", *R. D. I. L. C.*, vol. 6 (1925).
Tobin, H. J., "*Is Belgium Still Neutralized?*", *A. J. I. L.*, vol. 26 (1932).
de Visscher, C., "*Convention relative à la non-fortification et à la neutralité des Iles d'Aland*", *R. D. I. L. C.*, vol. 2 (1921).
——, "*Nouveau régime international du Rhin*", *R. D. I. L. C.*, vol. 1 (1921).
——, "*Révision de la convention de St. Gothard*", *ibid.*
——, "*Régime nouveau des détroits*", *R. D. I. L. C.*, vol. 4 (1923).
Woolsey, L. H., "Unilateral Termination of Treaties", *A. J. I. L.*, vol. 20 (1926).
"X", "*Annulation des traités bilateraux ou collectifs par la guerre*", *Revue de droit international privé et de droit penal*, vol. 11-12 (1915-16).

INDEX

Bei Fragen zur Produktsicherheit wenden Sie sich bitte an:
If you have any questions regarding product safety,
please contact:

Walter de Gruyter GmbH
Genthiner Straße 13
10785 Berlin
productsafety@degruyterbrill.com